Georg Lukács

Georg Lukács

The man, his work and his ideas

EDITED BY

G.H.R. Parkinson

VINTAGE BOOKS

A Division of Random House

NEW YORK

Contents

199.4391
L96p

1 Introduction *G.H.R. Parkinson*   1

2 Lukács' Concept of Dialectic *István Mészáros*   34

3 Lukács on Irrationalism *H.A. Hodges*   86

4 Lukács on the Central Category of Aesthetics   109
   G.H.R. Parkinson

5 Georg Lukács: the Concept of Totality *Roy Pascal*   147

6 The Marxist as a Literary Critic *A.G. Lehmann*   172

7 Lukács' Views on how History Moulds   191
   Literature *David Craig*

8 Lukács' Concept of 'the Beautiful' *Stanley Mitchell*   219

Selective Bibliography   237

Index   249

Contributors   255

Georg Lukács

1 Introduction

G. H. R. Parkinson

Although it is generally agreed that George Lukács is one of the most important Marxist theoreticians of this century, comparatively little has been written about him, and what has been written does not include any full-scale attempt to survey his work as a whole.[1] The absence of any attempt of this kind is not surprising; the task is a formidable one, by virtue of the sheer bulk and range of Lukács' work, which is the product of a very active literary career of more than fifty years, and which ranges over the fields of philosophy, sociology and literary criticism. The present volume, which is based on lectures given in 1968 in the Graduate School of Contemporary European Studies at the University of Reading,[2] is such an attempt. It is not claimed that the book covers every aspect of Lukács, but it does try to give an account of much of Lukács' work in all the three fields mentioned. The contributors to the volume follow no party line, and no attempt has been made to smooth out differences between them; it is an uninteresting author whose work is never the subject of disagreement. Each paper comments critically on a particular aspect of Lukács' work; the introduction which follows will be expository rather than critical. It offers a general sketch of Lukács' writings in the context of his political activity and attitudes, and is meant to provide a frame of reference which will be helpful to the reader of the more

[1] The book on Lukács by Henri Arvon (Paris, 1968) gives an all-round account of its subject, but is too short to be regarded as a full-scale study.

[2] I regret that it has not proved possible to include a lecture by George Lichtheim on Lukács, Marcuse and Adorno, and by Professor Alasdair MacIntyre on Lukács' concept of reification.

detailed discussions which follow it. Broadly, it concerns what Lukács has called his 'road to Marx', and the road that he has followed as a Marxist.

Lukács was born in Budapest on 13 April 1885 into a wealthy Jewish family of some social standing – his father had been awarded the hereditary title 'von Lukács' as a reward for his services as a financier.[1] Von Lukács wanted his son to follow him in the banking business, but met with a violent refusal.[2] Lukács has spoken recently[3] of his disdainful hatred of the life of capitalism, which, he says, springs from the period of his youth, and it may be assumed that this hatred was the reason for his refusal. Certainly, when still in his teens he was involved in activities which may well have seemed incomprehensible or even alien to the conventional businessman. In 1904 he helped to found the 'Thalia' dramatic society in Budapest; this was intended to present plays which were not in the current Budapest repertory, and to bring the theatre to the working class.[4] The society had existed for only a few years when its hired premises were closed by the police, with unconscious irony, on the grounds that they were a fire hazard. Before founding the 'Thalia', Lukács had joined in 1902 a socialist student club. This, the 'Revolutionary Socialist Students of Budapest', was organized by Ervin Szabó,[5] the most influential socialist theoretician in Hungary between about 1900 and his death in 1918. Szabó was an anarcho-syndicalist rather than a pure

[1] M. Watnick, *Soviet Survey*, 1958, No. 23, p. 62, n. 6.

[2] I. Mészáros tells the story of how Lukács symbolised his rejection of the business world by putting on his desk the portrait of his uncle, who had similarly rejected the 'activism' of everyday life and devoted himself to the interpretation of the Talmud. See *Georg Lukacs: Festschrift zum achtzigsten Geburststag*, ed. by F. Benseler, Neuwied, 1965 (abbreviated, 'Benseler'), p. 190.

[3] In the preface (March 1967) to *Geschichte und Klassenbewusstsein*. At the time of writing, this preface was not available in the German original, and is therefore cited from the Italian translation by G. Piana, published by Sugar Editore, Milan, 1967, as *Storia e Coscienza di Classe* (abbreviated, *Storia*). The present reference is to p. ix.

[4] Cf. *The New Hungarian Quarterly*, VIII (1967), No. 28, p. 208, which quotes Marcel Benedek, one of the founders of the 'Thalia'.

[5] R. L. Tökés, *Béla Kun and the Hungarian Soviet Republic* (New York and London, 1967), p. 20.

Marxist, though he borrowed some ideas from Marx;[1] similarly, Lukács was not yet a Marxist, though he was already studying Marx. He read the *Communist Manifesto* whilst still at his grammar school, and as an undergraduate he studied several works of Marx and Engels – he mentions in particular the first volume of Marx's *Capital*.[2] He adds that Marx's influence on him was originally limited to economics and sociology; he did not accept Marx's materialism, which he regarded as superseded by neo-Kantian theory of knowledge.

At this period, neo-Kantianism was the dominant trend in the philosophy of the German-speaking world, which included the educated classes of the Austro-Hungarian empire, and it is therefore not surprising that Lukács should have come under the influence of a type of neo-Kantian philosophy. There were two main schools of neo-Kantianism: the Marburg school, whose chief representatives were Cohen and Natorp, and the Heidelberg or South-Western school, whose chief representatives were Windelband and Rickert. For Cohen and Natorp, philosophy was the theory of the principles of science; they believed that Kant's philosophy needed modification in that thought was responsible not only for form, as Kant asserted, but also for content, which Kant ascribed to the influence of the unknowable 'thing in itself'. Lukács rejected this type of neo-Kantianism, on the grounds that he did not see 'how the problem of reality could be derived simply as an immanent category of consciousness'.[3] Windelband and Rickert were more concerned with problems of history and culture; the sociological neo-Kantianism of Simmel showed a similar concern, and it was neo-Kantianism of this type which influenced Lukács. He became Simmel's personal pupil, attending his lectures at Berlin in 1909–10; at Heidelberg in 1913 he studied under Rickert and Windelband and made the acquaintance of one of Windelband's pupils, Emil Lask, as well as of Max Weber.

[1] Tökés, op. cit., pp. 12ff.
[2] 'Mein Weg zu Marx', in *Georg Lukács: Shriften zur Ideologie und Politik* (abbreviated, *IP*), ed. by P. Ludz (Neuwied, 1967), p. 323. Besides offering valuable selections from Lukács' works, this volume also contains a useful chronological table of events in his life (pp. 709ff.).
[3] 'Mein Weg zu Marx', *IP*, p. 324.

However, the influence of neo-Kantian ideas on Lukács preceded his personal acquaintance with these philosophers and sociologists. Even before visiting Germany, he had completed in 1908 a book on the development of modern drama, in which he took Simmel and Weber as his models.[1] He had also written some of the essays which were to appear in his first important book, *The Soul and the Forms,* which was published in Hungarian in 1910, and in an expanded German version in 1911.

This is a work which was not so much a step forward on Lukács' road to Marx as an obstacle to be surmounted; as such, little need be said about it, particularly as Lukács soon abandoned the views it expressed.[2] The thesis of the work is that literary forms are the expression of certain mental contents, certain ways of seeing and feeling life, and that it is the business of the critic to attach each form to its corresponding content. Lukács might seem to have in mind an empirical inquiry into what people think and feel – a kind of social psychology, perhaps – but this is not what he means. He takes over from Rickert the distinction between the sensible world of science on the one hand, and on the other hand the non-sensuous objects of experience, such as art, which are known by 'understanding', and he argues that such understanding can be achieved only through flashes of intuition. Very little of this seems to survive in Lukács' later thought – the notion of intuitive knowledge was one to which he became particularly hostile[3] – though Morris Watnick has argued that the book contains an anticipation of Lukács' later rejection of naturalism,[4] and in Chapter 1 below Dr Mészáros notes that even in this early work, Lukács is

[1] *IP*, pp. 324, 709.

[2] *Storia*, p. xlii. Writing to a reviewer only a year after the book had appeared, Lukács stated that the work had become wholly foreign to him.

[3] See, e.g., *Die Zerstörung der Vernunft* (Neuwied, 1962), p. 372, and *Der junge Hegel* (Neuwied, 1968), pp. 531–2.

[4] Cf. *Soviet Survey*, 1958, No. 23, p. 63. It may be added that although Lukács now rejects *Die Seele und die Formen*, others continue to find it interesting. Lucien Goldmann argues that the work is dominated by the question, 'Under what conditions can human life be authentic?', and sees in it an important stage in the development of modern existentialism. (L. Goldmann: 'Georg Lukács: L'Essayiste', *Recherches Dialectiques* (Paris, 1959), p. 247, and 'Introduction aux premiers écrits de Georges Lukács', *Les Temps Modernes,* XVIII

concerned with the important dialectical notions of fragmentation and totality.

Lukács soon abandoned neo-Kantianism, because of what he considered its ahistorical character. Rickert and his school had opened a methodological gap between timeless value on the one hand, and the historical realization of value on the other. In *The Theory of the Novel*, written in the winter of 1914–15 and first published in 1916, Lukács rejected this view in favour of a historicizing of aesthetic categories.[1] The idea was derived from Hegel, and indeed Lukács regards this book as marking his transition from Kant to Hegel.[2] The book is by no means purely Hegelian; Lukács has noted the influence exercised on it by the *Geisteswissenschaft* movement, and in particular by Dilthey, the fascinating effect of whose *Das Erlebnis und die Dichtung* (1905) is expressly mentioned.[3] (It may be added that Dilthey's book on Hegel's youth (1906) did much to bring about the 'Hegel renaissance' early in this century.)[4]

Lukács now rejects *The Theory of the Novel* entirely; it is, he says, of interest only as a document of the pre-history of the important ideologies of the twenties and thirties.[5] The work has, indeed, serious defects. For example, something is seriously wrong with a theory of the novel that leads to the conclusion that Dostoevsky wrote no novels.[6] The book is also very limited; as Lukács notes,[7] it has no place for novelists such as Defoe, Fielding and Stendhal. However, it marks an important stage in the development of Lukács' thought, in that a number of his

[1] *Die Theorie des Romans* (Neuwied, 1965), p. 10.

[2] Op. cit., p. 6.

[3] Op. cit., p. 7; cf. p. 10.

[4] Lukács' account of Dilthey is discussed by Professor Hodges in Chapter 3 below.

[5] *Die Theorie des Romans*, p. 18. Cf. *Essays über Realismus* (Berlin, 1948), p. 157, where the work is declared to be reactionary in every respect, full of idealistic mysticism, and false in all its estimates of historical development.

[6] *Die Theorie des Romans*, p. 158.

[7] Op. cit., p. 8.

(1962–3), pp. 256–7.) Goldmann has also made considerable use of the last chapter of the book, an essay on the metaphysics of tragedy, in his book *Le Dieu caché: étude sur la vision tragique dans les 'Pensées' de Pascal et dans le théâtre de Racine* (Paris, 1955).

Georg Lukács

mature ideas can be found in it in embryonic form. Dr Mészáros and Professor Pascal (Chapters 2 and 5 below) note the presence in it of one of Lukács' key ideas, that of totality. Again, the idea that the process which constitutes the inner form of the novel is the journey of the problematic individual towards himself, towards self-knowledge, may be seen as an anticipation of Lukács' later view that all art is a means towards self-awareness.[1] Another point of resemblance between *The Theory of the Novel* and the views of the mature Lukács is perhaps still more important. Lukács came to hold that nature must be conceived historically, i.e. as something that develops,[2] and *The Theory of the Novel* takes a step towards this view by that historicizing of aesthetic categories which has already been noted – more specifically, by its view that the novel is an epic form that arises under specific historical conditions.[3] It is interesting, however, that Lukács' theory of the novel is not as rooted in what he would call concrete historical conditions as Hegel's was. Hegel relates the novel to social class: for him, the novel is the modern bourgeois epic. Lukács, on the other hand, says that the novel is the epic of the 'God-forsaken world', and seems to regard the decline of religious faith as occurring in a social vacuum.[4] This is far removed from Lukács' later views – and even, curiously, from some of his earlier ones; his book on the development of modern drama displays an awareness of the importance of social class in literature.[5]

The Theory of the Novel was written in a state of despair brought about by the war, of which Lukács, declared unfit for military service, was only a spectator. He regarded the prospect of an

[1] Op. cit., p. 79; cf. *Die Eigenart des Ästhetischen* (Neuwied, 1963), i. pp. 281, 529. (See also Parkinson, Chapter 4, Sec. 2 below.) The notion of the 'problematic hero' is developed by L. Goldmann, in *Pour une sociologie du roman* (Paris, 1964), pp. 16, 127, 239.

[2] E.g. *Die Eigenart des Ästhetischen*, i. p. 24.

[3] *Die Theorie des Romans*, p. 53.

[4] Lukács, op. cit., p. 87. Hegel, *Ästhetik*, ed. Bassenge (2nd ed., Frankfurt am Main, 1965), ii. 452.

[5] Lukács argues that bourgeois drama arises out of a conscious class-conflict; see *Zur Soziologie des modernen Dramas*, the introductory chapter of his book on the development of modern drama, in *Georg Lukács: Schriften zur Literatursoziologie* (abbreviated, *LS*), ed. P. Ludz, 2nd ed., Neuwied, 1963, p. 277.

ultimate German victory as a nightmare, but he was not much more enthusiastic about the Western powers.[1] News of the Russian revolution rescued him from his despair; it seemed to him that a road had been opened to humanity which led beyond war and beyond capitalism.[2] A year later, it seemed that it might be possible to repeat in Hungary what had happened in Russia. A coalition government under Count Károlyi came to power on 1 November 1918 initiating the 'bourgeois democratic' revolution in Hungary.[3] On 16 November the Communist Béla Kun and a few of his comrades returned to Hungary from Russia, and about a week later the Communist Party of Hungary was formed. Lukács joined the party in December,[4] and began a period of intense revolutionary activity. He was a member of the second or 'alternate' Central Committee, which took over the management of party affairs when Kun and some of his associates were arrested on 21 February 1919, and when the Károlyi government resigned on 21 March and the Hungarian Soviet Republic was proclaimed the next day, Lukács was given a post in the government.

Writing some fifty years after the event, Lukács remarks that he and his associates had a scanty knowledge of the Leninist theory of revolution.[5] This is clear enough from the fact that Kun agreed at the outset to a merger of the Communist Party of Hungary and the Social Democratic Party into a new Hungarian Socialist Party – a merger which brought an anxious telegram from Lenin, who was afraid that the new government would not be really communist.[6] In fact, communists often had to serve under Social Democrats; Lukács, for example, was Deputy People's Commissar for Public Education, the Commissar being the Social Democrat Zsigmond Kunfi. Lukács, however, defended the merger, arguing in the last section of his

[1] *Die Theorie des Romans*, p. 5.

[2] *Storia*, p. x.

[3] The description of events in Hungary in 1918–19 which follows is based largely on the detailed and scholarly account by R. L. Tökés, *Béla Kun and the Hungarian Soviet Republic*.

[4] 'Mein Weg zu Marx', *IP*, p. 327.

[5] *Storia*, p. x.

[6] Lenin, telegram of 23 March 1919: Collected Works, English translation, Vol. 29 (Moscow, 1965), p. 227.

Georg Lukács

Tactics and Ethics (1919) that with the existence of a dictatorship of the proletariat, there was no longer any justification for the existence of Communist and Social Democratic parties – the Social Democratic Party having been intended to help the proletariat to obtain power, and the Communist Party having been intended to help them to achieve class-consciousness.[1] Of Lukács' activity as a revolutionary, it is sufficient to say here that although he sometimes worked with the terrorist Szamuely – of whom he says dryly that he was 'little gifted from the theoretical point of view'[2] – he himself argued that organized class terror was unjustified, and protested in April and May 1919 against the taking of bourgeois hostages.[3]

The merger between communists and Social Democrats which Lukács had defended ceased to exist towards the end of June, when Kunfi and other moderates resigned, convinced that the revolution was in decline. Events proved them right; although a new government was formed, in which the communists had control, the Hungarian Soviet Republic came to an end on 1 August 1919. Béla Kun left for Austria at once; Lukács remained in Hungary for a time to organize underground work, but left for Vienna in September.[4]

Lukács has said of the Vienna of this period that it was in the full current of the international revolutionary movement. Not only did Hungarian communists take refuge there, but there were also communists from the Balkans and from Poland; Vienna also acted as a transit point for communists from Germany, France and Italy. So the review *Kommunismus,* of which Lukács was the chief editor and which appeared in 1920–1, became for a time the principal organ of what Lukács describes as 'extreme left tendencies'.[5] By 'extreme left' in this context is

[1] *IP*, pp. 38–9. [2] *Storia*, p. x.

[3] Tökés, p. 153. In June 1919 Kunfi attacked Lukács for terrorizing artists and literary men, but the attack is veiled and no details are given (cf. Tökés, p. 179). In the generally hostile account of Lukács as a commissar given by V. Zitta in *Georg Lukács' Marxism* (The Hague, 1964), pp. 92ff., one derives the impression of well-meaning *naïveté* on Lukács' part. It may not have been Lukács who was responsible for what turned out to be the politically disastrous prohibition of the consumption of alcoholic drinks, but it is significant that it should have been thought that he was (cf. Tökés, pp. 153–4).

[4] Tökés, p. 255. [5] *Storia*, pp. xi–xii; cf. *IP*, p. 786.

meant a messianic utopianism, which believed that the revolutionary socialist wave had not yet receded. *Kommunismus* proclaimed a total break with all institutions that derive from the bourgeois world; typical of this tendency was Lukács' essay 'On the Parliamentary Question', which opposed participation in bourgeois parliaments – a thesis which was severely criticized by Lenin in his *Left-Wing Communism: an Infantile Disorder*.[1] It was in this atmosphere that there appeared what is perhaps Lukács' most famous book, *History and Class-Consciousness*. The book was completed in 1922, and published in the next year. It consists of eight essays, most of them revised versions of previous work – two of them, 'What is Orthodox Marxism?' and 'The Change of Function of Historical Materialism' were written during the period of the Hungarian Soviet Republic. The only completely new works were the essays on organizational problems and on 'Reification and Proletarian Consciousness'.

A general introduction of the present type is not the place to attempt a critical estimate of *History and Class-Consciousness*; however, something must be said about the place of the work in Lukács' development. The Hegelian influence which was strong in *The Theory of the Novel* is also strong here, Lukács declaring that an adequate study of Marxist dialectic is impossible without a consideration of its relations to Hegel.[2] Lukács argues that Marx did not (as he put it in the preface to the second edition of *Capital*) merely 'coquet' with Hegelian terminology; instead, Lukács regards Marxism as a Hegelianism which, in Hegel's language, has been *aufgehoben*, sublated, retaining what is true in Hegel's thought, but remedying its contradictoriness and incompleteness.

Lukács takes the Hegelian concept of 'concrete totality', and says that this is the fundamental category of reality.[3] As he put it later, using Hegel's words (though at a time when he had

[1] See especially section 7 – 'Should we participate in bourgeois parliaments?': Collected Works, English translation, Vol. 31 (1966), pp. 56ff. Lukács' essay, 'Zur Frage des Parlamentarismus', may be found in *IP*, pp. 123ff.

[2] *Geschichte und Klassenbewusstsein* (abbreviated, *GK*), p. 8. References are to the first (1923) edition.

[3] *GK*, p. 28.

rejected *History and Class-Consciousness*), 'The true is the whole.'[1]
The concept of totality has continued to be an important one
for Lukács; not, however, the Hegelian concept with which it is
associated in *History and Class-Consciousness* – that of the
identical subject-object. Crudely, Hegel's philosophy may be
regarded as describing a movement from the abstract to the
concrete, from the sketchy and fragmentary to the concrete
whole. The same process may also be described as the self-
alienation of spirit, in nature and history, and the return of
spirit to itself in the knowledge that nature and history are
really its own products, and not objects which are alien to it.
The weakness of Hegel's doctrine, according to Lukács, lies in
what it asserts about this process of return. Hegel was unable
to find the identical subject-object, the spirit which is at one
with itself and no longer alienated, in history; for he thought
that history was unable to construct the living totality of the
system.[2] Consequently, he had to look beyond history, to the
realm of 'Absolute Spirit' – art, religion and philosophy.
Lukács argues that this is an error; the identical subject-object
is to be found in history in the shape of the proletariat, which
becomes an identical subject-object through its self-awareness.[3]

Lukács' reasoning seems to be as follows. From the assumption that the true is the whole, it follows that if any class is to
obtain self-knowledge, if it is to know what it is, then it must
have an accurate knowledge of society as a whole. Such knowledge might seem to be possible for any social class – the
bourgeoisie, for example, as well as the proletariat. Lukács goes
on to argue, however, that the bourgeoisie is not capable of
such knowledge; it is a minority interest, which has to pretend
that its rule is in the interest of all, and so it must gloss over the
true essence of bourgeois society. The proletariat, on the other
hand, is capable of seeing society from the centre, as a connected
whole.[4] All this might seem to imply that the proletariat has
grasped the totality of society, that it possesses absolute truth,
with the implication that Marxism (which is the philosophy of

---

[1] 'Reportage oder Gestaltung?' (1932), *LS*, p. 133. Cf. from the same year,
'Aus der Not eine Tugend', *LS*, p. 154.
[2] *GK*, p. 162.   [3] *GK*, pp. 14–15, 216.   [4] *GK*, pp. 78, 81.

the proletariat) is a complete and perfect system. This is far from being what Lukács means. When he speaks of the proletariat's self-awareness, of its class-consciousness, he is speaking of what he calls 'objective possibility'.[1] In his view, class-consciousness is not the sum, or even the average, of what the individual members of a class think, feel, etc.; it is what they would do in a situation of a certain type, if they were to grasp that situation properly. The situations in question are those whose essential character is determined by the position of men in the process of production; the rational, appropriate reaction to any such situation is class-consciousness. So to call the proletariat the identical subject-object is not to say that it has grasped the whole truth about society, but rather that it, and it alone, is capable of grasping that truth. One consequence of what Lukács has said must be noted. If his Marxism has as its basic concepts such notions as that of the identical subject-object and the self-awareness of a social class, it follows that it can have no place for a dialectic of nature, in the sense of a method which applies to purely physical objects and processes. Lukács expressly draws this conclusion; moreover, he claims that in doing so he is following the thought of Marx, and says that it was Engels, mistakenly following Hegel's example, who extended to the whole of nature a dialectical method which Marx applied only to historico-social reality.[2]

To complete this sketch of the nature of proletarian class-consciousness, something must be said about Lukács' concept of *praxis*. Lukács insists[3] that the relation between subject and object in the historical process is a dialectical one, by which he means that not only does the object act on the subject, but the subject also acts on the object. In other words, the subject does not merely reflect its object in a passive way, but it also acts on it, and this action is what Lukács calls *praxis*, practice. In the case of the proletariat, there exists what Lukács calls the unity of theory and practice, for the proletariat is the class whose self-assertion in the class struggle has as its condition an exact knowledge of the whole of society, with the result that theory is

[1] See especially *G K*, p. 62; also pp. 88, 92.
[2] *G K*, p. 17n.   [3] *G K*, p. 15.

geared immediately and adequately to the process of social revolution.[1] Under these conditions, theory has a revolutionary function; the materialistic dialectic, as Lukács says in the opening pages of *History and Class-Consciousness*, is a revolutionary dialectic.[2]

In effect, Lukács is here developing a point mentioned earlier. He has said that the proletariat (unlike the bourgeoisie) *can* grasp its own essence; now he is saying that it *must* do so, if it is to assert itself in the class struggle. This does not mean that Lukács thinks of Marxist theory as something which is developed in isolation from the class struggle, and is brought to the proletariat as a complete whole. On the contrary, he stresses the fact that the proletariat can reach self-consciousness only as a result of active struggle.[3] By this he seems to mean that when one speaks of 'theory' in the context of the class-consciousness of the proletariat one should not have in mind something fixed and rigid; theory is something which is constantly modified in the course of social history, modified to fit the actions of human beings. This means for Lukács that the predictions of Marxism are not like the predictions of the natural sciences, where what is predicted is independent of human decisions. He asserts, for example, that the success of world revolution is not scientifically guaranteed.[4] The certainty of its success is guaranteed only methodologically: namely, by action, by the success of the revolution itself. One may take him to mean by this that the statement, 'There will be a world revolution' is not like the statement 'The sun will rise tomorrow'; it is more like the statement 'I will go for a walk tomorrow'.

It will be noticed that nothing has so far been said about the content of that theory which is said to be united with practice; there has been talk of a concrete totality, but no detailed description of its nature. This is quite deliberate on Lukács' part. In his *Ludwig Feuerbach*, Engels had distinguished between

[1] Ibid., cf. *GK*, p. 34: the actions of the proletariat have the knowledge of the whole of society as an unavoidable presupposition. See also *GK*, p. 51; *praxis* is by its nature a penetration, a transformation of reality; but reality can be grasped and penetrated only as a totality, and only a subject which is itself a totality can do this.

[2] *GK*, pp. 14–15.   [3] *GK*, p. 55.   [4] Ibid.

method and system in Hegel, the method being valuable and the system far less valuable.[1] In much the same way, Lukács insists that Marxism – genuine Marxism, 'orthodox' Marxism – is a method, not a set of truths. Even if modern research were to disprove every proposition asserted by Marx (not that Lukács grants that it does, or will) Marxism would still remain as a method, the method of the revolutionary proletariat. It may be added that Lukács still thinks that this definition of orthodox Marxism is sound, and that it has relevance today.[2]

One of the categories of Marxist heresy is 'revisionism'; the term is imprecise, but broadly it refers to doctrines which claim to be faithful to the spirit of Marx, whilst saying the modern knowledge demands radical alterations in the content of Marxism. If the term is defined in this way, then *History and Class-Consciousness* comes very close to revisionism, and indeed it was denounced as a revisionist work at the fifth congress of the Third International (the Comintern) in June and July of 1924. The charge was brought by Zinoviev, who had been head of the Third International since its foundation in 1919 and who, with Stalin and Kamenev, formed the 'troika' which controlled the Soviet Union immediately after the death of Lenin.[3] Lesser figures joined in the attack; one of these was László Rudas, a founder member of the Hungarian Communist Party,[4] and another was the philosopher A.M. Deborin, who was to enjoy a short spell of power in Soviet philosophy a few years later.[5] Deborin argued that Lukács' attempt to interpret Marx by rejecting Engels had led him into philosophical idealism; he had

[1] Engels, *Ludwig Feuerbach*, Section I; Marx and Engels, *Selected Works* (London, 1950), Vol. ii, p. 329. Cf. Lukács, *Der junge Hegel* (Neuwied, 1968), p. 492.

[2] *Storia*, p. xxvii. The definition is given in *GK*, p. 13.

[3] Excerpts from Zinoviev's speech are given in German translation in *IP*, pp. 719 ff.

[4] Rudas was a member of the original Central Committee of the Hungarian Communist Party (Tökés, pp. 95–6). Like Lukács, he had been a member of the Socialist Students' Club organized by Szabó in 1902 (Tökés, p. 20n.) For Rudas' attack, cf. *IP*, p. 712, n.3.

[5] See G. Wetter, *Dialectical Materialism* (London, 1958), pp. 130 ff., and R. Ahlberg, 'The forgotten philosopher: Abram Deborin' in *Revisionism*, ed. by L. Labedz (London, 1962), pp. 126 ff.

rejected the idea of a dialectic of nature, and even where historico-social reality was concerned he was not really a materialist, since he made of consciousness a kind of substance.[1]

It has been suggested that these objections to *History and Class-Consciousness* are only on the surface, and that they conceal the real nature of the opposition to the work. Lukács' offence, George Lichtheim argues,[2] was that in the course of the book he blurted out the truth about the Communist Party – namely, that it was not really the most advanced section of the proletariat, but was a revolutionary élite of classless intellectuals who had imposed themselves upon an immature working class, on the grounds that they alone possessed the truth. Whether this is what Zinoviev really thought about Lukács' book is no longer ascertainable, but it is possible to attempt to answer the question whether this is what Lukács meant to say. A comparison with Rousseau is helpful here. Lukács' views on the Communist Party bear some resemblance to Rousseau's ideas about the general will; and just as it was possible for some of those ideas to be given a twist which led to Jacobinism, without Rousseau having intended any such doctrine,[3] in the same way some of Lukács' ideas about the party could be given an élitist interpretation, without his having intended it. For Lukács, the Communist Party is the conscious collective will (*Gesamtwille*) to real freedom.[4] The organizational separation of party from proletariat does not mean that the party wants to fight instead of the class, for the interests of the class (as the Blanquists did, for example). The separation is necessary so that the proletariat can see immediately its own class-consciousness, as an historical character (*Gestalt*). The purpose of the party is to assist and accelerate the development of class-consciousness in the proletariat; for the revolutionary process is equivalent to the process of the development of proletarian

[1] *IP*, p. 712n., and G. Planty-Bonjour, *Les Catégories du Matérialisme Dialectique* (Dordrecht, 1965), pp. 1–2.

[2] George Lichtheim, 'The Transmutations of a Doctrine', *Problems of Communism*, XV/4 (1966), p. 23.

[3] J. L. Talmon has discussed the relations between Rousseau and the Jacobins in *The Origins of Totalitarian Democracy* (London, 1952).

[4] *GK*, p. 318.

class-consciousness. But just as Rousseau had to distinguish between the 'general will' and the 'will of all', so Lukács notes that the party sometimes has to take up a position opposed to that of the masses, to show them the right way through the negation of their present will. It must not be supposed, however, that Lukács views the party as a kind of priestly caste, bringing wisdom to the proletariat, who have merely to receive passively what they are given; on the contrary, he insists that the party is in living interaction with the revolutionary class.[1] No doubt there is a possibility of élitism in all this, but it does not seem that this is what Lukács intended.

Initially, Lukács made no reply to the criticisms brought against *History and Class-Consciousness*, and occasional references to the work in essays published in 1925 and 1926 suggest that he did not immediately abandon, or at any rate wholly abandon, its doctrines.[2] However, he repudiated the work in 1933, and for many years afterwards expressed great hostility to it.[3] He has recently allowed the book to appear as part of Volume II of his collected works, and has contributed a long preface in which he makes it clear that his recantation was made for tactical reasons, and that although he still does not defend the whole book, he thinks that not all of it is mistaken. It will be convenient to discuss Lukács' recantation later, since this belongs to the politics of the early thirties, and to consider here his more recent, and franker, criticisms of his work.

It has already been mentioned that the idea of Marxism as a method, and of the importance of the concept of totality, are notions that Lukács still accepts. He also thinks it a merit of the

[1] Cf. *GK*, pp. 324, 328–9, 331. Similar views about the party can be found in Lukács' short book on Lenin, first published in 1924: Neuwied, 1967, pp. 25, 35. In his essay 'Der Begriff der "demokratischen Diktatur"' (Benseler, pp. 60 ff.; cf. *IP*, pp. xlvff.) P. Ludz also argues against an élitist interpretation of Lukács, producing evidence from works other than *Geschichte und Klassenbewusstsein*.

[2] See 'Die neue Ausgabe von Lassalle's Briefen' (1925), *IP*, p. 224, and 'Moses Hess und die Probleme der idealistischen Dialektik' (1926), *IP*, pp. 248, 283.

[3] See, e.g. his protests when Merleau-Ponty discussed the work in *Les Aventures de la Dialectique* (Paris, 1955); the book, said Lukács, had been deservedly forgotten. Cf. M. Watnick, 'Georg Lukács: An Intellectual Biography', Part II, *Soviet Survey*, 1958, No. 24, p. 57.

book that it drew attention to the problem of alienation (or more exactly, to the closely related phenomenon of reification) and, for the first time since Marx, treated this as the central point of the critique of capitalism.[1] Lukács notes (and this is certainly true) that it was through its discussion of alienation that the book exercised a profound influence on young intellectuals; however, he now regards this discussion as inadequate. Following Marx's account of 'The Fetishism of Commodities' in Volume I of *Capital*, Lukács had argued that bourgeois economic thought, when considering commodities, has failed to see that it is dealing with a social relation between human beings, and has supposed instead that it is dealing with a relation between things.[2] More generally, he argued that bourgeois thinkers operate with the notion of facts instead of with the notion of processes – another expression of reified thought. The proletariat, however, is able to understand reified forms in their true nature – namely, as processes between men.[3] So much, Lukács would probably still find unobjectionable; what he objects to is the fact that his discussion in *History and Class-Consciousness* took as its basis the identical subject-object, arguing that proletarian consciousness overcomes reification by becoming the consciousness of the process of evolution itself, and so appearing as the identical subject-object of history.[4] The reference to the proletariat, Lukács says, might seem (in Engels' phrase) to 'put Hegel back on his feet'; but he now doubts whether mere self-knowledge can end alienation, and thinks that what he offered in 1923 was 'a Hegelianism more Hegelian than Hegel.'[5] Lukács also finds his doctrine too Hegelian in that, like Hegel, he identified reification (*Verdinglichung*) with objectivity (*Gegenständlichkeit*); that is, he confused the subject-object relation as such with that type of

[1] *Storia*, pp. xxiii, xxvi.

[2] *GK*, p. 97. Cf. Marx, *Capital*, Vol. I; Marx-Engels, *Werke*, Dietz, Berlin, Vol. 23, p. 86; trans. by E. and C. Paul, Everyman's Library, London (1930), Vol.. i, pp. 43 ff.

[3] *GK*, pp. 201, 215.   [4] *GK*, p. 216; *Storia*, p. xxiii.

[5] *Storia*, p. xxiv. The quotation from Engels, to the effect that in materialist dialectic the Hegelian dialectic is '*wieder auf die Füsse gestellt*', is from *Ludwig Feuerbach*, Section IV.

thinking which, for example, turns a social relation into an object.[1] Lukács now holds that objectivation is unavoidable in human life – labour itself is an objectivation; it is only when social forms mutilate the essence of man that there arises the social relation of alienation. This duality, he asserts, is not recognized in *History and Class-Consciousness*.[2]

Lukács also thinks that the concept of revolutionary *praxis* in the book is exaggerated, corresponding to his messianic utopianism of the period.[3] Although justified in turning against the exaltation of mere contemplation, he failed to see that real *praxis* has labour as its original form and as its model – without this, the exaltation of *praxis* turns into an exaltation of idealistic contemplation. Lukács adds that his failure to see that labour is the source of *praxis* led him to deny, or at any rate to fail to grasp adequately, the fact that knowledge is a kind of reflection.[4] He failed to see that the most primitive labour presupposes a correct reflection of the reality in question, and that *praxis* can be a criterion of theory only because at its base there is a correct reflection of reality. Finally, Lukács thinks that he was wrong in separating Marx from Engels, and in trying to treat Marxism purely as a theory of society.[5]

Lukács regards the publication of *History and Class-Consciousness* as marking the end of a period of his development which began with the last years of the war. The next period, on Lukács' own estimation, covers the years 1923–8.[6] His publications during this period were comparatively few, and were largely

[1] *Storia*, p. xxv. Cf. Lukács' comments on *Geschichte und Klassenbewusstsein* (September 1962) in I. Fetscher, *Der Marxismus: seine Geschichte in Dokumenten* (2nd ed., Munich, 1967), p. 144.

[2] *Storia*, pp. xxv–xxvi. In *Der junge Hegel* (Neuwied, 1968, pp. 659ff.). Lukács distinguishes three kinds of alienation in Hegel: (1) the subject-object relation which is connected with all labour, with all economic and social activity, (2) the specifically capitalist form of alienation, which Marx was to call 'fetishism', (3) 'thinghood' (*Dingheit*), objectivity. It could be said, then, that in *Geschichte und Klassenbewusstsein* Lukács confused (1) with (2).

[3] *Storia*, p. xviii.

[4] *Storia*, p. xxvi. Cf. Fetscher, loc. cit.

[5] *Storia*, p. xvi.

[6] *Storia*, pp. xvi, xxxiv.

pièces d'occasion – they include an essay on Lenin (1924), written at the request of an editor,[1] reviews of a work by Bukharin (1925) and of editions of Lassalle (1925) and of Moses Hess (1926). The sparseness of his literary productions is due to the fact that he was much occupied with practical politics at this time. In itself, his political activity was unimportant – little more than a footnote to the history of world communism during these years. It deserves to be mentioned, however, because Lukács states that it influenced his thought, causing him to abandon his previous 'messianic utopianism'. The Third International, at its Congress in 1924, interpreted the condition of the capitalist world as one of 'relative stabilization'; the prospects of world revolution had dimmed, and the Party struggle in the USSR after Lenin's death in 1924 was mainly concerned with the issue of 'socialism in one country'. In this dispute, Lukács found himself on Stalin's side, on the side of those who affirmed the possibility of socialism in one country.[2] More important for Lukács, however, was a struggle inside the Hungarian Communist Party. The exiled Hungarian Communists had divided into two factions. One of these was the group led by Béla Kun, who had returned to Russia in 1920 and had become a high official in the Comintern. According to Lukács, Kun and his followers were characterized by the bureaucratism that Zinoviev had introduced into the Third International.[3] Lukács' support was given to the opposing group, led by Jenö Landler, a former trade-union leader and member of Kun's government in 1919. He is described by Lukács[4] as a man of notable intelligence; primarily a practical man, but with a great sensibility for theoretical problems. Landler died in 1928; in the same year, Lukács began to prepare the draft of the political theses for a Hungarian Party Congress to be held in 1929. His theses – the so-called 'Blum Theses', named after Lukács' pseudonym of the period – followed Landler's line of thought.

The argument of the Blum Theses was that conditions in

---

[1] *Storia*, p. xxxv.

[2] *Storia*, p. xxix.

[3] *Storia*, pp. xii–xiv. Cf. 'Noch einmal Illusionspolitik' (1922), *IP*, p. 165.

[4] *Storia*, p. xv.

Hungary were such as to make a direct transition to a Soviet Republic impossible, and that the Party must have as its immediate aim, not a dictatorship of the proletariat, but a democratic dictatorship of workers and peasants. Lukács has remarked[1] that it is hard to realize at the present moment how paradoxical this sounded in 1928. The Kun group denounced the theses as opportunist, and the support of Lukács' faction was only tepid. Learning that Kun was proposing to have him expelled from the Party as a 'liquidator', Lukács underwent in 1929 the 'self-criticism' demanded in an open letter of the Comintern Executive Committee to the members of the Hungarian Party.[2] He still believed in the rightness of his views, but the fate of Karl Korsch (criticized by Zinoviev in 1924, and expelled from the German Communist Party in 1926) had convinced him that, outside the Party, it was impossible to take an active part in the coming struggle with Fascism.

The defeat of the Blum Theses had a profound effect on Lukács. If his ideas were clearly right (and he was convinced that they were) and yet he had been unable to secure their acceptance, this meant that his capacity for practical politics was doubtful. He therefore decided to retire from a political career, and to concentrate on theoretical work. Lukács says that he has never regretted this decision, and has never in essence swerved from it – his assumption of a ministerial post in 1956 was intended to last only for a short time.[3]

The period between 1923 and the discussion of the Blum Theses was a transitional one in Lukcás' intellectual development; he was, as he puts it, trying to throw light on the way ahead, looking for a new orientation.[4] A decisive change occurred in 1930, when Lukács visited Moscow and worked at the Marx-Engels Institute. This enabled him to read, before publication, the text of Marx's Economic and Philosophical Manuscripts of 1844. Lukács says that it was the reading of this text which removed,

[1] *Storia*, pp. xxxii–iii. Excerpts from the 'Blum Theses' are given in *IP*, pp. 290 ff. Cf. *IP*, pp. 727 ff., 763 ff.

[2] *IP*, pp. 727 ff.

[3] *Storia*, p. xxxiv.

[4] *Storia*, p. xxxvi.

once and for all, the idealistic prejudices of *History and Class-Consciousness*. He adds that in the Blum Theses he had already eliminated the politico-social bases of his idealism, by which he presumably means that the more concrete analyses of economic and social conditions that he had undertaken had laid the foundations of a correct philosophical position; but it was the reading of the 1844 Manuscripts which destroyed the theoretical basis of *History and Class-Consciousness*.[1] He now found himself in that mood of enthusiasm and ferment which is appropriate to a fresh start, and large-scale projects were begun, or at any rate conceived, at about this time. He began an analysis of the connections between economics and dialectics, the first product of which was his book on the young Hegel, and which has since led to his essay on the ontology of social being.[2] The book on Hegel, completed in October 1938, was begun in Moscow and continued in Berlin (1931–3). In this book, Lukács argued that Plekhanov and others had overstressed the role of Feuerbach as a mediator between Marx and Hegel, and that there is in fact a direct link between the two.[3] Along with all this, Lukács wanted to construct a Marxist aesthetics. He had conceived the plan of writing an aesthetics long before, in the winter of 1911–12, and he worked on the subject at Heidelberg in the years 1912–14, encouraged by Ernst Bloch, Emil Lask and Max Weber. The work, which followed the lines of philosophical idealism, was abandoned by Lukács at the beginning of the war in favour of *The Theory of the Novel*; some idea of what it would have been like can be derived from an article, 'The Subject-Object Relation in Aesthetics', published in *Logos* for 1917–18. Now, in 1930, the idea of an aesthetics emerged again. When in Moscow in that year, Lukács made the acquaintance of Mikhail Lifschitz, who was interested in similar problems and who was to collect and edit the writings of Marx and Engels that bear on literature and art. Lifschitz was to become Lukács' lifelong friend, and together they discussed problems of Marxism and

[1] *Storia*, p. xl. Cf. Fetscher, op. cit., p. 145.

[2] *Storia*, pp. xxxix, xli.

[3] *Storia*, pp. xxii, xxxix. The date of completion of the book is given in *Storia*, p. xxxix, as 1937, but in the preface to *Der junge Hegel* (1st ed., Zürich, 1948, p. 26; 3rd ed., Neuwied, 1968, p. 9) as 1938.

art.[1] The writing of Lukács' systematic aesthetics was delayed for many years, but whilst in Berlin he wrote a number of articles for *Die Linkskurve*, the journal of the 'League of proletarian-revolutionary writers', in which he concerned himself with philosophical problems of mimesis and reflection in the arts.

When the Nazis came to power, Lukács had to leave Germany, and in 1933 he returned to the Soviet Union, where he was to stay until 1944. In 1933 there appeared in *Internationale Literatur,* a German language journal published in Moscow, Lukács' autobiographical sketch 'My Road to Marx', in which he criticized *History and Class-Consciousness* for containing idealist survivals and for being tainted with 'ultra-left subjectivist activism'.[2] Next year, Lukács criticized the book still more harshly and at greater length, saying that it was the summation of his previous syndicalist and idealist tendencies, and that it was not only theoretically false but also practically dangerous, since idealism was equivalent to Fascism.[3] This act of self-criticism has been described as 'the *mea culpa* of a man labouring under a sense of guilt for his own intellectual past', and has been explained as due to the shock produced by Hitler's rise to power.[4] However, in the recent preface to *History and Class-Consciousness,* Lukács gives quite a different account of his self-criticism. According to him, it was a calculated act, intended to make possible the spreading of his views on literature, which were not those of the official, Stalinist kind. Open opposition to the official views was impossible, but it was possible to wage a kind of guerrilla warfare against them, and Lukács claims that this is what he did between 1933 and 1939 in the journal *Literaturnyi Kritik.*[5] If he was to do this successfully, he must

[1] *Storia,* p. xli. On Lifschitz (to whom *Der junge Hegel* is dedicated), see *Die Eigenart des Ästhetischen,* i. p. 17. Lukács' early ideas for a treatise on aesthetics are described by him in *Die Eigenart des Ästhetischen,* i. p. 31.

[2] *IP,* p. 327. Lukács had already criticized the work briefly in 'Aus der Not eine Tugend', published in 1932 (*LS,* p. 148, n.3).

[3] See 'The Significance of *Materialism and Empirio-Criticism* for the Bolshevisation of Communist Parties', *Pod Znamenem Marksizma,* IV (1934), pp. 143 ff. Excerpts are given in Watnick, op. cit., Part II, p. 54.

[4] Watnick, op. cit., p. 55.

[5] *Storia,* p. xlii. On Lukács' 'guerrilla warfare' on behalf of his ideas, cf. '*Postscriptum 1957 zu: Mein Weg zu Marx*', *IP,* p. 648.

Georg Lukács

not be open to counter-attacks directed against *History and Class-Consciousness*, and so it was necessary for him to disown the work. It was easy for him to do this, since he considered the work to be intrinsically defective.

Such is the account that Lukács gave recently; but in fact his attitude seems to have been more complex than this. In a post-script (1957) to 'My Road to Marx' he makes it clear that, in paying lip-service to Stalinist orthodoxy before and during the Second World War, he felt that he was helping the fight against Fascism.[1] Not only was open opposition during this period impossible, but even if it had been possible it would have been wrong, since it would have given moral support to the enemy. Lukács illustrates this by a reference to his book on the young Hegel, which he had completed in 1938. During the war, it was asserted that Hegel was an ideologist of feudal reaction against the French revolution.[2] Lukács regarded this as a piece of nonsense (*Dummheit*), but as it was the official view it meant that his own book could not be published. However, he decided that it was more important to win the war than to fight for the correct interpretation of Hegel. In due course, the false view of Hegel was abandoned, and Lukács was able to publish his book.[3]

This is perhaps the place to consider the much discussed question of Lukács' attitude to Stalin. Lukács has been called a 'Stalinist' literary critic; his case has been described as one of 'genuine surrender to Stalinism'.[4] If the term 'Stalinism' is used here to mean a total adherence to all that Stalin said and did, then it is clear from what has already been said that Lukács is not a Stalinist. This is confirmed by many other passages from his writings, which show that he believes that Stalin made great

[1] *IP*, p. 648.
[2] Cf. I. Fetscher, '*Das Verhältnis des Marxismus zu Hegel*', *Marxismusstudien*, Series 3 (1960), pp. 122 ff.
[3] He says (*IP*, p. 648), 'without altering a line', but this cannot be correct, since he says at the beginning of the book that he has subjected the text to a thorough revision (*Der junge Hegel*, 1st ed., Zürich, 1948, p. 26; 3rd ed., Neuwied, 1968, p. 9). Presumably he means that he made no substantial changes.
[4] I. Deutscher, 'Georg Lukács and "Critical Realism"', *The Listener*, November 3rd, 1966, p. 659.

22

and sometimes cruel mistakes. For example, Lukács agrees with Khrushchev's view that the great trials of the thirties not only ended in unjust verdicts, but were also politically superfluous.[1] He notes Stalin's failures in international politics – for example, the disastrous effects of his assertion, at the end of the twenties, that the Social Democrats were the twin brothers of the Fascists, and of his assertion at the beginning of the Second World War that the war against Hitler was an imperialist war.[2] He notes, too, the damage done by Stalin's intervention in cultural matters. His attempt to make of the writer a mere screw in the machinery was harmful to literature, and his assumption that the answers to all problems were to be found in the Marxist classics, and above all in the writings of Stalin, made of Marxism a mere 'ideology' – a pseudo-theoretical justification of purely tactical measures.[3] Again, Stalin's methods had the overall effect of producing an atmosphere of constant mutual distrust. Lukács knows about this at first hand, since he spent some months of 1941 in prison, being released only after German and Austrian intellectuals had intervened repeatedly on his behalf.[4]

At the same time, Lukács does not believe that Stalin was wholly villainous. Stalin, in Lukács' view, had the great merit of having defended the theory of 'socialism in one country'.[5] Putting this theory into practice – creating socialism in one country, and that country an economically backward one, which also had to be defended against foreign intervention – had important social consequences. Heavy burdens were placed on the whole population, and these burdens could not be borne without some damage to proletarian democracy. Lukács regards it as the task of history to show when, and how far, Stalin's undemocratic methods went beyond the degree that circumstances demanded.[6] This evaluation of Stalin will not

[1] *Die Eigenart des Ästhetischen*, ii, p. 864.

[2] *IP*, pp. 608, 652, 666, 690, 764.

[3] Cf. *IP*, pp. 654, 667, 669. Discussing Stalin's effect on communist thought, Lukács cites a witticism of the Stalinist period: 'What is an idea? An idea is the link between quotations' (*IP*, p. 654).

[4] *IP*, p. 672; I. Mészáros, in Benseler, p. 197.

[5] *IP*, pp. 653, 661.

[6] *Die Eigenart des Ästhetischen*, ii, p. 864.

satisfy everyone. Trotskyists as well as anti-communists will find Lukács condemnation of Stalin too mild; on the other hand, the 'little Stalins' who existed in Stalin's day,[1] and who still exist, will find his censure too severe. But whatever the justice of Lukács' verdict, it is beyond doubt a sober and honest one.

To return to Lukács' stay in the Soviet Union between 1933 and 1944: during this period he worked in the Philosophical Institute of the Academy of Sciences in Moscow, and was also engaged in editorial work – he was for a time on the editorial boards of *Internationale Literatur* and of the Hungarian language journal *New Voice*. The war brought with it a new activity, in the shape of the delivery of lectures to high-ranking captured German officers.[2] Few books by Lukács appeared between 1933 and 1944, but his pen was far from idle. Besides working at his book on Hegel, he published many articles which formed the basis of books that appeared after the war: *Goethe and his Age* (1947), *Essays on Realism* (1948), *The Turning-Point of Destiny* (1948), *Russian Realism in World Literature* (1949), *German Realists of the Nineteenth Century* (1951), *Balzac and French Realism* (1952), *The Historical Novel* (1955) – all these have their origin in articles published whilst Lukács was in the Soviet Union. These books are all concerned with literary criticism; taken together, they constitute a large proportion of Lukács' work in this field. As Lukács' literary criticism is discussed in detail in the later chapters of this book, little need be said here about these essays. It has already been mentioned that Lukács claims that he carried on a guerrilla war against the official Soviet view of literature. This may be taken to refer to his opposition to the literary theory, referred to by him as 'naturalism', that lay behind the flatter products of 'Socialist realism'. Lukács' aim was to defend what he regarded as true realism, which goes beyond the limits of everyday reality and yet is always true in its social content.[3] This also led him to

[1] *IP*, pp. 659, 689.

[2] Cf. '*Aristokratische and demokratische Weltanschauung*', *IP*, p. 405.

[3] *Balzac und der französische Realismus*, *LS*, p. 345; *Studies in European Realism* (New York, 1964), p. 43.

attack the *avant-garde* artistic trends of the time, such as expressionism and surrealism, and involved him in a controversy with a fellow-Marxist philosopher and old friend, Ernst Bloch.[1] In his attack on the *avant-garde*, Lukács spared no one; he was as severe on communist writers such as Ehrenburg and Brecht as he was on James Joyce.[2] We shall return later to the question of Lukács' attitude to modern, or modernist, art.

With the end of the European war in 1944, Lukács returned to Hungary; he had been away from his native country (apart from a brief and illegal stay in 1929) for some twenty-five years. So began a new phase in his life; it was a phase in which Stalin and (after his death) the memory of Stalin was still dominant in the western communist world, and it lasted until February 1956. Lukács was soon occupying important posts in Hungary, chiefly in the cultural field; he became a member of the Praesidium of the Hungarian Academy, and Professor of Aesthetics and of the Philosophy of Culture at the University of Budapest. He did not hold any important post in the Party – it may be assumed, on the basis of what has been seen already, that he did not seek one – but he became a member of the Hungarian National Assembly.

Intellectually, the period 1944–56 brought no great changes. As already mentioned, some of the time was occupied with the publication of books, much of the material for which had already appeared in articles written whilst Lukács was in the Soviet Union. Lukács also produced an answer to the newly fashionable philosophy of existentialism in his *Existentialism or Marxism?*, published in Hungarian in 1947 and in a French translation in 1948. He also published his *Sketch of a History of Modern German Literature*, which was based on articles written in 1945, and which appeared in book form in Hungarian in

[1] Cf. 'Es geht um den Realismus' (1938), in *Essays über Realismus* (Berlin, 1948), pp. 128 ff.

[2] On Joyce, see, e.g. *Essays über Realismus*, p.136; on Ehrenburg, see 'Reportage oder Gestaltung?' (1932), *LS*, p. 133. Lukács' views on Brecht are discussed by L. Illés, 'Die Freiheit der künstlerischen Richtungen und das Zeitgemässe', in *Littérature et Réalité*, ed. by B. Köpeczi and P. Juhász (Budapest, 1966), pp. 83 ff.

1946 and in German in 1953; also the first version of his book on Thomas Mann, which appeared in Hungarian in 1948 and in German in 1949. Perhaps the major new work of the period is *The Destruction of Reason,* a long essay on the history of German philosophy first published in 1954, and designed to show 'Germany's way to Hitler in the region of philosophy'.[1] The book has been violently criticized, even by some who are on the whole sympathetic to Lukács; it has been called, for example, a 'regrettable' work, 'hommage "philosophique" an génie de Staline'.[2] Lukács, however, has never taken back anything that it contains. Here it can only be said that (as Professor Hodges suggests, Chapter 3 below) an undeniably journalistic last chapter may have diverted attention from the real merits of the rest of the work.

The work written during this period that produced the sharpest reaction in communist circles was a book, *Literature and Democracy,* published in Hungarian in 1947.[3] To put this reaction in the proper context, it is necessary first to say something about the Hungarian politics of the time. The communists who returned to Hungary in the wake of the victorious Soviet armies were led by Mátyás Rákosi,[4] a former member of Kun's government (Kun himself had perished in a Stalinist purge). Gradually, with the aid of Soviet occupation forces, they obtained control of the country. Opposition parties were either dissolved or merged with the Communist Party, and by May 1949 the communists' power was such that they were able to hold elections on a single-list basis. On 20 August a constitution modelled on that of the USSR came into force.[5]

Communist control of Hungary was accompanied by a struggle for power within the Party between Rákosi and Rajk. László Rajk, formerly Minister of the Interior, and then

[1] *Die Zerstörung der Vernunft* (Neuwied, 1962), p. 10.

[2] K. Axelos, preface to the French translation of *Geschichte und Klassenbewusstsein* (Paris, 1960), p. 3.

[3] There is no complete translation of this work, but excerpts have been translated in *IP*, pp. 376ff., 434ff.

[4] Cf. F. A. Váli, *Rift and Revolt in Hungary* (Cambridge, Mass., and London, 1961), p. 33. The account of Hungarian politics which follows owes much to Dr Váli's work.

[5] Váli, pp. 31–2, 40.

Minister of Foreign Affairs, was arrested on 8 June 1949, and after a show trial was sentenced to death on 24 September.[1] At roughly the same time, Rákosi and his followers asserted themselves in the cultural field. László Rudas, who had attacked *History and Class-Consciousness* in 1924, published an attack on *Literature and Democracy* in a review in July 1949. The real reasons for the attack are not clear, but exception may have been taken to Lukács' remarks about 'sectarian bureaucrats'.[2] Lukács produced a somewhat tepid self-criticism in the next issue of the review, and this called forth attacks in the Party newspaper by József Révai,[3] Minister of Culture and chief editor of the paper, and later by his deputy Márton Horváth.[4] Fresh attacks in 1951 by a new Minister of Culture, József Darvas, led to Lukács' withdrawal from public life. Lukács has since made it clear that his self-criticism was a purely tactical move.[5] He thinks that his book was defective in many ways, but that it was a step in the right direction, towards the realization of his aims at the time – namely, making the transition to Socialism in a new, gradual way, founded on persuasion. The controversy which it aroused showed him the hopelessness of a fruitful discussion with 'the ideologists of dogmatism', and Lukács now regards his withdrawal from public life and his exclusive concentration on theoretical work as a gain.

The period 1944–56 ended quietly for Lukács. He may have benefited from the 'thaw' in the communist world which followed Stalin's death in March 1953; whatever the reason may have been, his former pupil József Szigéti paid tribute to him in the Party newspaper on the occasion of his seventieth

[1] Váli, pp. 60ff.

[2] *IP*, p. 402; cf. p. 396.

[3] Révai had played a minor role in the Hungarian Soviet Republic, and later became Kun's secretary in the Comintern (Tökés, op. cit., p. 257).

[4] Révai's attack can be found in a German translation in *Georg Lukács und der Revisionismus* (Berlin, 1960), pp. 9ff.; an English version has been published as *Lukács and Socialist Realism* (Fore Publications, London, 1950). For Horváth's article, see *IP*, pp. 753ff., and *Communist Review*, May 1950. The attacks on Lukács are described by T. Aczél and T. Méray, *The Revolt of the Mind* (London, 1960), pp. 72ff.

[5] 'Postscriptum 1957 zu: Mein Weg zu Marx', *IP*, p. 651; cf. the preface to Lukács' *Werke*, Vol. V (1964), p. 5.

birthday in 1955, the Aufbau-Verlag in East Berlin brought out a *Festschrift* in his honour, and he was made a corresponding member of the German Academy of Sciences.

In February 1956 Khrushchev delivered his now famous attack on Stalin at the Twentieth Congress of the Communist Party of the Soviet Union. Lukács has spoken of the shock created by this Congress,[1] which he clearly regards as a turning point in the history of modern communism. It did not, however, produce any immediately dramatic results in Hungary; although lip-service was paid to the 'principle of collective leadership' announced at the Twentieth Congress, the rule of Rákosi went on as before.[2] One apparently insignificant concession to liberal ideas was made. On 17 March 1956, the Party approved the formation of a debating club, the 'Petöfi Circle', within the framework of the Federation of Working Youth. Perhaps the intention was to provide a safety-valve, to reduce dangerous pressure in Hungary; if so, the plan was a disastrous failure, for the Petöfi Circle provided a platform for attacks on the régime, and it does not seem an exaggeration to say, with a historian of the events of 1956,[3] that the intellectual prelude to the Hungarian revolution took place there.

Lukács spoke in a philosophical debate organized by the Petöfi Circle on 15 June,[4] at which he said that the dogmatism of the Stalin era had done severe damage to Marxism, which was now viewed with contempt by many of the intelligentsia. In a lecture given on 28 June,[5] 'The Struggle between Progress and Reaction in Contemporary Culture', he again attacked dogmatism, and spoke on behalf of 'peaceful co-existence', during which communists should use only ideological means to further the development of socialism in each capitalist state. The Petöfi Circle was suspended by the Party at the end of June, but in mid-July Rákosi himself had to resign, being succeeded as First Secretary of the Party by Ernö Gerö. In an atmosphere of increased intellectual freedom, Lukács gave an interview to

---

[1] Preface to *The Meaning of Contemporary Realism* (London, 1963), p. 7.
[2] Váli, p. 216.   [3] Váli, p. 220.
[4] Cf. *IP*, pp. 593 ff.   [5] *IP*, pp. 603 ff.

the Party newspaper[1] (published on 14 October 1956) in which he said that administrative interference with the expression of ideas must cease, and that the whole question of Party control must be re-examined, to find a middle way between its total abolition on the one hand, and sectarianism on the other.

The Hungarian revolution began nine days later, on 23 October. It is impossible to chart here the complex course of this revolution, which was ended on 4 November by Soviet intervention. It must be sufficient to say that Lukács was made a member of the Central Committee of the Party on 24 October, and Minister of Culture in Imre Nagy's Patriotic Government on 27 October. He was also chosen as a member of a preparatory committee whose task was to direct and organize the 'new' Hungarian Communist Party, announced on 1 November by János Kádár, who had succeeded Gerö as First Secretary on 25 October. Lukács soon lost his post in the Government, not being included in a new cabinet formed by Nagy on 3 November; this may have been because of the reservations that he is reported to have had about Hungary's withdrawal from the Warsaw Treaty on 1 November.[2]

After the suppression of the revolution, Lukács was deported to Rumania, but was allowed to return to Budapest in April 1957. He did not perform any act of self-criticism, and although he was not prosecuted for his part in the revolution he was expelled from his chair at the University of Budapest and from the Communist Party. Repeated attacks were made on him in 1957 and 1958, begun by Szigéti (at this time, Deputy Minister of Culture) and continued by Béla Fogarasi, the leading Party philosopher.[3] The Soviet philosophical journal, *The Problems of*

[1] *IP*, pp. 633 ff.

[2] For Lukács' activities during the Hungarian revolution, see Váli, pp. 281, 290, 299, 303–4, 364, 559 n.13.

[3] Szigéti's article, translated as 'Noch einmal zur Lukács-Frage' (1957/8) appears in *Georg Lukács und der Revisionismus*, pp. 137 ff. Fogarasi originally attacked Lukács in the Hungarian Academy of Sciences on 22 October, 1958 (Váli, p. 413); cf. 'Der revisionistische Charakter einiger philosophischer Konzeptionen von Georg Lukács', in *Georg Lukács und der Revisionismus*, pp. 303 ff. Another who joined in the attack was Elemér Balogh, who criticized in particular *Die Zerstörung der Vernunft* (Cf. E. Balogh, 'Zur Kritik des Irrationalismus', op. cit., pp. 213 ff.).

Georg Lukács

Philosophy joined in, criticizing *The Young Hegel* and *The Destruction of Reason*.[1] By way of summing-up, the Aufbau-Verlag, which had published Lukács' works in German since the war, published in 1960 a collection of attacks on him (including those by Szigéti and Fogarasi), entitled *Georg Lukács and Revisionism*.

The more tolerant 'new course' which has been followed by the Hungarian Communist Party since 1961 did not involve an immediate softening in the official attitude towards Lukács. In December 1963 he was attacked by Ádám Wirth, secretary of the Party's philosophical collective, for supporting a programme of universal democracy, as opposed to the doctrines of class struggle and of proletarian revolution; these charges were echoed in the *Hungarian Review of Philosophy* in March 1964. In 1965, however, the official attitude changed. In that year, the Hungarian Academy of Sciences compiled a bibliography of Lukács' works, and the *Hungarian Review of Philosophy* published as the leading article of its fourth issue of the year a translation of the chapter on alienation from *The Young Hegel*.[2] It is reported that Lukács was re-admitted to the Hungarian Communist Party in 1967.[3]

Lukács' enforced retirement since 1957 has by no means been an unmixed evil, for it has enabled him to devote himself to the writing of major works on ethics, aesthetics and social theory. At the present moment, the only one of these that has appeared is Part I of his aesthetics, *The Specific Nature of the Aesthetic* (1963), a major theme of which is discussed in Chapter 4 below. A book on the ontology of social being has been completed and is expected to appear in Autumn 1969; in the meantime, some hints of Lukács' line of argument in this work may be found in *Conversations with Georg Lukács*, edited by Theo Pinkus; this is the text of discussions held in September 1966 between Lukács, Hans Heinz Holz, Leo Kofler and Wolfgand Abendroth. Mention must also be made of a short but important work

[1] *Voprosy filosofii*, 1958/10, pp. 15 ff. Excerpts in a German translation in *IP*, pp. 775 ff.

[2] See E. Laszlo, *Studies in Soviet Thought*, IV (1964), pp. 240–41; V (1965), p. 319; VI (1966), p. 42.

[3] H. Arvon, *Georges Lukács* (Paris, 1968), p. 182.

of literary criticism, *The Meaning of Contemporary Realism*; this is a transitional work, begun before the Twentieth Congress but completed after it.[1]

An adequate discussion of this latest phase of Lukács' work would extend far beyond the limits of this introduction; here, there is room only for a sketchy discussion of one topic – namely, the difference that the Twentieth Party Congress has made to Lukács. It has clearly affected what he has written, in the sense that it has enabled him to say frankly what he could say before only in enigmatic language, if at all. But it must also be asked whether it has affected his thinking – whether, for example, it has led him to relax the rigidity of some of his earlier views. Here the answer is not so clear, for it may be that the rigidity was only apparent, an orthodox covering for unorthodox doctrines. *The Specific Nature of the Aesthetic* is relevant in this connection. One of the many notable features of this work is Lukács' declaration that he adheres to the 'great traditions' of previous thought.[2] He says that hitherto (and especially in the Stalin period) the emphasis has been on what distinguishes Marxism from the great traditions of human thinking. He agrees that there is a 'leap' that separates Marxist dialectic from its most advanced predecessors, such as Aristotle and Hegel, but says that it is wrong to isolate what is radically new in Marxism and to neglect the aspect of continuity in the development of human thought. This is certainly a more liberal attitude than that of some Marxists; the point here, however, is that this is not new with *The Specific Nature of the Aesthetic*. Lukács is only making explicit an attitude which was present in his book on Hegel, in which he implicitly contradicted Stalin's view that there was a radical break in historical development between Hegel on the one hand, and Marx and Engels on the other.[3]

[1] Lukács began work on the book in Autumn 1955, using previous lectures as a basis; the latter part of the book was written immediately after the Twentieth Party Congress. The preface was begun in September 1956, but only completed in April 1957. The book was published in Italian in 1957 and in German in 1958. (*The Meaning of Contemporary Realism,* English translation, pp. 9 ff.)

[2] *Die Eigenart des Ästhetischen,* i. p. 18.

[3] Cf. I. Fetscher, 'Das Verhältnis des Marxismus zu Hegel' *Marxismusstudien,* Series 3, 1960, pp. 122 ff.

Georg Lukács

It will have been noticed that, in the passage just mentioned, Lukács regards Aristotle as a predecessor of Marxist dialectic. The fact that Aristotle joins Hegel and Marx as an influence on Lukács' thought is another striking feature of *The Specific Nature of the Aesthetic.* Incidentally, this is not as strange as might at first appear, for at least one Hegelian scholar has found it useful to introduce Hegel by way of a consideration of Aristotle.[1] It may also be mentioned that Lukács is apt to bend Aristotelian concepts to fit his own purposes, rather than to try to interpret Aristotle's thought faithfully. The addition of Aristotle to the Lukácsian canon is an indication of a widening of philosophical interests; once again, however, this does not seem to be new with *The Specific Nature of the Aesthetic.* The work is not wholly a product of the period after Lukács' return from exile; it incorporates ideas from articles which Lukács wrote in 1954 and 1955, and which he has published as a separate book, as a kind of prolegomena to aesthetics.[2] In these articles, an interest in Aristotle is already evident. It is perhaps in the field of literary criticism that there has been a change in Lukács' ideas since 1956. In Chapter 5 below, Professor Pascal suggests that in *The Meaning of Contemporary Realism,* Lukács has succeeded in freeing himself from his previous view that all modernist literature is decadent, and is willing to concede that there is some virtue in writers such as Kafka. Lukács himself denies that there has been any basic change in his ideas, but there need be no contradiction here. He probably means that his basic critical values – for example, the view that realism is of primary importance in the arts – have not altered, and this is no doubt the case. But there does seem to have been a change, in that Lukács is now prepared to count a writer such as Kafka as a realist, and therefore as worthy of the critic's approval.[3] However, it has already been mentioned that although *The Meaning of Contemporary Realism* was completed after the Twentieth Congress, it was begun before it, so it is not certain that this

[1] G. R. G. Mure, *An Introduction to Hegel* (Oxford, 1940).
[2] *Über die Besonderheit als Kategorie der Ästhetik* (Neuwied, 1967). For the origins of the book, see the postscript, pp. 389 ff.
[3] Cf. *The Meaning of Contemporary Realism,* English translation, pp. 9–10, 77.

32

trend towards greater liberalism in Lukács' critical views is to be ascribed to the influence of the Congress.

This account of Lukács' writings, seen in the context of his political activity, has of necessity been schematic. It may perhaps have given some idea of the range of his thought; the papers which follow will show something of its richness. If, in conclusion, one were to try to sum up Lukács as a man, one could hardly find better words than a quotation which Lukács has mentioned more than once.[1] In Feuchtwanger's *Jew Süss* the Rabbi Jonathan Eybeschütz says, 'It is easy to be a martyr; it is much more difficult to appear in a shady light for the sake of an idea.' A tough and determined fighter for his ideas, Lukács has refused the way of the martyr and, in his apparent submission to Stalinist orthodoxy, has been willing to appear 'in a shady light' for their sake.

[1] *The Historical Novel*, English translation, p. 292; *Essays über Realismus* (Berlin, 1948), p. 107.

2 Lukács' Concept of Dialectic

István Mészáros

'*Der Zwiespalt von Sein und Sollen ist nicht aufgehoben*' – *Die Theorie des Romans*
(The division between 'is' and 'ought' is not transcended – *The Theory of the Novel*)

The problems of dialectic occupy a central place in Lukács' thought.[1] To give a detailed account of his ideas on the various

[1] Two of his greatest philosophical works make this clear even on the title page: *Geschichte und Klassenbewusstsein* (History and Class Consciousness) bears the subtitle *Studien über marxistische Dialektik*, and *Der Junge Hegel* (The Young Hegel) is subtitled *Über die Beziehungen von Dialektik und Ökonomie* (On the Relations between Dialectic and Economics). Similarly, one of his major philosophical essays is entitled: *Moses Hess und die Probleme der idealistischen Dialektik* (Moses Hess and the Problems of Idealistic Dialectic). But Lukács' concern for the problems of dialectics goes well beyond these works, important though they are on their own. Thus his work *Über die Besonderheit als Kategorie der Ästhetik* (On the 'Specific' as a Category of Aesthetics) investigates, in its broadest connections, a central category of dialectics; *Die Zerstörung der Vernunft* (The Destruction of Reason) systematically explores the contrasts between 'irrationalism' – in its most developed, German version – and 'dialectical rationality', insisting on the validity of the latter as opposed to all forms of 'irrationalistic mystifications'; *Die Eigenart des Ästhetischen* (The Particularity of the Aesthetical Element), Lukács' massive *Aesthetic*, contains several chapters in which the discussion of some central issues of a materialistic dialectic predominates; and his last great systematic work, *Zur Ontologie des gesellschaftlichen Seins* (Towards an Ontology of Social Being), on the evidence of his own accounts of it, is centred around the problems of dialectics. (In fact the latter is the first attempt at producing a systematic Marxist dialectical Ontology.) But fully to comprehend the extraordinary wealth of his ideas on dialectics in all its details one should also take into account, in addition to the major systematic works, the innumerable references to the manifold aspects of dialectics contained in his essays and articles on History, Politics, Economics, History of Philosophy, History of Aesthetics, History of Literature, Epistemol-

34

aspects of dialectic would be quite impossible in view of the fact that his work – the result of seven decades of feverish activity – runs into many thousands of pages and embraces an enormous variety of topics. It is therefore necessary to single out a few central problems, even if this method carries with it the risk of over-simplification.

Two quotations from his works can be contrasted with each other as a point of departure. The first[1] emphasizes, in a dramatic tone of voice, that the outcome of the objective economic forces that dialectically clash with each other is open-ended, and as far as mankind is concerned everything depends on which of the opposite alternatives is realized by man himself:

Whether the result of these objective determinants is *the highest*

---

[1] *Gespräche mit Georg Lukács.* Rowohlt, Hamburg, 1967, p. 109. Unless mention is made to the contrary, translations from the German in this paper are the work of the editor, to whom grateful acknowledgment is made. Translations from the Hungarian are my own.

---

ogy, Aesthetics, Ethics, Sociology, Party matters, Cultural Policy, Ideology, etc.

The main reasons behind his constant preoccupation with the problems of dialectics could be briefly characterized as follows:

(i) The prevalence of 'vulgar Marxism' in the organized working class movement; dogmatic attacks on dialectics and glorifications of pedestrian, mechanistic materialism in a variety of its versions; ideological and political-organizational trends expressing the same mechanistic dogmatism. (Lukács' rigorous defence of Hegel must be understood in this connection: as a defence of the universal methodological validity of the dialectical approach.)

(ii) Problems of dialectics are assigned a central place in Marx's 'intellectual Testament' – the tasks he formulated in the field of theory but could never realize himself: that is, the systematic elaboration of the principles of Marxism in History, Logic, Aesthetics, Ontology, Epistemology, Ethics, etc. (E.g. the issue of paramount importance – the relationship between 'system' and 'history' – is a problem of dialectic *par excellence*.) Lukács, perceiving his tasks in this respect, had to return time and again to the problems of dialectics.

(iii) The problematic character of dialectic and of 'dialectical rationality' in an age in which mankind is repeatedly menaced with self-destruction. The Hegelian 'ruse of Reason' (*List der Vernunft*) as the objective dialectical law of historical development, and its Marxian version as 'ruse of history', seem to be inevitably problematical at a time when human history is in danger of 'outwitting itself', darkening thus the perspectives of numerous philosophical and artistic trends. Lukács' unceasing reassertion of the validity of dialectic is to be considered against this background, even if his answers often over-emphasize one side of this complex of problems, radically condemning all kinds of 'irrationality' and 'decadentism'.

level of humanity or a *maximum of inhumanity* – this depends on us, this depends on human beings. Economic development cannot produce this by itself.

The second quotation,[1] by contrast, anticipates a positive solution. It goes as follows:

Even today, many obstacles remain. From the time of its birth, the revolutionary workers' movement has had to avoid ideological wrong-turnings of the most varied kind. So far, it has always succeeded in this, and it is my profound conviction that *it will succeed in future.* Allow me, then, to conclude this sketch with a somewhat modified saying of Zola: '*La vérité est lentement en marche et à la fin des fins rien ne l'arrêtera.*'

The contradiction is striking; and yet it is more apparent than real. Here we are confronted with a central characteristic of Lukács' conception of dialectic. An attempt at elucidating and resolving this contradiction, to the extent to which it is possible to do the latter, is therefore a main task of this essay.

1

It is always dangerous, if not arbitrary, to parcel up philosophers as 'the young X' and 'the mature X' for the sake of opposing one parcel to the other. The main outlines of a fundamental synthesizing idea not only may, but also must, be present in the philosopher's mind when he works out in a particular writing some of its concrete implications in particular contexts. This idea may, of course, undergo significant changes; the particular contexts themselves require constant re-elaborations and modifications in accordance with the specific characteristics of the concrete situations that have to be taken into account. But even a genuine conversion from 'idealism' to 'materialism' does not necessarily imply a radical rejection or repression of the original synthesizing idea.

A striking case in point in the twentieth century is Georg Lukács. His post-idealist works reveal in his approach to all

[1] '*Postscriptum 1957 zu: Mein Weg zu Marx.*' In: *Georg Lukács: Schriften zur Ideologie und Politik.* Lutcherhand, Neuwied and Berlin 1967, p. 657.

major problems the same structure of thought, despite the fact that he had genuinely left behind him his original idealistic positions. Those, however, who could not distinguish between the general structure of a philosopher's thought and its idealistic or materialistic articulation insisted that he 'always remained a Hegelian idealist' and – following their own preferences – either praised or blamed him for this. In doing so they were also implicitly ignoring the fact that Marx himself was a revolutionary well before he became a materialist, and he did not cease to be one afterwards.

It goes without saying that the continuity in question is a dialectical one: 'the unity of continuity and discontinuity', i.e. the 'supersession-preservation' (*Aufhebung*) of a previous stage in an increasingly higher complexity. Nevertheless it must be emphasized that there can be no originality without this – relative, dialectical – unity of thought as far as its general structure is concerned. For the precondition of any synthesis is some kind of synthesis as the active principle of selection of the first, even if the new synthesis apparently has nothing to do with the initial one. As Goethe said, 'to be able to do something one must already be something',[1] which applies to the philosopher not less than to the artist or to anybody else. This is why one cannot properly understand a philosopher's thought without reaching down through its many layers to that original synthesis which structured it, dialectically, in all its successive modifications. (This is all the more important in cases – like Hegel, Marx, Lukács, Sartre, etc. – in which at some stage there seems to be a radical break with the past. But 'radical break' is not the same as 'qualitative change'. The latter can characterize the totality of one's development, the former is confined to certain aspects of it, however important in some respects – e.g. sociologically – they might be. A 'total conversion', in so far as it is not confined to the ideological content of one's thought but is claimed to embrace the person's general structure of thought, is very doubtful even as regards 'religious fanatics'. It is by no means accidental that disappointed religious communists turn into religious anti-communists. 'Total

[1] Quoted by Thomas Mann in his *Essay in Autobiography*.

conversion' is the privilege of a second intellectual infancy that
may follow a total amnesia.)

Lukács' identification with Marxism signified a qualitative
change in his development. It did not happen, however, overnight; it could not be characterized with the categories of
'radical break' and 'radically new' against which Lukács, in his
defence of dialectic, waged a lifelong battle. On the contrary,
the roots of this change ought to be sought a long way back, in
his youthful dialectical synthesis and in its internal tensions. It
can be no task of this essay to attempt to work out a typology
of structures of thought in which Lukács could be situated.
(The concepts that ought to be pursued in this respect range
from 'formalism', 'monism', 'dualism', 'objectivism', 'subjectivism', etc. to 'fanaticism', 'fatalism', 'opportunism', 'opposition-
alism', 'rebelliousness', etc. etc.) It is necessary to stress,
however, that we are not concerned here with some timeless
psychological entity – a metaphysical fiction – but with a
characteristic that can be explained only in concrete socio-
historical terms. The formation of a philosopher's structure of
thought has for its basis that ontological commitment – anima-
ted by a moral impetus – which is inseparable from the issues of
his particular situation. The trends of development which he
perceives have their own 'internal logic' and objective – though,
of course, relative – continuity. This latter may, or may not,
correspond to the dynamism of the philosopher's development.
Rapid historical changes require greater and more radical
adaptations through qualitatively differing reassessments than
relatively quiet and long drawn out transformations, and it is by
no means certain that the individual is able to match the
rhythm of historical dynamism. (The 'conflict of generations'
often has for its ground the inability of the older generation to
readjust its own historical perspectives in accordance with some
major changes which have occurred, or are about to emerge,
and are perceived, however one-sidedly and with an unwarranted
impression of finality, by the representatives of the younger
generation.)

Yet: whatever the limits of adaptability of the individual
philosopher might be, the point is that he does not learn from

books the important issues of his time, but lives them; that is, if he is a man of significance. Intellectual influences, therefore, ought to be treated with utmost care. For the significant philosopher follows Moliére's advice in taking 'son bien où il le trouve' and moulds all that which he has taken – not simply found – into a coherent whole of his own. Obviously here, again, the relationship is a dialectical one: it would be foolish to deny that the assimilated influences are *influences*, and have their effect on his further orientation as constitutive elements – though '*aufgehoben*' ones – of his principle of selection and synthesis. Nevertheless in this relationship the historical situation itself has the primacy over the intellectual influences. What separates the important philosopher from the clever eclectic is the historical irrelevance of the latter's merely academic synthesis as compared to the ultimate practical significance of the first.

The major influences on Lukács can be characterized with the following names: Georg Simmel, Wilhelm Dilthey, Emil Lask, Ervin Szabó, Hermann Cohen (and other representatives of the Marburg school of neo-Kantianism), Max Weber, Hegel, Marx, Rosa Luxemburg and Lenin. This list itself shows that the lion's share was taken by German culture, especially in the years of his intellectual formation. And yet, Lukács turned out to be the most radical critic of the internal contradictions of German thought and literature. A vast amount of his massive production is dedicated to the problems of German history and culture, but even the smallest article is written from a distance.[1] The backwardness of Hungarian philosophy left him no alternative to seeking orientation elsewhere, and attaching himself to the mainstream of German philosophy was, in the circumstances, the most obvious thing to do. The class into which he was born – the Hungarian Jewish bourgeoisie – was facing, at the time of

[1] Although many of Lukács' works deal with German topics, and although his attachment to German culture – in particular to the German philosophical heritage – is really very profound, his writings on German problems are unmistakably those of an 'outsider'. In fact his work as a whole cannot be understood without the Hungarian cultural and historical setting that greatly affected not only his early development but also, in more ways than one, his later orientation.

Georg Lukács

Lukács' intellectual formation, a very complex situation. On the one hand, through its increasing economic power it was speedily emancipating itself in social standing from its subordination to the so-called 'historical class'; on the other, it also succeeded in asserting its independence from the Austrian ruling classes. At the same time, however, it found itself confronted by a new social force: the challenge of the organized working-class movement. The belated development of Hungarian capitalism, the enormous inertia of feudal and bureaucratic-statal interests, the contradictions between the two major partners of the Austro-Hungarian monarchy, the special complications of Jewish emancipation, the increasing resistance of national minorities under Hungarian domination, these were the major factors in Lukács' situation. Many of his contemporaries, looking towards the west, simplified the tasks in the rather unrealistic programme of 'bringing up to date' capitalistic Hungarian society. (Significantly, the two principal periodicals were called *The West* and *Twentieth Century*.) Lukács went a long step further: he emphasized the profound crisis of the bourgeoisie and its culture in general and thus conducted a constant polemic, even if in an indirect form, against the problematic and illusory character of the programme of 'up-to-dating'. As one of his first significant efforts he organized – at the age of nineteen – a theatre company called 'Thalia' whose function was to bring culture to the working classes, which it did over a period of almost five years, until the frightened Hungarian Government's interference killed it. While Lukács fully recognized the great cultural-intellectual merits of both *The West* and *Twentieth Century* – he actively supported them with his regular contributions – he also realized the socio-political as well as philosophical limits of the trends expressed in them. Not only did he do this as a very young man, but also a great deal earlier than his intellectual contemporaries irrespective of age, with the exception of the syndicalist theoretician Ervin Szabó and the supremely great poet Endre Ady.

Here we reach a point of great importance: Lukács' relation to Ady. Their personal contacts were almost non-existent, so that Ady's impact on the young Lukács issued primarily from the reading of his poems. While his contemporaries were at odds

40

with the intricately mediated meaning of Ady's symbolic poetry, recognizing in its author only the formal-linguistic innovator, the young Lukács was the first to focus attention on the organizing core of this poetry: the elemental passion of a democratic revolutionary.[1] The objective affinity of their search for a solution brought Lukács into the immediate vicinity of Ady, enabling him to grasp, already in its embryonic form, the true significance of a trend which was to become fully developed only several years later. Just as much as Ady, he felt the devastating inertia of the Hungarian situation in which the interaction of the heterogeneous contradictions mentioned above tended to emasculate all forces of social dynamism, maintaining the suffocating grip of conservative immobility. (It was still fresh in Lukács' memory that even their theatrical experiment was deemed dangerous by the guardians of the anachronistic *status quo*.) The rebellion against this kind of hopeless inertia and immobility had to take the form of pathetic denunciations, full of the cosmic undertones one finds in the 'last warnings' of the prophets of doom; the more so since neither Ady nor Lukács opposed the inert anachronism of their situation, the equally (though in a different way) anachronistic ideal of bourgeois stability so dear to the heart of the anglophile Don Quixotes of the western-orientated Hungarian bourgeoisie.

Ady's sombre prophetic Messianism, with its dramatic appeals formulated in terms of '*either* salvation *or* total disaster', expressed with the highest lyric intensity the dilemmas of those who, in their efforts to find a solution to their particular problems on a European scale, had to perceive the deepening crisis of the social order on a global scale. How simple it was, by comparison, for Petöfi when, in 1848–9 and before, he could appeal to the example of France in his programme, aiming at the radical overcoming of Hungarian feudalism: the clear and straightforward character of his poetry bears witness to this. For Ady, however, there was no alternative to singing in this voice:

[1] '*Új magyar líra*.' (New Hungarian Lyric Poetry) In: *Huszadik Század* (Twentieth Century) Vol. 2 (1909) pp. 286–92 and 419–24.

41

Saltier are the tears here,
And the pains hurt more.
The Magyar Messiahs are Messiahs
A thousand times, and more.

They die a thousand deaths,
But their crosses bring no salvation,
For they could do nothing,
They were condemned to achieve naught.

What could be set against such inertia of powerlessness? Only a dramatic appeal to an *'ought'* emerging from the succession of heightened alternatives:

New flames, new faiths, new furnaces, new saints,
Either you are real, or vanish again in the mist of nothing.

Either this faith of ours turns into reality,
Or, bereft of reason, we are doomed to the last.

Thirty years after the publication of his first essay on Ady, Lukács quoted the lines:

Will it last long, still longer
The old fate, the old curse?
Lingering, inert, red Sun
I implore Thee.

and commented: 'for Ady the democratic revolution existed, and could only exist, as *desire, hope and dream*.'[1] He might have written the same words about the young Lukács. Their perspectives were essentially the same in a fundamental respect: in that the solution could appear on their horizon only in the form of an 'ought', articulated in alternatives of the utmost dramatic intensity. The poetic qualities of the young Lukács' style – *The Soul and the Forms, Aesthetic Culture, The Theory of the Novel* – which were to disappear later, find their explanation in these perspectives, in this horizon. In the course of the 1917–18 social upheavals his perspectives changed, and what was earlier a 'desire, hope and dream' turned for him into a concrete,

---

[1] *'Ady, a magyar tragédia nagy énekese.'* (Ady, Great Poet of the Hungarian Tragedy) 1939, p. 28 of the volume *Az Irástudók Felelsösége* (The Intellectuals' Responsibility), Moscow, 1944.

practical task, representing a 'scientific challenge' directly associated with the tangible issues of economic and social organization and programming. At this point the old style had to give way to the matter-of-fact, prosaic, practice-orientated style of a peculiar brand of economic-philosophical and politico-historical reasoning.

2

And yet, the supersession of the youthful perspectives remained a relative one. As we shall see later, the concern for 'ought' and the enunciation of dramatic alternatives has remained with Lukács ever since. His identification with Marxism has given, it goes without saying, a qualitatively new setting to this concern. The stylistic change went parallel to the transference of 'ought' to a different level, and it was by no means achieved overnight. (*History and Class Consciousness* is his major work of transition, preceded by essays like *Bolshevism as a Moral Problem, Tactics and Ethics, The Role of Morality in Communist Production,* etc., which show as regards both style and issues a significant affinity with his earlier works. The book on *Lenin,* written in 1924, is markedly different in this respect.) The problems associated with 'ought' have become progressively mediated in his works – Lukács would say 'concretized' – and topics have been brought into the foreground which have apparently very little to do with 'ought', save in the form of negative polemics. Nevertheless his original confrontation with '*Sollen*', with 'ought', has remained a fundamental structuring dimension of Lukács' entire thought.

It cannot be stressed enough: we are not concerned with the influences of neo-Kantianism, etc. The young Lukács reached out for them in the spirit of his own situation and assimilated them in his own way, in a comprehensive synthesis not in the least recognizable in the work of any one of his friends and teachers. Max Weber, to name but the most significant of them, was well aware of the impressive originality of the young Hungarian philosopher, and regarded him more as an intellectual equal than a pupil. As we have seen in his relation to Ady, the overriding factor was the common objective situation – the perception of which produced a profound affinity of perspectives.

Paradoxical as it might seem, the historical backwardness of Hungarian developments proved to be the vantage point of a profoundly original synthesis. It was not simply that Hungary was socially backward. Russia was on the whole no more advanced, but in her development she was catching up with the most advanced countries in socio-political dynamism. In a complex historical situation it is never simply the economic and social maturity of a given country that is the cause of radical changes but the favourable configuration of the various causal factors into a dynamic overall pattern.[1] Both Russia and China have amply proved this point. Hungary, by contrast, was characterized by a very different overall configuration. In that country there were many forms of ideological and political movements, from reactionary conservatism to liberalism, from populism to Marxist-orientated syndicalism, and from nationalism to bourgeois radicalism. Their interactions, however, because of the underlying objective stalemate of the heterogeneous social contradictions, could only emphasize the massiveness of general social impotence and immobility. Those who rebelled against the latter had to aim – in ideological terms – at the transcendence of all the existing forms of impotence-enhancing partial opposition. This rebellion took place with various degrees of socio-philosophical awareness and political radicalism. Nevertheless a concern for universality was an integral part of it. It produced not only some peaks of twentieth-century European culture – like Ady, Lukács, Bartók, Kodály, and Attila József – but also an almost incredible number of outstanding individuals in every field of culture and across the whole spectrum of ideology.[2]

[1] See pp. 65–6 of this essay, on Lukács' conception of the complex causality at work in the structure of totality.

[2] A group of intellectuals used to meet regularly on Sundays in a private circle, until it was broken up by the upheavals at the end of the war. The undisputed intellectual head of this circle was Lukács, and several of its members later acquired world fame. To name but a few: Frigyes Antal, Béla Balázs, Béla Fogarasi, Arnold Hauser, Zoltán Kodály, Karl Mannheim, Wilhelm Szilasi, Charles de Tolnay, Eugene Varga, John Wilde.

As to Lukács, the possibility of transformation was conceived by him in terms of 'either a complete fulfilment or no substantial change at all'. When, in his youth, he turned away from the perspectives of socialism he did this with the justification that although 'the only hope could be in the proletariat, in socialism . . . it seems that socialism does not possess the religious power which is capable of filling the entire soul: a power that characterized primitive Christianity.'[1] The measure and magnitude of expectations was set in these terms and when in 1917–18 he identified himself with socialist perspectives he did not give up an iota from the radicalism and totality of this measure. This is where we can see clearly the essential continuity of his development in a dialectical sense: i.e. the reformulation of an all-pervasive conception in terms of a new social instrumentality.

Of course the change of perspectives took place in the middle of a grave international crisis – the end of the First World War and the October Revolution – which he observed from a rather inert national setting. Even after the Hungarian revolutionary events it remained true that in the country there existed no powerful social agency which could have materialized the changes desired and advocated by Lukács. Understandably, therefore, his social philosophy bears the marks of the sociopolitical vacuum to which it was related, in sharp contrast to the tremendous realism that characterized almost every single line of Lenin's writing. Lenin reads even Hegel's *Logic* – in the interval between two revolutions – in order to derive concrete stimuli for the solution of the urgent immediate *practical* tasks he faces in planning and organizationally preparing the October revolution. Lukács reads even Lenin in order to concretize, but always in *theoretical* terms, his own general philosophical synthesis. Lukács repeatedly postulates the unity of theory and practice; Lenin lives it in a specific form. But such contrasts cannot be simply explained with reference to differences, real or alleged, in intellectual talents. References of this kind rather beg the question, ignoring the fact that the realized intellectual talent is the result of the interaction between whatever gifts the individual might have had and his situation. The striking

[1] 'Esztétikai kultúra.' (Aesthetic Culture) In: *Renaissance, 1910*.

contrasts are basically due to the fact that while Lenin's entire predicament is dense with concrete practical tasks, Lukács' practical possibilities can only be compared to a rarefied atmosphere. Even at the time of the shortlived Hungarian revolution of 1919 the margin of real possibilities is almost infinitesimal as compared to the magnitude of the tasks and problems. The old inertia, helped by the international situation in the aftermath of the October revolution, prevailed again, 'condemning to achieve naught' those who tried to rebel against it. And the political movement of an emigration which lacks a solid backing in its own country of origin is, in practical terms, but the original rarefied atmosphere still more rarefied.

This situation has given an ambivalent character to Lukács' perspectives. If he wanted to render more concrete his general conception, in an effort of translating it into a feasible practical programme for him, there was no alternative to associating himself with the increasingly more Stalinist-dominated Communist International. (Although he remained always in an internal opposition both in his Party and in the Comintern, he could not avoid, as we shall see, the problematic effects of this association however necessary it was.) On the other hand the weakness of the practical-political predicament also turned into an advantage for him. It enabled him to tackle and elaborate some fundamental philosophical categories of the greatest ultimate practical significance – e.g. 'totality' and 'mediation' (*Vermittlung*), to be discussed later. It also enabled him to anticipate the objective logic of stalinistic developments as early as the spring of 1919, in the framework of a general theoretical consideration into which he has 'trans-substantiated' an immediate and, as far as the Hungarian circumstances are concerned, hopeless practical task. The issue is important enough to warrant the long quotation that follows.[1]

It is clear that the most oppressive phenomena of proletarian power – namely, scarcity of goods and high prices, of whose immediate consequences every proletarian has personal experience –

---

[1] 'Az erkölcs szerepe a komunista termelésben.' (The Role of Morality in Communist Production.) Reproduced in the volume cited in Note 1 on p. 36. The quotation is from pp. 79–80 of this volume.

are direct consequences of the slackening of labour-discipline and the decline in production. The creation of remedies for these, and the consequent improvement in the individual's standard of living, can only be brought about when the causes of these phenomena have been removed. Help comes in two ways. Either the individuals who constitute the proletariat *realize* that they can help themselves only by bringing about a voluntary strengthening of labour-discipline, and consequently a rise in production; or, if they are incapable of this, *they create institutions which are capable of bringing about this necessary state of affairs.* In the latter case, they create a legal system through which the proletariat *compels* its own individual members, the proletarians, to act in a way which corresponds to their class-interests: *the proletariat turns its dictatorship against itself.* This measure is necessary for the self-preservation of the proletariat when correct recognition of class-interests and voluntary action in these interests do not exist. But one must not hide from oneself the fact that *this method contains within itself great dangers for the future.* When the proletariat itself is the creator of labour-discipline, when the labour-system of the proletarian state is built on a *moral* basis, then the external compulsion of the law ceases *automatically* with the abolition of class-division – that is, the state withers away – and this liquidation of class-division produces out of itself the beginning of the true history of humanity, which Marx prophesied and hoped for. If, on the other hand, the proletariat follows another path, it must create a legal system which cannot be abolished automatically by historical development. Development would therefore proceed in a direction *which endangered the appearance and realization of the ultimate aim.* For the legal system which the proletariat is compelled to create in this way *must be overthrown* – and who knows what convulsions and what injuries will be caused by a transition which leads from the kingdom of necessity to the kingdom of freedom by such a *détour*? ... It depends on the proletariat whether the real history of humanity begins – that is to say, *the power of morality over institutions and economics.*

This quotation gives clear expression to practical and political misery in the shape of an abstract moral postulate – the moralizing direct appeal to the consciousness of the proletariat.[1] It also

[1] At the beginning of this essay (cf. p. 36) we quoted a passage written in 1957, in which Lukács expressed his faith in the positive solution of the problems of the socialist movement. The same faith is expressed, in almost identical

Georg Lukács

shows Lukács' great power of insight as regards the objective dialectic of a certain type of development. Lenin, by comparison, was far too busy squeezing out the last drop of practical socialist possibilities from the objective instrumental set-up of his situation to indulge in theoretical anticipations of this kind in 1919. By the time he started to concentrate on the dreadful danger of Stalinistic bureaucratization and the prevalence of the 'institutions of necessity' over the ideals of socialism it was too late. It is pathetic to see Lenin, a genius of realistic strategy, behaving like a desperate utopian from 1923 to the moment of his death, insistently putting forward hopeless schemes – like the proposal to create a majority in the Central Committee from working-class cadres in order to neutralize the Party bureaucrats – in the hope of reversing this dangerous trend, by now far too advanced. Lenin's great tragedy was that his incomparable, instrumentally concrete, intensely practical strategy in the end defeated him. In the last year of his life there was no longer a way out of his almost total isolation: the development he himself, far above anybody else, had helped to set in motion had made him historically superfluous. The specific form in which he lived the unity of theory and practice proved to be the limit even of his greatness.

In this issue we find manifest the general dilemma of the relationship between Politics and Philosophy. We shall return later to this question. In this connection the point to be stressed is that Lukács defined his own position in the unhappy correlation between direct practical instrumentality as manifest in the Soviet developments – the only *real* one over a long historical period, whatever its contradictions – and the universal perspectives of socialism in general. He attempted the impossible task of bridging the gap between the two, not out of selfish opportunism – one can hardly imagine a more selfless person than him, as has been recognized even by his political oppo-

terms, thirty-eight years earlier when he writes at the end of 'The Role of Morality in Communist Production':

It is impossible for the proletariat, which has hitherto remained true to its world-historical vocation under much more difficult conditions, to abandon this vocation at the very moment that it is finally in a position to realize it in action. Op. cit., p. 81.

nents[1] – but because of the objective external and internal limitations of his general position. The practical rarefaction of his
own political predicament and the limitations of the instrumentality of 'Socialism in one country' forced him to focus attention
on the far-away perspectives of 'soul-filling socialism'. Paradoxically this also enabled him to identify and elaborate some
general issues of the greatest ultimate practical significance
that were hardly, if ever, noticed before him. At the same time,
in the course of his efforts to indicate the concrete social agencies
which could translate his ultimate perspectives into practical
reality, the internal logic of his general position has more than
once compelled him to take for a solution something that was
far from it. (His references to the 'asiatic form of socialism'
amounted to no more than pinpointing the handicaps Soviet
society should get rid of in order to remain the model of socialist
development.) Thus the two poles of his thought reciprocally
conditioned each other, often producing in his syntheses an
abstract immediacy on the one hand and a pseudo-concreteness
on the other, in so far as far-away perspectives were transferred
by him into the present or near future. (Especially in his writings
on People's Democracy.)

Not that he was unaware of the gap between the given
practical instrumentality and the general perspectives. He spent
by far the greatest amount of his energies in trying to work out
those 'mediations' which should bridge that gap. (The numerous
works he has written in the course of his never-ending confrontation with the problem of mediation (*Vermittlung*) acquire their

[1] In 1919, when Horthy's men pressed the Austrian Government to extradite
Lukács, a group of intellectuals published an appeal to save him:

He had given up the seductions of the pampered life which was his inheritance, in favour of the position of responsible, solitary thought. When he
turned to politics, he sacrificed what was dearest to him, his freedom of
thought, to the reformer's work which he intended to fulfil . . . Saving Lukács
is no party matter. It is the duty of all who have personal experience of his
human purity, and of the many who admire the lofty-minded intellectuality of
his philosophical and aesthetic works, to protest against the extradition.

In *Berliner Tageblatt*, 12 November 1919. Signed by Franz Ferdinand Baum-
garten, Richard Beer-Hoffmann, Richard Dehmel, Paul Ernst, Bruno Frank,
Maximilian Harden, Alfred Kerr, Heinrich Mann, Emil Praetorius, Karl
Scheffler.

full meaning only in this connection.) He never ceased to talk about the task of 'overcoming' (*Überwindung*). But his '*Überwindung*' could never be other than a *theoretical* one on the premise of the theoretical – not merely tactical – acceptance of the instrumental validity of 'Socialism in one country'. Although later he greatly improved upon his just-quoted position, he has never fully realized that the alternative between 'free insight, producing voluntary activity' and 'the institutions of necessity' is a hopelessly abstract and, therefore, false alternative; that one form of instrumentality can realistically be opposed only by another form of instrumentality and institutions. He tried, instead, an '*Überwindung*' in the form of a synthesis between the 'free insight' and 'necessity' – in his theory of the 'Leninist Party' as the 'bearer of proletarian class-consciousness'[1] – and thus in his 'ought-ridden' abstract-theoretical solution of the problem ended up with idealizing an 'institution of necessity'. The possible alternatives which objectively implied the revision of his premise had to remain completely outside his horizon. (It is highly significant that the profoundly original perspectives of both Gramsci and Mao Tse-tung, despite their massive implications for the development of the socialist movement as a whole, have found no positive resonance whatsoever[2]

---

[1] *Geschichte und Klassenbewusstsein*. Malik Verlag, Berlin 1923. p. 54. Lukács' later formulated 'partisan-strategy' is still well within the limits of the same conception of an institutional framework. By contrast, Gramsci's idea of the 'hegemony of the proletariat' is a qualitatively different concept.

[2] Lukács' assessment of the Chinese situation is extremely problematical. It is based on the false premise that the destiny of mankind will be decided by the greater ideological 'force of attraction' (*Anziehungskraft*) of one of the '*two* systems'. Both elements of this premise are unrealistic. The idea of an ideological '*Anziehungskraft*' minimizes the role of objective internal contradictions. (This problem will be discussed in the last section of the present essay.) If however the institutional framework of one of the 'two systems' is taken for granted, there remains no room for criticism except appeals concerning the possible improvement of the ideological 'force of attraction' of Soviet-type socialism. More important is, however, the assumption according to which 'two systems' are involved in the '*internationalen Klassenkampf der Koexistenz*' (international class-struggle of co-existence). In reality the military stalemate that forces 'co-existence' on the two political-military power blocs sets free the development of a multiplicity of transitional systems, with internal dynamisms – and contradictions – as well as objective interests of their own. Consequently it is impossible to reduce this complexity to the scheme of 'two systems'. The

in a man of such intellect and sensitivity as Lukács. His one-sided judgments on Trotsky find their explanation in the same limitations.)

That the validity of Lukács' perspectives as attached to a narrow instrumentality is historically superseded is obvious enough. What needs repeated emphasis is that his perspectives are characterized by a dialectical bipolarity. As we have seen, not only the problematically-immediate – i.e. the already superseded – conditioned the 'far-away perspectives', but also the latter determined his interpretation of the concrete situations and of their significance. This means not only that the critical assessment of his works, including the most polemical ones, requires the constant awareness of the historical circumstances and dialectical interconnections. It also means that one should look out for those aspects of his *oeuvre* which, due to the historical validity of many of his perspectival formulations, represent a deep-rooted, concrete, topical as well as enduring achievement. For this complex bipolarity of his perspectives has provided him with a margin of activity that enabled him to produce – primarily in the 'mediated' field of Aesthetics and in the more abstract spheres of Philosophy – works of exemplary value.

---

artificial unity of 'two power blocs' (in the past corresponding, in fact, to two systems), viewed at the social level, belongs irrevocably to the past. No amount of 'ideological clarification and persuasion' can explain away the objective differences of interest and of internal dynamism that involve even the sharpest-oppositions among the multiplicity of transitional systems. This historical change requires a much more complex strategic assessment of the trends of socialist transformation and rules out the acceptance of Lukács' model of the 'ideological force of attraction' of Soviet-type socialism. At the same time it must be stressed that no matter how problematical Lukács' approach to the Chinese problem may be, the duality of his perspectives enables him to raise some fundamental theoretical issues connected with the dialectical category of 'mediation'. Irrespective of the concrete historical framework to which he applies his theoretical considerations – the contemporary Chinese situation – his reflection on the inherent relationship between 'sectarianism' and 'lack of mediations' has a general methodological validity in its applications to the ideological sphere. (See his essay: 'Zur Debatte zwischen China und der Sovjet-union. Theoretisch-philosophische Bemerkungen.' In: *Georg Lukács: Schriften zur Ideologie und Politik*. pp. 681–706.)

Georg Lukács

3

Lukács' concept of '*Sollen*', or 'ought', is far more complex than it would seem at first sight. The dominant note of his formulations (*Fragestellungen*) is a 'longing for objectivity' and, in accordance with it, a never-ending explicit polemic against 'ought'. Yet he is intensely aware of the problematic character of any cult of objectivity in our age, and therefore qualifies his statements in such a way that the 'overtones' of his analyses to some extent reassert the validity of 'ought' in an indirect form. This is why his attitude must remain a '*longing for* objectivity', and never an unproblematic self-identification with it – whether under the heading of the category of 'life' (*Lebensphilosophie*) or of those of 'economic reality', 'productive forces', 'class', 'history', etc.

Also, this is why already the young Lukács feels the greatest sympathy for Thomas Mann who remains his twentieth-century literary hero ever since. In an essay written in 1909, after praising Mann's dialectical and artistic power of seeing 'the connection between all things' (*den Zusammenhang von allem mit allem*) as well as his great sense of objectivity, Lukács makes the general point that 'objectivity can perhaps never exist without a certain irony. The most serious regard for things is always somewhat ironic, for somewhere or other the great gulf between cause and effect, between the conjuring of fate and the fate conjured, must become obvious. And the more natural the peaceful flow of things appears, the truer and deeper this irony will be. Admittedly it is only in *Buddenbrooks* that this emerges so clearly and, as it were, from a single source. In the later writings this irony of Mann takes on differing forms, yet its deepest root remains this feeling of dislocation from, and longing for, the great natural vegetative community.'[1] The philosopher feels the same dislocation from, and the same longing for, an objective synthesis and unity in a world in which the gulf between 'cause and effect', 'intention and result', 'value and reality' (*Wert und Wirklichkeit*) appears to be ever increasing,

[1] 'Royal Highness.' In: *Essays on Thomas Mann*, translated by Stanley Mitchell, Merlin Press, London 1964, pp. 135–7.

although of course for him 'irony' cannot bring a solution. And whatever the envisaged particular solution may be, throughout all its modifications in the course of Lukács' development the underlying original programmatic challenge remains a major structuring factor of his thought for the rest of his life.

Lukács' entire work is characterized by incessant attempts at finding a way of removing the tragic menace implicit in the 'either – or' situation (the possibility of the dominion of 'a maximum of inhumanity'). His 'longing for objectivity' is in the spirit of a constant struggle against 'bad objectivity'. From the very beginning he realizes that a direct appeal to '*Sollen*' ('obligation') on the lines of '*Individualethik*' ('Individual ethics'), is hopelessly inadequate, and therefore he opposes to it the imperative of some objective force. But the 'unity', the 'supersession of opposites' – if claimed at all – is built on an imperatival foundation. Thus '*der Zwiespalt von Sein und Sollen ist nicht aufgehoben*' – 'the division between "is" and "ought" is not transcended'. It is only given a dialectical, and increasingly more concrete, assessment.

The reason for this can be found in a certain duality in Lukács' conception of Ontology. Even the most recent Lukács – the author of a massive *Social Ontology* – insists on a duality, on a dual causality, and on an ultimate autonomy of 'decisions between alternatives' (*Alternativentscheidungen*). The gist of his argument is as follows:

There are causal connections which work *as spontaneous causes,* and there are causal connections which are set in motion in a specific way by a teleological initiative, whereby they still preserve their causal necessity . . . I come now to another basic ontological problem of social development, which is linked with the fact that society is an extraordinarily complicated complex of complexes, in which there are two opposite poles. On the one hand there is the *totality of society*, which ultimately determines the interactions of the individual complexes, and on the other there is the complex individual man, who constitutes an *irreducible minimal unity* within the process. By their interaction, these poles determine the process. In this process, man finally becomes man; . . . the aspect of freedom acquires a significance which is ever greater, ever more comprehensive, embracing the whole of humanity ... I assert, therefore, that however much all these problems have been made possible by economic factors, they can be translated into reality only through men's *decisions between* alternatives.[1]

The *purely objective development* of labour creates, it is true, an ever-diminishing minimum of necessary labour; but that it is capable of turning labour into a need of life is not part of this ontology. Rather, at a determinate stage, men must make labour a need of life.[2]

The question is not whether one agrees with Lukács or not. It is rather that on the basis of his Ontology the positive outcome can only be envisaged as the impact of a '*Sollen*': the autonomous choice of their potential humanity by the individuals (the '*unauflösbare Minimaleinheiten*') who become aware, after an arduous work of theoretical demonstration and persuasion, that they *can* and *ought to* change their way of life:

> It must be one of our major tasks to offer a theoretical proof of the fact that all these circumstances and reifications are only phenomenal forms of real processes. By this, we shall *gradually make men understand* that they *ought* to experience their own life too as an historical process.[3]

> It is important, therefore, *to awaken* the *genuinely* independent personality, whose *possibility* has been created by previous economic development.[4]

And here we arrive at the question of resolving, in so far as it is possible, the apparent contradiction referred to at the beginning of this essay. If the objective development produces 'open-ended' alternatives, clearly there can be no other power to bring about the desired solution than the 'work of consciousness upon consciousness'. (This, in Lukács' eyes, opens up a great field of activity for the intellectual – also putting a tremendous moral responsibility[5] on his shoulders.) If, however, this work of illumination and persuasion is to succeed, it cannot do without

[1] '*Gespräche mit Georg Lukács*,' pp. 105–10.
[2] Ibid., p. 101.
[3] Ibid., p. 94.
[4] Ibid., p. 45.
[5] An ever-recurring theme of Lukács' writings is the question of the responsibility of the intellectuals. It predominates in several of his volumes. E.g.

54

the assertion that '*la vérité est lentement en marche et à la fin des fins rien ne l'arrêtera*'.

4

So far the stress has been laid mainly on the unity of Lukács' thought; now it is necessary to show, however briefly, the inner logic of his development: the modifications of his position within the ultimate unity and the determinations behind them. In the confines of this essay there is no space for more than the bare outlines. But however summary and schematic the result may be, it is necessary to trace them in order not to distort the overall picture.[1]

The Soul and the Forms – a volume of essays written between 1908 and 1910 – is Lukács' first major intellectual achievement. It is a work of great sensitivity, dense with allusions and inexhaustible ambiguities. It has no unifying topic, and yet the

---

[1] I have discussed some related aspects of Lukács' work in 'Die Philosophie des "tertium datur" und des Koexistenzdialogs', *Festschrift zum Achtzigsten Geburtstag von Georg Lukács*, Luchterhand, Neuwied-Berlin 1965, pp. 188–207.

Az irástudók felelössége (The Intellectuals' Responsibility), *Irodalom és demokrácia* (Literature and Democracy), *Új magyar Kultúráért* (For a New Hungarian Culture), *Schicksalswende, Existentialisme ou marxisme, Fortschritt und Reaktion in der deutschen Literatur, Die Zerstörung der Vernunft*, etc. A characteristic quotation from one of his essays:

'The intelligentsia stands at the crossroads. Ought we – like the intelligentsia of France in the 18th century, and of Russia in the 19th – to prepare the way and fight for a new and progressive world epoch, or ought we, like the German intelligentsia of the first half of the 20th century, to be helpless sacrifices, weak-willed assistants to the assistants of a barbaric reaction? There is no question as to which attitude is *worthy*, and which is unworthy, of the essence, the knowledge and the culture of the intelligentsia.' 'Von der Verantwortung der Intellektuellen.' In: *Schicksalswende*, Aufbau-Verlag, Berlin 1956, p. 245.)

He lays an enormous emphasis on exploring the moral aspects of general philosophical and aesthetic problems. Significantly his massive *Aesthetic* – everywhere full of moral references – reaches its climax in the chapter on 'Der Befreiungskampf der Kunst' (The Liberating Struggle of Art). (See *Die Eigenart des Ästhetischen*, Luchterhand, Neuwied-Berlin 1963, Vol. 2., pp. 675–872.) Thus for Lukács a work of art devoid of moral significance, not surprisingly, cannot pass the test of lasting artistic significance.

overall impression is that of having read *one* work, not an occasional collection of essays. (Lukács' post-1913 collections are very different indeed in this respect.) The compositional principle of these early essays – including those which compose *Aesthetic Culture* – is heavily weighed down on the subjective side. The chosen topics are more grounds for a 'take-off' than objective points of reference. Paradoxically it is the absence of a sharply defined central theme that unites these essays, not its presence. Only the partial themes are well lit and properly in focus. But the dialectical contrasts of the sharply focused partial theme produce an overall *chiaroscuro* effect: that of a vaguely contoured, unresolved complexity. One might say that these essays are 'variations on a missing theme'. The synthesizing theme – which is originally there only as a vague intuition, as an undefined and inarticulate 'longing for objectivity' – is being born before our eyes. As it takes shape through its partial aspects, bringing into life at the same time the challenge of the supersession of that partiality, it foreshadows the necessary destruction of the young Lukács' essay form.

The question of fragmentation appears time and again, under many of its aspects. 'Human knowledge,' writes Lukács, 'is a *psychological nihilism*. We see a *thousand relations,* yet never grasp a *genuine connection.* The landscapes of our soul exist nowhere; yet in them, every tree and every flower is concrete.'[1] Again, 'The man of George's lyrics . . . is a solitary man, freed from all social ties.'[2] And again:

> Kassner sees *syntheses* only, as it were, with his eyes closed; when he looks at things he sees so much, such delicate details, so much that can never be repeated, that *every synthesis must appear as a lie,* as a deliberate falsification. If he gives in to his longing, if he closes his eyes so that he can see things *together – in the realm of values* – his honesty immediately compels him to look at them again, and once more they are separated, isolated, without air. The oscillation between these two poles determines Kassner's style.[3]

When, against such a background, he says of the George poems

[1] *Die Seele und die Formen.* Egon Fleischel & Co., Berlin 1911. p. 189.

[2] Ibid., p. 190.

[3] Ibid., p. 54.

that 'One day, perhaps, even these poems could become folk-songs',[1] that amounts to nothing more than a gratuitous hope: the weakest of all possible 'oughts'. Nevertheless this does not alter in the least the fact that the challenge itself has appeared on the horizon, carrying with it the growing realization that there can be no solution in terms of value-postulates. Lukács sets out to find solutions to partial problems. He finds none, but emerges victorious from his defeat. For what he achieves is the metamorphosis of his original problems into a qualitatively higher complex of more concrete questions. Armed with the graphic awareness that the concreteness of the 'trees and flowers devoid of landscape' is a meaningless concreteness, he is now in a position to attack the all-important issue of 'totality'. The price he has to pay for this unintended achievement is the definitive abandoning of the early essay form, with all the immediate attractiveness attached to it.

The consummation of this essay form takes place in *The Theory of the Novel*, in 1914–15. It was originally intended as an introduction to a massive systematic work that has never been brought to completion. (Hundreds of pages of manuscript exist deliberately unpublished: Lukács once described to me this attempt of his at a systematization as a 'six-legged monster'.)[2] It turned out to be a great accomplished essay *malgré lui*. The appearance of systematization in *The Theory of the Novel* should not deceive us: the real structure – the fundamental compositional principle – is essayistic, in the spirit of the early essay form. The analysed works do not preserve their own physiognomy; they are 'sublimated' into pillars of an intellectual (a *'geisteswissenschaftliche'*) construction. The full potentiality of the early essay form is brought to its fulfilment and stretched to its extreme limits in *The Theory of the Novel*, due to the qualitatively higher complex of problems it sets out to solve as compared with the earlier volumes. In the course of its fulfilment, however, this early essay form is also made to burst,

[1] Ibid., p. 177.

[2] In 1963, when I returned to him some three hundred foolscap pages of the manuscript that survived in Arnold Hauser's custody, though glad about the survival of an old document, he found that it would be a waste of his time re-reading it.

and thus it is permanently transcended in Lukács' development. The element of objectivity – in the *Problematik* of 'totality' inherited from *The Soul and the Forms* – floods it and proves to be far too massive for its fragile structure. There will be no more return to it, nor could there be; only occasional expressions of a feeling of *nostalgia* for a necessarily and (in Lukács' view) rightly lost formal accomplishment. The peculiar appeal of *The Theory of the Novel* is inseparable from the historical resonance of a widespread feeling of nostalgia for the accomplishment displayed in it. *The Theory of the Novel* is *no longer* within the bounds of a (disciplined) subjectivity, and *not yet* the conscious acceptance of the methodological impersonality that follows from the recognition of the ultimate determining power of 'objective totality'. (This means also the conscious subordination of one's compositional aspirations to the task of tracing the chaotic intricacies and 'orderless' complexities of the objective order.) It is a once-only work which is characterized by the contradiction between the highest intensity of awareness of the power of objectivity, and the uncompromising radicalism of its rejection. The unique appeal of this work is that the contradiction is 'transcended' in it – if only subjectively – through formal accomplishment, compositional rigour, poetic imagery and passionately heightened style.[1] Ideologically it is situated in some sort of a 'limbo' immediately at the confines of the vision of a capitalistic hell. No wonder that the champions of a romanticized limbo of intellectual existence have turned it into their myth.

---

[1] One short quotation should suffice to give an idea of the type of style in question:

Blessed are the ages for which the starry heavens are the map of the roads which can be travelled and which are to be travelled, and whose roads are illuminated by the light of the stars. Everything is new for them, and yet familiar; adventurous, and yet their own property. The world is wide, and yet it is like their own home, for the fire which burns in the soul is of the same nature as the stars. They are sharply separated – the world and the ego, the light and the fire – and yet they will never be eternal strangers to one another; for fire is the soul of every light, and every fire clothes itself in light.

Die Theorie des Romans. Ein geschichtsphilosophischer Versuch über die Formen der grossen Epik. P. Cassirer, Berlin 1920, p. 9.

The 'new world-epoch' (*neue Weltepoche*) that appears on the horizon of *The Theory of the Novel* is no more than a vague intuition: even in the final references to Dostoevsky it remains a mysterious hint, an ought-ridden question mark. It is forced into the picture by the inner dialectic of his arguments, by the realization that:

> The process which constitutes the inner form of the novel is the problematic individual's journey to himself; the road from gloomy captivity in reality which merely exists, which is heterogeneous and is meaningless for the individual – the road from this to clear self-knowledge. When this self-knowledge is attained, the ideal that has been discovered does, it is true, appear in the midst of life as the meaning of life; but *the division between 'is' and 'ought' is not transcended,* and cannot be transcended in the sphere in which this is enacted, namely in the life-sphere of the novel.[1]

Nevertheless when in the unfinished manuscript Lukács tries further to concretize this problem of '*Aufhebung*' within the confines of his vision of this period, he finds that he never gets beyond a cancerously growing work leading nowhere. This manuscript is characterized by enormously long 'run-ups' to jumps materializing in landings right on the spot of the 'take-off'. The significance of this unfinishable manuscript for Lukács' development was that it intensified his awareness – which he felt even at this level of abstraction – of being right in the middle of a blind alley. One of the maxims Lukács used to recommend was: 'do not stop half-way but follow uncompromisingly the idea to its conclusion; the sparks produced by the collision of your head with the wall will show you that you have reached the limits'. He learned it from Georg Simmel, in his 'privatissimo' seminar, and accepted it as both subjectively and objectively valid. He never experienced a higher intensity of sparks than in this period of the unfinished synthesis, but he fully explored in all directions the limits of adaptability of the Hegelian categories. His unpublished manuscript graphically displays the inadequacy of these categories for coping with the specific complexities of our historical situation, despite the passionate efforts of a great intellect to bring them 'up-to-date'. For this

[1] Ibid., p. 75.

reason alone, if not for others, it well deserves to see the light of the day.

The deep personal crisis was helped to a solution by the dramatic intensification of events: the October Revolution, the military collapse of the Austro-Hungarian Monarchy and the eruption of a general socio-economic and political crisis. Seeing the 'new world-epoch' of *The Theory of the Novel* emerging as a concrete material force, he hailed it with enthusiasm and with great immediate expectations. His first attempts at a radical reassessment bear the marks of an impatient, hasty unification – in theory – of the newly identified material force and his principle of a morally founded practical synthesis. The way he greets the unification of the Hungarian Communist and Social Democratic Parties is highly characteristic of this mood:

> Today the (unified) party is the expression of the unified will of the unified proletariat; it is the executive organ of the will which is forming itself out of new forces in the new society. The crisis of socialism, which was expressed by the *dialectical opposition between the two types of workers' parties,* has at last reached its end. The proletarian movement has *finally* entered upon a new phase, the phase of its power. The mighty deed of the Hungarian proletariat consists in the fact that it has finally led the world revolution into this new phase. The Russian revolution has shown that the proletariat is able to take power and to organize a new society. The Hungarian revolution has shown that this revolution is possible without fratricidal strife between proletarians. With this, the world revolution reaches an increasingly advanced stage. It redounds to the honour of the Hungarian proletariat that it has been able to create *from itself* the power necessary for this leading role – for *leading its leaders,* and the proletarians of all countries.[1]

Similarly, as we have already seen (pp. 46–7), the solution of a well identified dilemma of socialist power is envisaged in terms of a moral postulate versus institutions. The early destruction of the Hungarian experiment put an understandable end to this mood. There follows afterwards a passionate *prise de conscience*

---

[1] *'Taktika és etika.'* (Tactics and Ethics.) In: *Georg Lukács: Schriften zur Ideologie und Politik.* p. 40.

of the highest intellectual intensity, whose rightly famous – though often misunderstood or misinterpreted – monument is *History and Class-Consciousness*. This work is not only a profoundly original and largely successful attempt at a Marxist supersession of Hegel (apart from certain aspects of the thorny issue of 'Subject-Object' – relations), but also raises a host of concrete institutional and organizational problems in close conjunction with the most general philosophical ones. E.g.:

> *The Workers' Council* is the *politico-social conquest of capitalist reification.* In the situation after the dictatorship, it ought to overcome the bourgeois separation of legislative, executive and judiciary; similarly, in the struggle for power it is called upon to end the spatio-temporal fragmentation of the proletariat, and also to bring together economics and politics into the true unity of proletarian activity, and in this way *to help to reconcile the dialectical opposition of immediate interest and ultimate aim.*[1]

Thus although the imperatival element is still very strong, the recognition of the mediatory potential of a historically concrete institution is a significant step forward from the earlier position.

In the twenties Lukács' energies are divided between political tasks and philosophical studies. In politics his position is by no means a happy one, receiving attack after attack from Comintern functionaries and sectarian leaders of his own Party. And after the defeat of his 'Blum-theses' even his peripheral political activity comes to a close. From then onwards his activity is confined to theoretical work and, during a short interval after the war in Hungary again, to the politics of culture. The philosophical studies, in the form of closely argued reviews, carry on the investigations left off in *History and Class-Consciousness.* (The most important of them are the articles on Bukharin, Lassalle and Moses Hess. The little book on Lenin is in a class of its own, characterized by a clear synthesis of some central problems of dialectic – elaborated in *History and Class-Consciousness* – with a remarkable sense of political reality.) One can notice in them the impact of a growing assimilation of political economy, though the peak in this respect is represented by a major systematic work written in the thirties: *The Young Hegel,*

[1] *Geschichte und Klassenbewusstsein.* p. 93.

Georg Lukács

On the Relations between Dialectic and Economics. (As a programme the central theme of this book first appears in *Moses Hess and the Problems of Idealistic Dialectic.*)

The thirties bring back the literary essays but, of course, in a fundamentally different form. As to their structure, they are much closer to the systematic monograph than to the traditional essay. Their composition is dictated by the objective connections of the works in question as seen in the general framework of Lukács' conception of the world, however complex and 'side-tracking' they might be. The author of these essays takes upon himself the task of tackling problems which the young Lukács would have *a priori* excluded from his field of interest. The central notion that both guides these essays and emerges from them in an increasingly more concrete form is the concept of 'specific'. Its universal philosophical equivalent – 'mediation' – has been repeatedly tackled in the preceding period. Without the successful tackling of this general problem the new literary essays would have been devoid of a principle of internal cohesion which could ultimately prevail over their manifold ramifications and involved complexities. On the ground of this general point of reference Lukács was enabled not only to plunge into the most heterogeneous aspects of the works of art discussed– from the political and sociological ones to the moral and epistemological aspects – as they presented themselves in their concrete individuality, but also to synthesize them into a well-identifiable particular aesthetic picture. As the field of his concrete investigation enlarged, so his general aesthetic categories gained in concreteness and complexity. Thus the 'condensed monographs' have dialectically prepared the ground for a general aesthetic synthesis as well.

By the time, however, that he could start writing the latter, important changes in the world perspectives of socialism – the programme of 'destalinization', the Hungarian explosion, China and later Cuba, etc. – brought with them new complications. They brought out into the open a latent contradiction in Lukács' essays. For the intense 'mediatedness' that characterizes them is by no means simply an adequate fusion with the specific character of the works he discusses, although to a lastingly significant extent it is that too. It is at the same time also an '*incognito*' for politico-philosophical polemics into which he has been pushed as a result of his forced retirement from politics and the hardening conditions of life under Stalin, as well as a resignation to the narrowing down of perspectives and to the inevitability of what he called a 'historically necessary *détour*'. In so far as the 'side-trackings' in his literary analyses are due to this 'incognito' and 'resignation', his own objective compositional principle of the essays is evidently violated, no matter how important the excursions themselves might be in other respects. (All the more because some important formal aspects of the analysed works are inevitably pushed into the background in the course of such incursions and excursions.) More important, however, is the fact that the preparatory work to the later synthesis turns out, even in the light of Lukács' own perception of the changing perspectives, to be temporally conditioned to a more than acceptable extent. One of the measures of Lukács' greatness is that he finds the moral strength and intellectual power to face up to the challenge of a 'new beginning', even past the age of seventy.

There is here a more than superficial similarity to the crisis of the post-*Theory of the Novel* period, even if coupled with essential differences. The first result of his attempt at a synthesis is the book *On Particularity as a Category of Aesthetics* (*Über die Besonderheit als Kategorie der Ästhetik*). It was planned originally as an Introduction to the major aesthetic work. As it turned out, it had to be kept separate from the latter. The essential difference from the years around 1915 is, however, that the new personal crisis – again, against the background of an objective historical crisis – has been attacked and resolved, to the extent that it was possible for him so far, within the perspectives of Marxism. This fact has enabled him to complete the new work; the massive volumes of *Die Eigenart des Ästhetischen*. But this work clearly bears the marks of an unresolved situation: it is much more like a '*Rohentwurf*' (rough draft) than an accomplished synthesis. It reveals heterogeneous layers of the development of his thought, left side by side. Also, the extensive new 'groundwork' – made necessary by the realization of the temporal shortcomings of the earlier preparations as well as by an acute awareness of the unfilled gaps – is being done in front of our eyes and incorporated in its immediacy into the general synthesis. This latter characteristic – and not the level of abstraction – sadly cuts off this fundamental work from the reading public.[1] Another major work of searching re-examination and synthesis is the just completed *Ontology of Social Being*, known so far only from Lukács' own accounts of it. On the evidence of the latter one can only hope, but by no means anticipate, that the completed work itself succeeds in superseding the internally determined '*Rohentwurf*' character of his *Aesthetic*.

5

The central categories of Lukács' dialectic are the closely interrelated concepts of 'totality' and 'mediation'. Adequate discussion of them would require a very detailed analysis which is, unfortunately, out of the question here. We have to content ourselves, again, with tracing the bare outlines of Lukács' formulations and solutions of these problems.

As we have seen, the passionate revolt of the young Lukács against the prevailing forms of capitalistic fragmentation and isolationism had brought with it very early expectations as regards a possible solution, and postulates of an uncompromisingly comprehensive character. But we have also seen that even in *The Theory of the Novel* the concept of totality remained an abstract regulative principle, despite the heightened awareness of its crucial importance. It was in *History and Class-Consciousness* that Lukács first succeeded in raising, at the highest level of generalization, the issue of 'concrete totality'.

He emphasized that

It is not the predominance of economic motives in the interpretation of society which is the decisive difference between Marxism and bourgeois science, but rather *the point of view of totality*. The category

---

[1] It is to be hoped that one day a re-worked and substantially condensed version of this great '*Rohentwʌrf*' (rough draft) will appear.

of totality, the all-round, determining *domination of the whole over the parts* is the essence of the method which Marx took over from Hegel and, in an original manner, *transformed* into the basis of an entirely new science.[1]

And he added, after his criticism of the 'individual standpoint' of bourgeois theory: '*The totality of the object* can be posited only when *the positing subject* is itself a totality.'[2] Although the opposition of 'individual standpoint' and 'the standpoint of totality' is still an abstract one, it enables him to work out the Social Ontology of *History and Class-Consciousness*. He asserts that '*Concrete totality* is therefore the *true category of reality*',[3] and concretizes it as 'socio-historical process' (*gesellschaftliches Geschehen*),[4] and formulates the task of the supersession of the theoretical-intellectual-artistic fragmentation as a necessary dimension of the practical unification of 'Subject and Object'. (When, in the already quoted recent work, he defines social totality as a 'complex of complexes', he offers a much more concrete general framework of reference which promises an *Ontology* far superior to that of *History and Class-Consciousness*.)

However, 'social totality' without 'mediation' is rather like 'freedom without equality': an abstract – and empty – postulate. 'Social totality' exists in and through those manifold mediations through which the specific complexes – i.e. 'partial totalities' – are linked to each other in a constantly shifting and changing, dynamic overall complex. The direct cult of totality, the mystification of totality as an immediacy, the negation of mediations and complex interconnections with each other, can only produce a myth and, as Nazism has proved, a dangerous one at that. The other extremes of undialectical separation: the cult of immediacy and the negation of totality, of the objective interconnections between the individual complexes, is also dangerous, producing disorientation, the defence of fragmentation, the psychology of the meaninglessness of one's actions, the cynical rejection of morally inspired activity, and the powerless acceptance of one's conditions, however inhuman they might be. No wonder that Lukács rejects them both.

[1] *Geschichte und Klassenbewusstsein.* p. 39.
[2] Ibid., p. 40.   [3] Ibid., p. 23.   [4] Ibid., p. 27.

Georg Lukács

His 'tertium datur' is a historically concrete, dialectical conception of totality. He writes in 1947: 'The materialist-dialectical conception of totality means first of all the concrete unity of interacting contradictions . . . ; *secondly*, the *systematic relativity* of all totality both *upwards* and *downwards* (which means that all totality is made of totalities *subordinated* to it, and also that the totality in question is, at the same time, *overdetermined* by totalities of a higher complexity . . .) and *thirdly*, the *historical relativity* of all totality, namely that the totality-character of all totality is changing, disintegrating, confined to a determinate, concrete historical period.'[1] The significance and limits of an action, measure, achievement, law, etc., cannot be therefore assessed except in relation to a dialectical grasp of the structure of totality. This in turn necessarily implies the task of a dialectical grasp of the complex mediations which constitute the structure of totality.

The early Lukács was unable to formulate the concept of 'concrete totality' because he was not in a position to envisage those mediations which could transcend the 'details, fragments, isolated things' of the 'immediately given' in the ultimate unity of a dynamically changing dialectical totality. The picture of an unmediated, segmented, non-interconnected, statically frozen conglomeration of discrete things could only generate an equally static concept of totality: a nostalgic value-postulate of unity. By the time of writing *History and Class-Consciousness* the vision has changed qualitatively. Discussing the problem of 'ultimate aim' (*Endziel*) Lukács writes:

It is also no *ought*, no *idea*, which would be associated with the 'real' process in a regulative way. Rather, the ultimate aim is the *relation to the whole* (to the whole of society, regarded as a process), through which every individual moment of the struggle first receives its revolutionary significance. It is a relation which *dwells within* every moment in its simple and sober everydayness, but which first *becomes real through its becoming conscious,* and which

---

[1] 'A marxista filozófia feladatai az új demokráciában.' (The Tasks of Marxist Philosophy in the New Democracy. Text of a lecture delivered at the Congress of Marxist Philosophers in Milan, on 20 December 1947.) Budapest, 1948, pp. 11–12.

(by *making manifest the relation to the whole*) gives reality to the moment of daily struggle, *raising it to reality* out of *mere factuality*, mere existence.[1]

The problematic aspects of Lukács' conception of 'Subject-Object-relations', characteristic of this period of his development, can be detected in this passage. But also it can be clearly seen that this concept of totality is already a dynamically mediated one, though of course it cannot go beyond the limitations imposed on Lukács by the lack of a greater concreteness in his conception of 'mediation' at the time.

In Lukács' development the concept of 'mediation' has been taken up over and over again. The fight against the meaninglessness of 'immediacy' (*Unmittelbarkeit*) is characteristic of Lukács' approach right from the beginning: one cannot fail to see this in *The Soul and the Forms* and in *Aesthetic Culture* – not to speak of *The Theory of the Novel*. 'Aestheticism', 'naturalism', 'impressionistic descriptions', etc., are rejected by him because of their fragmented character: their inability to produce the picture of a coherent whole. At the same time 'symbolism' is also rejected, because the picture it produces is that of an artificial, false, abstract-subjective totality, in so far as the immediacy of detail is directly – and with subjective arbitrariness – elevated to the status of universal significance, comprehensiveness. (The earlier quoted passage concerning Thomas Mann's irony is revealing also in this respect.) The common denominator between 'naturalism' and 'symbolism' is, of course, the missing mediation, and thus their close interrelatedness, despite their superficial contrasts at various levels – subject-matter, linguistic characterization, external form, etc. – is understood, even if at this stage only as a hunch, rather than a coherently developed insight. The young Lukács does not possess the conceptual apparatus that would enable him to transform that hunch into a systematic theoretical vision. The abstractness of his own general level of inquiry – the categories of 'the soul and the forms' (*die Seele und die Formen*), 'value and reality' (*Wert und Wirklichkeit*), 'the height of being' (*Gipfel des Seins*), 'appearance and essence' (*Schein und Wesen*), 'life and work of art'

[1] *Geschichte und Klassenbewusstsein.* pp. 36–7.

Georg Lukács

(*Leben und Kunstwerk*), 'pure constraint on the pure will' (*der reine Zwang auf den Reinen Willen*), 'the pinnacle of being' (*der Hohepunkt des Daseins*), etc. etc. – prevented him from identifying those concrete mediations which could transcend the rejected immediacy by moving towards a concrete totality, and not towards some abstract 'metaphysical essence', as happens in the early works. The contradiction between grasping the meaninglessness of immediacy and Lukács' inability to solve conceptually the complex problems involved in the dialectical relationship between mediation and totality results in a false conception of the critic's role:

> The critic is the man who sees what is fateful in the forms, whose strongest *experience* is that *spiritual content* which the forms conceal within themselves, *indirectly* and unconsciously.' 'The essay is a court, but what is essential and value-determining in it is not the *judgement* (as in the case of the *system*), but the *process of judging*.[1]

Thus the elements of truth are pushed to the point of mysticism, in order to hide, however unconsciously, the ultimate contradiction that what is being opposed to the fragmented immediacy of 'naturalism', 'symbolism', etc. – by means of the categorial apparatus of *The Soul and the Forms,* etc. – is a mystical immediacy of frozen, metaphysical essences. If one starts – as Lukács does – from the premise that philosophy can offer the 'icy finality of perfection',[2] the margin of the critic's activity is an illusory one. The 'process' he opposes to the 'icy finality of perfection' as displayed in philosophy is 'predetermined' by those metaphysical 'soul-contents' which the critic is supposed to 'strongly experience', 'directly live', and thus to free from that 'mediatedness', and 'unconscious hiddenness' which inevitably characterize them as they assume the forms of 'sensible immediacy' (*sinnliche Unmittelbarkeit*). The critic is given the task of opposing the 'soulless immediacy' of naturalism, etc., as well as indicating those forms of 'sensible immediacy' which are penetrated by 'soul-contents', i.e. in which a 'metaphysical immediacy' takes on a directly perceptible form. But in the end

[1] *Die Seele und die Formen.* pp. 17 and 38.
[2] Ibid., p. 4.

there is no criterion of judgment, neither for the rejected immediacy nor for the romanticized one. This is why the 'process of judging' must be mystified *per se* and opposed to the 'judgment' characteristic of the 'system'. The critic's role as an intermediary between the 'forms' and the 'system' is an illusory one, for the metaphysical entities of the 'system' are taken for granted and are assigned the metaphysical value-quotient of the 'finality of perfection'. The problem of mediation, despite the recognition of the 'bad immediacy' of naturalism, symbolism, etc., remains unresolved. And this is what defeats the young Lukács in the end, forcing him to search for a solution where it cannot be found: in a mystically inclined opposition to 'the system'.

But even if the young Lukács failed to master the problem of concrete totality through the grasp of the concrete mediations that constitute it, one should not underestimate the fact that the negative side of the issue – in the form of the repeated polemics against the immediacy of aestheticism, impressionism, naturalism, symbolism, etc. – is tackled with great rigour and sensitivity. We can recognize here, in fact, a major theme of Lukács' later aesthetic writings: the analysis of the profound structural affinity between naturalism and symbolism as regards their inability adequately to transcend the level of crude immediacy. The paradoxical phenomenon of naturalism verging on symbolism, or even turning into symbolism, on the one hand, and symbolism falling back on naturalistic positions on the other finds its explanation in the structural affinity of missing mediations. Clear definitions in this regard can only be found in the later Lukács, but this complex of problems has been inherited from the author of *The Soul and the Forms*.

The road towards greater concreteness as regards the concrete mediations of concrete totality led through the earlier mentioned crisis in the years 1914–17. What is significant in this context is that in this period the earlier unquestioned 'system' is submitted to searching examination and is found hopelessly wanting, so much so in fact that it had to be abandoned. Thus the 'icy finality of perfection' at a closer look turned out to be the lifeless perfection of a frozen dialectic: the transformation of the categories of an originally dialectical quest for the transcendence of immediacy into the frozen essences of a metaphysical immediacy. No wonder that the 'six-legged monster' could not be brought to an organic conclusion: every new attempt at remedying its defects could only add a new frozen member, thus underlining the contradictions of the conception as a whole. And the help Lukács could receive from the Hegelian philosophy was here of no use whatsoever. For, as he later realized, Hegel tried to tackle this complex of problems:

... as purely theoretical, as logical. ... As a result, the *mediating categories achieved independence* as real 'essences'; they freed themselves from the *real historical process,* from the basis of their genuine comprehensibility, and so turned into a *petrified new immediacy.*[1]

A system of this kind could be of no help, except in an indirect way, i.e. by displaying the contradictions of such an approach. Lukács himself had to abandon first the premises of his earlier system before he could find a satisfactory solution to the problem of immediacy-mediations-totality. His encounter with Marxism brought home to him the fact that the crucial intermediary link of all human phenomena is man's 'practico-critical activity', with its ultimate reference – a reference 'in the last analysis' – to the sphere of economics. His reckoning with the Hegelian philosophy in *History and Class-Consciousness* – especially in its central piece on *Reification and the Consciousness of the Proletariat* – is unequivocal and conclusive in this respect. It forcefully makes the point that the Marxist critique of political economy is methodologically based on the Hegelian programme of the 'dissolution of immediacy' which for Hegel had to remain an abstract and unrealizable programme, because of the socio-historical limitations of his standpoint. At the same time it is repeatedly stressed that the crux of the matter is the complexity of 'concrete mediations': if the latter are suppressed, the result is inevitably something negative, or even dangerous, like 'vulgar Marxism', 'economism', 'ethical utopianism', '*Proletkult*', 'sectarianism', 'schematism', 'naturalism', 'revolutionary romanticism' (a version of 'symbolism'), 'voluntarism',

---

[1] 'Moses Hess und die Probleme der idealistischen Dialektik.' In: *Georg Lukács: Schriften zur Ideologie und Politik.* p. 268.

'subjectivism', 'Stalinism', etc. etc. What is common, according to Lukács, to all these trends and manifestations is the neglect or suppression of the categories of mediation.

Thus in Lukács' conception the role of economics, far from being mechanical and one-sidedly deterministic, is dialectically active: it is given the role of the structurally and methodologically ultimate frame of reference. This does not mean, of course, that now we have acquired a 'magic wand' in the shape of a mechanical 'common denominator'. On the contrary, the assertion about the importance of economics becomes meaningful only if one is able to grasp the manifold specific mediations in the most varied fields of human activity, which are not simply 'built upon' an 'economic reality' but also actively structure the latter through the immensely complex and relatively autonomous structure of their own. Only if one grasps dialectically the multiplicity of specific mediations can one understand the Marxian notion of economics. For if the latter is the 'ultimate determinant', it is also a 'determined determinant': it does not exist outside the always concrete, historically changing complex of concrete mediations, including the most 'spiritual' ones. If the 'demystification' of capitalist society, because of the fetish-character of its mode of production and exchange, has to start from the analysis of economics, this does not mean in the least that the results of such economic inquiry can be simply transferred to other spheres and levels. Even as regards the culture, politics, law, religion, art, ethics, etc., of capitalist society one has still to find those complex mediations, at various levels of historico-philosophical generalization, which enable one to reach reliable conclusions both about the specific ideological form in question and about the given, historically concrete form of capitalistic society as a whole. And this is more evident if one tries to transfer the inquiry to a more general level, as becomes in fact necessary in the course of the structural analysis of any particular form of society, or of any specific form of human activity. One cannot grasp the 'specific' without identifying its manifold interconnections with a given system of complex mediations. In other words: one must be able to see the 'atemporal' (systematic) elements in temporality, and the

Georg Lukács

temporal elements in the systematic factors. It is in relation to this point that Lukács stresses the fundamental differences between Marx and Hegel, while emphasizing the great achievements of the latter:

> Hegel's tremendous intellectual contribution consisted in the fact that he made *theory* and *history dialectially relative* to each other, grasped them in a dialectical, reciprocal penetration. Ultimately, however, his attempt was a failure. He could never get as far as the *genuine unity of theory and practice*; all that he could do was either fill the logical sequence of the categories with rich historical material, or rationalize history, in the shape of a succession of forms, structural changes, epochs, etc., which he raised to the level of categories by sublimating and abstracting them. Marx was the first who was able to see through this false dilemma. He did not derive the *succession of categories* either from their *logical sequence*, or from their *historical succession,* but recognized 'their succession as determined through the relation which they have to each other in bourgeois society'. In this way, he did not merely give dialectic the real basis which Hegel sought in vain, he did not merely put it on its feet, but he also raised the critique of political economy (which he had made the basis of dialectics) out of the fetishistic rigidity and abstractive narrowness to which economics was subject, even in the case of its greatest bourgeois representatives. The critique of political economy is no longer one science along with others, is not merely set over the others as a 'basic science'; rather, it *embraces the whole world-history* of the 'forms of existence' (the categories) of human society.[1]

This conception of economics as the dialectical comprehension of all the categories of human society, through their complex transformations in history, could not be further away from a mechanistic vision. For the immense variety of categories can be interrelated in a coherent whole only if the 'model' of general assessment is that of multiple transitions and mediations, qualified both historically and systematically.

Lukács' philosophical achievements reach as far as his conception of mediation (totality) allow him to go. It goes without saying, however, that his conception has been profoundly affected by his historical predicament as a critic, politician and philosopher. The issue of mediation is not just one among many,

[1] Ibid., pp. 286-7.

nor is it simply an abstract philosophical problem, however complex and 'abstract' many of its aspects might be. When Lukács strongly criticizes Feuerbach's 'ethical utopianism'[1] as the result of a myopic rejection of the Hegelian category of 'mediation', he is also fighting a battle against a utopian trend in the existing socialist movement. Similarly his criticism of 'vulgar Marxism', 'economism', 'sectarianism', 'naturalism', '*Proletkult*', 'schematism', 'revolutionary romanticism', 'Zhdanovism', 'voluntarism', 'subjectivism', 'Stalinism', etc., has always a mark of historical urgency, just as much as his polemics directed against the other side, against 'irrationalism', 'decadentism', 'the myth of immediacy', etc. etc. Lukács lives and works at a time when 'the mystifications of capitalistic immediacy' have already penetrated the organized socialist movement ('economism', 'revisionism', etc.), and when the society that emerged after the victorious October Revolution is being conditioned and affected in more ways than one by the 'irrational' moves of this system of 'reified immediacies'. The theoretical task is seen as a challenge of great practical significance. This is how Lukács assesses, for instance, the sectarian approach:

> The sectarian world-view which politically underrates the *mediatory role* of the *immediate interests* (incentives) in the realization of world historical tasks creates the same kind of dogmatism at the level of the individual's conception of the world: a dogmatism that dismisses all the mediatory factors.[2]

It is obvious enough that the issue is not an academic one, for the dismissal of 'all the mediatory factors' is not far from the tragedy of the concentration camps. In *History and Class-Consciousness, Moses Hess, The Young Hegel, Essays on Realism, The Category of Besonderheit, Die Eigenart des Ästhetischen,* we observe Lukács' theoretical quest for a deeper understanding of the complexities of mediation in a world dominated by the dangerously narrow perspectives that arise on the foundations of reifying immediacies. The quest acquires its

[1] See several passages of his essay on Moses Hess.

[2] *Új magyar kultúráért.* (For a New Hungarian Culture) Szikra, Budapest 1948. p. 134.

practical pathos in this context: as a philosopher's answer to an historical challenge. And no matter what one might think of some parts of *The Destruction of Reason*, its really fine and gripping chapters acquire their significance in the same context.

Lukács' achievements are outstanding in those of his works in which the inquiry can legitimately remain at a more abstract level. In such works he systematically explores the intricate problems of mediation under its manifold aspects as no philosopher before or beside him. The outcome is not only the solution of numerous complex aesthetic issues, but also the formulation of some fundamental and challenging problems in the fields of Epistemology, Ethics, Ontology and Philosophy of History.

However, the general theoretical nature of his conception of mediation proves to be a self-imposed trap in certain situations; namely in circumstances in which even a simple inventory of the socio-historical ingredients at work would reveal much more than Lukács' far-fetched and completely unrealistic theoretical assessment of the presumed new historical trends. As an example, let us quote his discussion of the characteristics of the 'new democracy', i.e. of the 'People's Democracy':

> The true democracy – the new democracy – produces everywhere real, *dialectical transitions* between private and public life. The turning point in the new democracy is that now man participates in the interactions of private and public life as an *active subject* and not as a *passive object*. . . . The ethically emerging new phase demonstrates above all that one man's freedom is not a hindrance to another's freedom but its precondition. The individual cannot be really free except in a free society. . . . The now emerging self-consciousness of mankind announces as a perspective the end of human 'prehistory'. With this, man's self-creation acquires a new accent; now as a trend we see the emergence of a unity between the individual's human self-constitution and the self-creation of mankind. *Ethics is a crucial intermediary link in this whole process.*[1]

As we can see, this analysis is hopelessly off-target as a concrete assessment of a particular historical situation: it is, in fact, a succession of general philosophical postulates represented as

[1] Op. cit. in Note 1 on p. 66.

actually existing social trends. In this it strongly resembles the earlier quoted passage, written at the beginning of 1919, on the occasion of the unification of the two Hungarian workers' Parties (see p. 60): the same approach, the same attempt at directly linking – without the necessary 'mediations' – a particular historical situation with far-away 'world-historical perspectives'. We are confronted here with philosophico-moral anticipations, with the reassertion of the validity of some fundamental moral postulates, with an invitation to realize some basic tenets of the Marxist programme – in a situation in which the political power-requirements of translating a programme into reality seem to be satisfied – but not with a realistic grasp of the specific features and contradictions of a social formation.

The unreality of the 1919 analysis might have been explained as due to Lukács' political inexperience, although – as we have seen – even then things were much more complex than that. Almost thirty years later, at the time of writing about 'the new democracy', the hypothesis of political inexperience is definitely a non-starter. After all, in the meantime Lukács lived through not only the dramatic months of the Hungarian Soviet Republic, followed by the long years of political emigration both in the west and in Moscow, but also he had to experience personally the political prisons of the Stalinist system. If despite all this he nourishes the illusions we have just seen, this cannot be explained with a tautological reference to the illusions themselves. Rather: an explanation ought to be attempted in terms of the philosopher's life and its interactions with the system of his ideas.

As has already been mentioned, the limits of Lukács' philosophical achievements are set by his own conception of mediation or, to be more precise, by the defects of this conception: by the unwarranted intrusion of 'immediacy' into his general world-view. This can be clearly seen in both the 1919 and the 1947 quotations in the direct transference of a particular social pattern to a most general world-historical level. This, however, in itself is no explanation. The question that needs answering is: why does such undialectical transference occur in some specific connections of Lukács' thought, despite his unrivalled general awareness of the crucial importance of mediations?

To find an answer to this question one must try to understand the abstract character of the political dimension of his conception of mediation. The major determinants in this respect cannot be confined to the already mentioned socio-political immobility that dominated the years of Lukács' intellectual formation in his native country. Nor could they be exhausted with a reference to the rarefied atmosphere of politics in a weak emigration (i.e. in a political emigration devoid of a broadly based social support in its country of origin) in which Lukács tried to overcome the handicaps of his beginnings. The *'übergreifendes Moment'* (overriding factor) was the fundamental change in the organized international socialist movement in the twenties, following the changes in Soviet internal development as a result of Stalin's victory. Parallel with these developments the political trend represented by Lukács within the Hungarian Party was defeated by the end of the twenties, and with the defeat of his so-called *'Blum-theses'* – in 1928 – he ceased to play any significant political role. (Even during the post-war years of the 'new democracy', before he was attacked by Révai and others for his 'deviations', his role was strictly confined to the politically subordinated realm of culture. He was not allowed in the large body of the Central Committee, let alone given a place in the effective organ of political direction, the *Politbüro*.) His *History and Class-Consciousness* was strongly attacked, by Comintern officials and others, and later too attacks and intrigues continued to restrict his range of action even before the final blow of the defeat of his 'Blum-theses'. These are the personal aspects of his political non-evolution. More important were, however, the general trends of development, quite independently of their personal repercussions which in the philosopher's mind could have been ascribed to the excesses of narrow-minded party functionaries. We can single out here only one aspect of this development: the practical disintegration of all forms of effective political mediation, from the Workers' Councils to the Trade Unions. Even the Party, in the course of its adaptation to the requirements of Stalinistic policies, had largely lost its mediatory function and potential. If Lukács' idea of the Party as formulated in *History and Class-Consciousness* contained a great deal of idealization, in the changed circumstances this idealization has become overwhelming. All the more because in *History and Class-Consciousness* the institution of the Workers' Councils still appeared as a necessary form of mediation and its effective instrumentality. Now, however, its place had to be left empty, as indeed all the other forms of political mediation too had to leave a vacuum behind them. In this respect the twenties not only did not bring a political evolution but unmistakably marked a phase of involution in political realism.

This is where one can see the contradictions between the limited immediacy of political perspectives and the universality of a socialist programme in Lukács' conception. Since the political intermediaries – and instrumental guarantees – are missing, the gap between the immediacy of socio-political realities and the general programme of Marxism has to be filled by means of assigning the role of mediation to ethics, by declaring that 'ethics is a crucial intermediary link in this whole process'. Thus the absence of effective mediatory forces is 'remedied' by a direct appeal to 'reason', to man's 'moral responsibility', to the 'moral pathos of life', to the 'responsibility of the intellectuals', etc. etc. So that – paradoxical as it might seem – Lukács finds himself in this respect in the position of 'ethical utopianism', despite his repeated polemics against it, and despite his clear realization that the intellectual roots of ethical utopianism can be pinpointed in the lack of mediations. (Lukács' significant overrating of the role of the intellectuals in contemporary society belongs to the same complex of problems.)

The direct extrapolation from the prevailing form of unmediated instrumentality to the universal perspectives of socialism, and vice versa, confers a certain abstractness on more than one of Lukács' analyses. And no wonder. For the 'concrete mediations' that constitute 'concrete totality' are closely interrelated (and reciprocally interpenetrating) partial totalities; they acquire the character of a totality from the reciprocal interpenetration of the various modalities and forms of mediation.

77

Thus the abstractness of the political dimension in one's conception of this dialectical system of mediations leaves its marks, though of course not in the same way and degree, on the various complexes of problems, whether in Aesthetics or in Ontology, in Epistemology or indeed in Ethics itself to which that problematical role of 'should-be mediation' is assigned. (It is not difficult to see, to take only one example, that in order to be able to fulfil its 'mediatory function' Ethics needs the support of the very instruments and effective forces of mediation which it is supposed to replace in Lukács' conception.)

Similarly, it is rather inconsistent of Lukács that, while he condemns Zhdanovism and its 'unmediated' theory of 'revolutionary romanticism', he accepts the narrow and unmediated instrumentality that necessarily produces it. His analyses of this cultural-ideological phenomenon remain inevitably abstract in the sense that the concrete social determinants of Zhdanovism cannot be revealed. The discourse is confined to the ideological sphere, and at times the actual causal relations are even reversed: it appears as if the aberrations and contradictions of the ideological level were responsible for the ills of social development and therefore the remedies should be found at that level, by means of an intense ideological clarification. (Of course they were also responsible for those ills; but basically they were determined by them, they were specific manifestations of them.) 'Sectarianism' represented a similar issue. Here too Lukács' correct recognition and penetrating dialectical analysis of the missing mediations in the sectarian approach could not alter in the least the fact that sectarianism as an ideological form was determined by the actual absence of effective mediatory forces and institutions from the social body: it reflected this state of affairs, it did not cause it. (Of course it also contributed to the solidification and perpetuation of the social structures which necessarily brought it into being.) To envisage remedies simply by means of an ideological clarification, however rigorous, against this background of social determinations reminds one of the attempts directed at disposing of religious alienation by means of noble atheistic sermons.

The actual absence of socio-political mediatory forces and

institutions in Soviet development greatly affected Lukács' perspectives, undermining the possibility of practical-political criticism: from the end of the twenties, criticism was condemned to become abstract-theoretical and generic-ideological. (Its practical side was narrowly circumscribed by the only feasible instrumentality: the Stalinist Party as the final arbiter over the fate of the competing ideological positions.) To make things worse, Soviet society had become internationally isolated and confronted with extreme hostility by the incomparably more powerful capitalist world. In these circumstances it became ever more difficult to envisage concrete material forces of socio-political mediation as an effective form of practical criticism of the prevailing trend of Stalinism. Soviet development thus increasingly acquired the character of a 'model' of socialism, despite the obvious violations of some elementary principles of socialism, however paradoxical this might seem. Its complete international isolation – which in fact greatly contributed to the weakening and ultimate disintegration of the internal forces of mediation and thus to the bureaucratic violations of socialist principles – restricted the margin of action of all those who in an ever more polarized world (one should not forget the dramatic rise of European Fascism) refused to turn against the only existing social system that professed socialist principles and *de facto* became the 'model', however paradoxical and problematic, of socialism. In this restricted field of action their discourse – in the absence of both external and internal mediatory and conditioning forces of a socialist character – was confined to the ideological sphere. Since the historically conditioned narrow instrumentality of Soviet developments had to be directly linked with the universal perspectives of socialism in the idea of 'Socialism in one country', the general moral perspective itself had to be turned into a mediatory force. Needless to say this could be done only at the level of theoretical abstraction. This is why in the end *'der Zwiespalt von Sein und Sollen ist nicht aufgehoben'*, for the philosophically postulated mediatory force, in order to become reality, would itself need actual, effective mediatory forces and instruments. An anticipated moral postulate, as mediator

79

between the ultimate postulates of the universal perspectives of socialism and the immediacy of a given situation, is and necessarily remains a pseudo-mediator, an ideological postulate, an ultimate '*Sollen*'. And to mediate between '*Sein und Sollen*' by means of another '*Sollen*' amounts to not mediating at all. For the '*Zwiespalt von Sein und Sollen*' cannot be superseded through postulating another '*Sollen*' which is then projected and superimposed on the immediate reality of 'the new democracy', for instance. The numerous unfulfilled optimistic anticipations of Lukács' writings – later recognized as unfulfilled by the philosopher himself – find their explanation in this contradiction inherent in his position and thought.

Needless to say, the 'ought-ridden' character of Lukács' solutions is not simply the manifestation of personal limitations. The basic determinants are those of the concrete historical situation which set the ultimate limits to any personal achievement. Lukács' significance consists in his ability to explore the objectively given field of action to its extreme limits, creating thus a life-work simply incommensurable with philosophical achievements produced within the Soviet world. Paradoxically, in this the same '*Sollen*' that circumscribed the limits of his achievements proved to be his greatest asset. For he never accepted the immediately given in its crude immediacy, i.e. he never abandoned for a moment the ultimate perspectives of socialism. As was mentioned earlier, his perspectives were characterized by a duality, in the form of linking the everyday issues with the broadest general aims of a socialist mankind. In this duality of perspectives the dominating factor always remained the incessant advocacy – however 'ought-ridden' – of the ultimate socialist goals and values. Though this has given an abstract character to so many of his analyses, it also enabled him to keep alive, with the greatest intellectual rigour, socialist ideals and use them as a general framework of criticism of the immediately given. True, this criticism always remained confined to the ideological sphere – even after the officially-announced programme of 'destalinization'. But in the latter he achieved more than anybody else, thanks to the validity of his 'ought-ridden' ultimate postulates and perspectives.

If the contradictions of Lukács' position now appear to be obvious, this is because the historical perspectives themselves have significantly changed. To what extent Lukács can keep pace with such change, remains to be seen. (That he made great efforts to do so, both in his *Aesthetics* and in his *Social Ontology*, is clear enough, however problematic the results might be.) What matters in this connection is that his old perspectives, personally and historically valid in the sense which has been shown, now irrevocably belong to the past. There is no room here for an adequate discussion of these problems. It must be stressed, however, that the question of the 'mediation of socialism with socialism' has ceased to be an abstract moral postulate and has become an often rather confusing, disconcerting and even disorienting reality. We are faced today with objective tensions and contradictions within the socialist world. The issues that have thus arisen cannot even be tackled, let alone solved, with ideological labels like 'sectarianism' which Lukács tried to stick, in one of his recent essays, on to the body of Chinese development. Some fundamental reassessments would be required in the present situation; all the more because another new, and perhaps the most important, historical factor – the profound structural crisis of the most advanced capitalistic countries and the potential new social dynamism closely connected with it – raises the question of socialism in a radically different way. It seems, however, that Lukács is unable to reformulate the question of mediation as an institutionally safeguarded internal necessity of socialism, because this would imply the presence of objective contradictions within and between socialist systems: a sharp contrast to his advocacy of 'Reason' and 'ideological clarification' as a solution to the existing problems. On the other hand, he seems to be too ready to accept the prospects of 'many decades' of social stagnation and immobility in developed capitalist countries, naïvely expecting a 'turn towards socialism' in these countries as a result of the 'force of attraction' of Soviet-type socialism that succeeded in freeing itself 'from the remnants of Stalinism'. Thus the solutions are, again, confined to the ideological sphere.

The total unreality of Lukács' position is graphically displayed in a context where he praises the Kennedy-type 'Brains-Trust as an organizational form' as valid also for socialism. His words are as follows:

> A Kennedy knew for certain that he was no theoretician and no man of science, but (in contrast with European, and specifically with German development) he did not identify the expert with the top-level bureaucrat. He knew that from *this* expert he could discover nothing of importance, but that what he needed was a set of intellectuals and theoreticians. (Whether or not Kennedy chose correctly, is unimportant here.) These theoreticians were to do nothing but devote their knowledge and their thought to the exposure of general problems, so that the politician could derive from this material the slogans for his movement. Now, I believe that the specific position of Marx and Lenin in socialist countries has led to a fantastic over-estimation of the theoretical value of the Party's First Secretary.
>
> With the Brains-Trust, 'a new organizational principle has appeared, namely, a *duality* and a co-activity of theory and political practice, which is no longer unified in one person – and which happened to be unified only once, if at all – but which, on account of the extraordinary widening of the tasks, *can be brought about today only in such a dual form.*'[1]

It is pathetic to see this great demystifier of our century yielding to sheer mystification. Almost every single element of this assessment is hopelessly out of touch with reality. George Kennan, perhaps the best brain of Kennedy's Brains-Trust, has a much lower opinion of this 'organizational form'. He knows that its actual working principle is: 'Leave your brains and ideals behind you when you enter this Brains-Trust', that is if your ideals happen to differ from those of the 'top-level bureaucrats' (*'hohen Bürokraten'*). (He wrote after his resignation from the Kennedy team that the only occasion when those bureaucrats could not prevail over him was when he donated his blood after the Skopje earthquake: they could not prevent *that* from happening.) Also, the issue is not whether we abound in men of the stature of a Marx or a Lenin. (Though again significantly the names of both Gramsci and Mao Tse-tung are omitted.) The rarity of intellectually creative political talent is

[1] 'Gespräche mit Georg Lukács,' pp. 78–9.

not some 'original cause', but rather the *effect* of a certain type of social development, which not only prevents the emergence of new talent, but destroys the talent available through political trials (cf. the numerous Russian intellectuals and politicians liquidated in the thirties), through the expulsion of men of talent from the field of politics (Lukács, for instance), or through bending them to the acceptance of the narrow practical perspectives of the given situation (e.g. the great talent, by the highest standards, of a József Révai). Lukács himself was denounced as a 'professor' when he tried to integrate politics and theory,[1] and he had to leave the field of politics as a result of successive attacks. He accepted this turn of events with resignation. Now, however, he invents a theory to justify the permanent 'duality' and separation of theory and politics: the 'widening of the tasks' (*'Verbreitung der Aufgaben'*). The earlier resignation now becomes a mystified virtue through the assertion of its alleged necessity. *'Der Zwiespalt von Sein und Sollen ist nicht aufgehoben'*, it merely seems to be. For the advocated 'organizational form' as the synthesis between theory and practice only appears to be a practical reality; it is in fact a mere utopian postulate. It is no more than a pious hope to expect the frustrated Kennan's bureaucrats to give way to his insights and proposals, just as much as it is a mere wishful thinking to expect the solution of the great structural problems of international socialism to come from the self-conscious and willing recognition by Party First Secretaries that they are neither Marxes nor Lenins. If it is true, as it well may be, that we are today confronted with an 'extraordinary widening of tasks'

---

[1] When Lukács, in 1924, was attacked by Zinoviev – who later himself fell a victim to Stalinism – in the company of Antonio Graziadei and Karl Korsch, it was held against him that they were 'professors'. (Lukács in fact had his first University Chair in 1945.) The attack went like this:

'If a few more of these professors come and dish out their Marxist theories, then the cause will be in a bad way. We cannot, in our Communist International, allow theoretical revisionism of this kind to go unpunished.'

(See pp. 720–21 of *Georg Lukács: Schriften zur Ideologie und Politik*.)

The fight against intellectuals in the Comintern was justified in the name of preserving Marxism against revisionism. In fact it signified the replacement of some fundamental tenets of Marxism by the theses of a narrowly practicist and rigidly dogmatic version of revisionism.

('*ausserordentliche Verbreitung der Aufgaben*'), this makes it all the more urgent and vital to insist on the reciprocal interpenetration of theory and politics, theory and practice, rather than to offer a justification of their alienation and 'necessary duality' by idealizing an organizational form, a non-existent or unworkable 'Brains Trust.' Nothing could be more illusory than to expect the solution of our problems from the 'Brains-Trust' of abstract intellectuals and narrowly pragmatic politicians. The alleged '*Verbreitung der Aufgaben*' needs for its solution the reciprocal interpenetration of theory and practice in all spheres of human activity and at all levels, from the lowest to the highest, and not the sterile stalemate of academics and politicians at the top. In other words the task is a radical democratization and restructuring of all social structures and not the utopian reassembly of existing hierarchies.

As we have seen, the thread of an unresolved duality leads, in one form or in another, through Lukács' entire development. We have also seen the close connection between the structure of his ideas and some fundamental trends of development of an age of which Lukács is one of the greatest representatives. If we are reluctant today to accept some basic tenets of his social ontology, this is not because of some sudden conceptual inspiration, but because we feel its inadequacies as regards the possibility of answers to our practical problems. Reluctant to accept the 'many decades' of social immobility he prophesies, we are forced to question the elements of dualism in his social ontology. This we must do with great caution; not only because his systematic work on Social Ontology still awaits publication and the samples from it, contained in his *Gespräche*, are inevitably summary and schematic, but also because the animating element of our own questioning is a hope, not a certainty. The emerging new historical perspectives seem to sustain this hope, but they do not warrant its transformation into a self-reassuring certainty. Lukács' notion of a '*rein objektive Entwicklung der Arbeit*' (*purely objective* development of labour) that necessarily produces '*ein immer kleineres Minimum der Arbeit*' (an ever-diminishing minimum of necessary labour) seems to us rather problematical. It does not raise, in the first place, the question of the *limits* of such *'rein objektive Entwicklung'*, granted that we accept this notion as an element of ontological discussion. (The question of limits is a vitally important one; its absence creates a wide gap that can only be filled by trust. E.g. *'La vérité est en marche'*, etc.) Secondly, by postulating a *'rein objektive Entwicklung'* within a *dual* causality, we are pushing things to their extreme poles, in order to find an 'ontological place' for the recommended mediatory function of Ethics. In fact an answer to the question of limits might yield a unified and integrated system of causality which would fill the 'ontological gap' reserved by Lukács for his *'Sollen'* ('ought'), for the never ceasing moral appeals of his thought.

At the same time it ought to be stressed that though the general historical perspectives have changed, the socio-political trends that form the basis of many of Lukács' formulations are still very much alive today and are being transformed only in the dialectical sense of 'continuity in discontinuity'. Thus his discourse concerning the undialectical 'immediacies' of various ideological trends retains its general methodological validity, and at times even its urgent topicality, in the relevant ideological sphere. Also it should not be forgotten that the dilemmas Lukács had to face in his efforts at defining his position in relation to Marx's postulate of the unity of Philosophy and Politics, Theory and Practice, were not simply personal dilemmas but representative of a difficult age in which the given problematical perspectives seemed to prevail for a long time over the historical orientation of the socialist movement. Opinions may differ as to the practical validity of some of Lukács' conclusions. But no one should fail to see the representative monumentality of his undertaking.[1]

[1] This essay will form part of my forthcoming book: *Life and Work of Georg Lukács* (to be published in 1970).

3 Lukács on Irrationalism

H. A. Hodges

1

This paper is in the nature of a review of one of Lukács' books, which is entitled *Die Zerstörung der Vernunft* (The Destruction of Reason). The book was written during Stalin's lifetime and published in 1953, the year of his death; but the introduction which he wrote for the second edition in December 1960 says that he has not found it necessary to alter anything that was in the first edition. It is in fact noticeable that he has not found it necessary to withdraw, or even qualify, his acceptance of Lysenko as a first-class geneticist.

As regards the content of the book, it is a history of irrationalism. Something which can be called irrationalism is a discernible trend in philosophy in all countries from about 1800 until the present time, but more especially in what Lukács calls the imperialist period, that is since about 1890. From a Marxist point of view it is a reactionary type of philosophy. In this book Lukács writes the history of it, concentrating his attention chiefly upon Germany, though there are references to parallel phenomena in other countries. (It is surprising at first sight to find Croce listed among its representatives; but Lukács has his reasons.) Lukács concentrates upon Germany, I think, for three reasons: firstly because that is the country whose intellectual history he knows best, secondly because Germany does hold a central position in the history of philosophy during the whole period in question, and thirdly because Germany is the country where irrationalism bore its finest flower – Adolf Hitler. The main body of the book is a demonstration of how irrationalism prepared the ground for Hitler and almost ushered him on to the scene. There is a final chapter describing the continuance of irrationalism in philosophy after Hitler's fall, but that was quickly written and (as Lukács says himself) more journalistic than scholarly in manner. The substance of the book ends with Hitler.

What then is irrationalism? How does Lukács conceive it? As a Marxist he inherits a faith in reason and progress as two things which cannot be separated from one another. It is a faith which comes down from the age of the encyclopedists. Humanity is capable of progress without assignable limits, but this depends on the overcoming of ignorance, prejudice and superstition. Reason is that activity of the human mind which overcomes these obstacles and so promotes progress. Any doctrine which opposes or sets limits to reason opposes progress, and that is the oustanding feature of the movement of thought whose history Lukács gives us. Irrationalism resists progress both in science and in the social order, using the weapons of the intellectual to that end. A politician resists progress by political action; an intellectual resists progress by attacking the very conception of progress, by putting forward a doctrine according to which there can be no such thing as progress, or at least by arguing that the road of progress does not lie where it actually does, viz. along the line to socialism.

Irrationalism shows itself both in the theory of knowledge and in the picture of the universe which a philosophy presents.

In the theory of knowledge the first form of it is any doctrine which denies the existence or knowability of an independently existing physical world, that is to say any form of idealism or phenomenalism. Lukács is somewhat surprisingly respectful to objective idealism, i.e. Hegel's kind of idealism, because it embodies at least an attempt to get away from subjectivism and agnosticism and to assert knowledge of reality – though the reality which it presents to us is a reality in which in the long run we cannot believe. Apart from that qualification, which is a tribute to Hegel's subjective intention rather than to his objective achievement, it may be said that all idealisms and all phenomenalisms are irrationalist because they deny knowledge by denying either the existence, or at least the accessibility, of an independent object. This judgment, of course, strikes at most modern philosophers, because of the strong vein of subjectivism which has run through philosophy ever since Descartes.

A second way in which irrationalism shows itself in the theory of knowledge lies in stressing the inherent limitations of scientific method. Here Lukács brings in the important Hegelian distinction between *Verstand* and *Vernunft*. *Verstand* means the abstract intellect as manifested most notably in mathematical and natural-scientific thinking. This, as is often pointed out by philosophers, theologians and poets, is apt to lead either to contradictions and antinomies, or to conceptions which do not do justice to the experienced reality to which they profess to refer. Now in Hegel, when you find that *Verstand* brings you up against this kind of difficulty, what you do is to appeal to *Vernunft*, which means dialectical thinking. You transcend the abstractness of *Verstand* by a dialectical forward move, and so generate concepts which are adequate to do what until now *Verstand* was not able to do. For example, Lukács often refers to the crisis in biology round about the year 1800, when it was becoming clear that mechanistic concepts were not adequate to explain or even to describe the behaviour of living matter. Until that date it had been generally supposed that to be scientific was to be mechanistic, and therefore it seemed to follow that science can never deal with living matter. That is the view which the poets and theologians mostly held. But the true view was that you must make a dialectical change in your explanatory concepts, and realize that the next dialectical step beyond the mechanistic whole is the organic whole. You will find the theory of this set forth in the third section of Hegel's *Logic*. That in general is what dialectic is; it is the transition from a concept which has proved itself too abstract for the facts to a concept which is concrete enough, rich enough in content, to cover them. Irrationalism takes the form of refusing to do this, of denying that it can be done. The irrationalist points to the frustration of science in face of certain problems with which its present methods are not adequate to deal, and then assumes that the limits of present-day science are the limits of human possibility in knowledge. He denies or ignores the possibility of dialectical advance. Sometimes indeed we are told that it is possible to go beyond our abstract scientific thinking, but only by recourse to some kind of intuitive insight. Bergson is famous as a spokesman for this doctrine, but it is one which he shares with many others. Intuition is the irrationalist substitute for dialectic, and wherever you find a philosophy which claims that intuitive insight is the only way in which certain things can be known, you are in the presence of an irrationalism. The appeal to intuition is irrational, in the ordinary sense of the word, because intuition is by its nature not a form of argument, and dialectic is a form of argument. But it is irrational in another sense too: the appeal to intuition is always accompanied by the claim that some people have a capacity for it and others have not. The appeal is therefore to a privileged few; it is, what Lukács constantly calls it, an aristocratic theory of knowledge.

A third way in which irrationalism shows itself in the theory of knowledge is in denying the possibility of scientific explanation in history and the social studies. The physical world – yes, there are natural laws and we can find them out, but there are no laws in history and therefore no explanation or prediction in the scientific sense. Historical knowledge is something in principle different from natural science. It aims not at the general but at the individual, the unique. It gives something which is indeed called 'understanding', but that means a kind of intuitive apprehension which has nothing to do with scientific explanation. Such is the doctrine of historical knowledge put forward in Germany by writers like Windelband and Rickert, and in Italy by Croce.

Irrationalism in the world picture means holding not that there is no objective reality, or that we cannot know it, but that we can know it, and know it to be meaningless. Granted this, we may either find a way of living with the meaningless, or we may deliberately construct a myth in order to give the world a meaning, considering that it is better to live consciously with a myth than to live a meaningless life in a meaningless world.

2

Of irrationalism, thus understood, Lukács constructs a detailed
and in many ways convincing history. I shall talk first about the
overall picture he presents, before I turn to his treatment of two
authors with whom I am more specially qualified to deal.

Philosophy has no history of its own. You cannot write the
history of philosophy, any more than of religion or law, in
terms of itself. All these are among the cultural superstructures
of society, and what goes on in them is unintelligible except by
reference to the economic substructure. To write the history of
philosophy, therefore, it is not enough to take each philosophical
system as a set of contentions, to be argued about abstractly and
judged on their inherent merits; we must see each philosophy as
a historical phenomenon, and relate it to those causes in the
economic substructure which have led to its arising at the time
when it does. This, as Lukács says, has never yet been done.
No one could be expected to do it except a Marxist, and no
Marxist has. There is as yet no Marxist history of philosophy.
Lukács' book is in fact a pioneering work in this respect, a
massive contribution towards a Marxist history of philosophy.
The histories of philosophy written by bourgeois thinkers are
useless to a Marxist. They class together things which the
Marxist would see to be quite different in their nature, and they
fail to draw distinctions which are fundamental. They are
superficial and subjective in their principles of interpretation.

Lukács' account, then, is based on an analysis of the economic
events, and the events in the field of the class struggle which
have followed from them, during the period since about 1800.
This of course is divided into sub-periods, the first of which
begins in 1789 with the first great French Revolution and goes
on until 1848. The great French Revolution was a bourgeois
revolution. It was then for the first time that the bourgeoisie
seized political and social power, being fully conscious of what
it was doing and what it wanted to do with the power when it
had it. It was an age of optimism and a rather naïve belief in
progress on the part of the middle class. The bourgeoisie at the

time rightly regarded themselves as the spearhead of human progress. They had not analysed, of course, down to the sub-structure, and their doctrines of progress were idealistic, but still they were right to hold them. But from 1815 onwards, when not only the French Revolution, but the Napoleonic sequel (which also had its liberal side) had been liquidated, we come to the Restoration period, the period, in Lukács' words, of feudal reaction. It is here that Lukács begins his tale.

He begins with an account of Schelling. 'Why Schelling?' That, I think, will be many people's reaction to finding him here at the head of the history of irrationalism. For one tends to think of Schelling as a radical and forward-looking young man who unfortunately had shot his bolt by 1800, after which date everything of value that he had said was incorporated in Hegel. That is what Hegel thought. One does not ask what Schelling did with the remaining fifty years of his life. But it is a fact that ten years after Hegel's death, at a time when Hegel's philosophy was the prevailing influence among philosophically interested youth in Germany, the authorities in Berlin brought Schelling out of his obscurity and gave him a platform in the University there, in the hope that he would undermine Hegel's reputation and influence. He was to do this in the interests of the reactionary régime then in power. Being a feudal and aristocratic régime, which still saw its chief enemy in the free-thinking bourgeoisie, it of course promoted not only political reaction but theological reaction too; Hegel's Absolute was to be replaced by something more like orthodox theism. Schelling did the work which he was summoned to do, though it could add nothing to the contribution he had once made, fifty years earlier, to the contemporary philosophical movement. But in the works of this his last period he laid down some of the conten-tions which were to be characteristic of irrationalism. Dialectic is not, as Hegel pretends, an organ of positive discovery. It is valid as a negative way of analysis, to bring out the inadequacies of scientific concepts; but to go beyond them to more adequate ones is not a rational progression of thought, but a flash of intuitive insight, of which not all are capable. Dialectic deprived of its positive value; intuition as the vehicle of true understanding;

the truth accessible only to an élite – here in Schelling are three of the leading features of irrationalism.

If anyone hesitates to accept this unfavourable picture of Schelling merely on Lukács' authority, it is worth mention that Croce too, in his *Logica*, can find no good thing to say of Schelling's 'second philosophy', and expressly characterizes it as irrationalistic.

Upon Schelling follows Schopenhauer, the first bourgeois philosopher who openly takes up a stand against the working class as well as against feudalism and monarchism. Twice over Lukács tells the story of how, in the revolutionary year 1848, when the workers were out in arms in the streets of Berlin, Schopenhauer lent his field glasses to a Prussian army officer so that he might see better to shoot working men.

The substance of his philosophy is a doctrine of the meaninglessness of life and history. For in place of the Absolute of the post-Kantian philosophers, which all of them held to be in some sense of the word 'rational', the absolute reality in Schopenhauer is a creative Will which is essentially irrational, and so meaningless; and consciousness, to which reason belongs, is in Schopenhauer, as in many Indian philosophies, essentially painful and a thing to be avoided. As far as knowledge is concerned, what natural science knows is truly known, but it is a superficial knowledge, knowledge merely of phenomena. Behind these phenomena stands the irrational creative Will, but this is understood only by an intuitive vision. The business of the enlightened person who has seen, with Schopenhauer, through the veil of phenomena, is as far as possible, by the cultivation of moral virtue and the arts, to weaken in himself the life impulse which is the source of all human misery.

Lukács draws attention to three typically bourgeois features in Schopenhauer's life and thought. First, the famous independence of mind which Nietzsche so admired in him (*niemandem war er untertan!*) was in fact nothing more than the consequence of possessing an unearned income, and when this income seemed threatened by the revolutionary workers his philosophical calm gave way to panic. Second, for all its appearance of deep disillusionment, his philosophy leaves intact the scientific inquiries upon which the bourgeoisie depends for its productive technologies and the comforts of life. It only denies our right to draw any conclusions from scientific discoveries as to the real nature of things or the meaning of life; for in that way lies revolution. Third, although Schopenhauer presents his philosophy as entailing a way of life, it makes no costing demand upon its author; it enables him to sit in his study, in idleness and luxury, and indulge in high thinking without having to take a stand about anything.

Upon him follows Kierkegaard, who also belongs to the pre-1848 period. Kierkegaard is above all the individual revolting against the restraints of society. The Hegelianism which he chooses as his enemy, the Hegelianism popular in Denmark in his time, is the philosophy in which society, the State and the *Sittlichkeit* of the nation-State is regarded as the 'moral substance', of which the individual is merely a passing mode. Kierkegaard revolts in the name of the reality and significance of the individual. He knows no way of securing the reality and significance of the individual except by giving him a close link with God. But he also knows and openly says that there are no rational grounds for believing in God. His solution is that we are to come to that belief by an existential leap. We hear a lot from Kierkegaard about existential leaps, and one of the things that we hear is that they are essentially leaps in the dark.

Need Lukács say more? But he has more to say. He observes that the position in which Kierkegaard's own existential leap lands him, which is a kind of Christianity, differs from most kinds of Christianity in that it involves him neither in a Creed nor in a Church. He is under no obligation to believe anything in particular, nor to belong to any particular community – in fact he goes all out to assail the religious community existing in Denmark in his time. Nor is he called upon to take any social or political action. He simply goes about in what he calls his incognito, the 'knight of faith' who looks just like a clerk, but who by virtue of faith is all glorious within. It is a strange kind of faith too. Lukács calls attention to a curious likeness between the religious frame of mind in which Kierkegaard ends and the 'asthetic' frame of mind with which his whole line of thought begins. The content of both is 'despair'.

It is interesting that these last two philosophies should have taken shape before 1848; for it was not until 1848 that the proletariate appeared as a political force, walking the streets with arms in its hands, and armed too with a doctrine and a programme. Schopenhauer and Kierkegaard anticipate in their philosophies the social conditions of a later period. That, according to Lukács, is why Schopenhauer, who had been little noticed during his creative period which was before 1848, acquired public recognition and became an influence after that date. The bourgeoisie had suddenly realized that his philosophy, which denigrates and builds defences against the popular masses, was what they needed. Kierkegaard did not come to his full recognition until the 1920s and 1930s; so far ahead of his time was he.

The next period in the social history of Europe runs from the revolutions of 1848, with the proletarian action in Berlin and Paris, through the Commune of 1871, until 1890. This is a transitional period, in which the class struggle has not yet attained its highest intensity, but it has already become clear to all that the proletariate is now the revolutionary class and that the bourgeoisie have a common interest with the feudal and monarchical elements in society in resisting it. The philosopher of this period is Nietzsche, who comes out not merely as an opponent of the working class, but with an openly confessed and virulent hatred of it. Lukács warns us against listening to apologists who would have it that the things Nietzsche says about the ruthlessness and heartlessness with which the masters of society must maintain their position are not literally meant. Make no mistake, says Lukács, Nietzsche meant what he said exactly as he said it. And this society from which humanity has departed is set in the framework of a universe which has no place for a lasting betterment of man's lot. It is a universe of perpetual recurrence, which is Nietzsche's way of excluding the possibility of any genuine progress, any real novelty. Nietzsche also initiates the attack on the conception of truth itself: the truth is whatever is useful to the master class.

We come to the imperialist period, which begins in 1890. If any English hearer or reader wonders what happened in 1890 to make it a significant date, the answer is the dismissal of Bismarck and the lapsing of the anti-socialist laws in Germany. These usher in a period which is marked by the growing intensity of the class struggle and a growing reflection of that struggle in the world of culture, a growing despair of reason and a growing feeling of the need for a *Weltanschauung* or a myth, to make life endurable.

The prevailing philosophical tendency of this period is what in German is called *Lebensphilosophie*. It stems from Dilthey, to whom Lukács does full justice as a scholar and as a sincere seeker after objectivity; but the after-effects of Dilthey's teaching were such as he himself would have been horrified to see. As Lukács tells the story we see a series of philosophers and sociologists of rapidly dwindling intellectual and moral stature: Georg Simmel, Max Scheler, Max Weber, the so-called *Hegelrenaissance* of the 1930s, and finally the existentialists Heidegger and Jaspers. In this part of the story Lukács' language becomes more virulent than in most of the earlier parts of the book. He is speaking of things he has witnessed in his lifetime, and his personal feeling comes out strongly. This virulence of language rises to its height in the section which deals with Heidegger and Jaspers. Again and again on successive pages the words 'philistine' and 'philistinism' come up. No phrases are sufficient to express his contempt for this philosophy, and in his account of the post-war situation he adds some acid remarks on the personal behaviour of Heidegger and Jaspers during and since the Hitler period in Germany.

The imperialist period is the heyday of irrationalism, both in intellectual matters and in social life. It is the period when it becomes axiomatic that value judgments have nothing rational in them and that science itself, since it depends on presuppositions, is exposed to the relativities of personal and social outlooks. It is a period when, with this growing irrationalism rotting away the foundations of knowledge and of all values, mythmaking becomes open and confessed. It is the period in which Weber brings before us the conception of the charismatic leader, and so prepares the niche in which Hitler is to stand.

At this point, before going on to examine Lukács' treatment of two particular authors, I should like to comment a little on the general picture he has drawn.

There really is an irrationalist trend in nineteenth- and twentieth-century philosophy. It is not the only important trend in philosophy during the period, and Lukács admits that it is not, but it is real and deserving of serious study. It is also true that many of the doctrines advanced by writers belonging to this trend have had an unsettling effect upon the mind of the general public, in so far as it has come to know of them. It is not only Marxists who have seen in Nietzsche a dangerous thinker, and we are familiar with the complaints so often brought in this country against the analytical philosophy which is associated with Oxford. Its doctrines could hardly be more different from those of German *Lebensphilosophie*, but the charge brought against them is the same: disintegration of the world-picture and a sense of meaningless in things.

Unpleasing as this trend is to many people, it may yet be that it points to truths which need to be explored. Philosophy in the eighteenth century and earlier had tended to overemphasize the powers and achievements of reason, and the nineteenth and twentieth centuries have seen, perhaps, a necessary and healthy reaction against this lack of balance. There are many non-rational factors at work in human experience and activity – in aesthetic perception and imagination, in moral judgment, in political and religious belief and commitment, even in scientific and philosophical thinking itself. Rationalists may not like this, Marxists may suspect the motives of any who mention it, but it is true. Non-rational factors can in fact be detected in Marxism itself. Nay, the word 'reason' or 'rational' itself is often used emotively, as a cheer-word, and a careful examination of the ways in which it is applied might be disconcerting. At any rate not all would agree that devotion to the Marxist dialectic is a criterion of rationality.

It has been given to our age to explore this aspect of human life more deeply and fully than was ever done before, and the result is indeed unsettling. But it is also laid upon us to face the music honestly, and to find a way to go on being human without yielding to a Leader, or a Party, or a doctrine which is set above criticism. Because Lukács has yielded, he cannot see the situation as it is, and his interpretation of it, while often shrewd, remains in the end an outsider's comment.

3

I should now like to look more closely at what Lukács says about two writers, Wilhelm Dilthey and Karl Mannheim: Dilthey because I once did some work on him, and Mannheim because I often met and talked with him during the last years of his life.

In Wilhelm Dilthey, Lukács sees the undoubted source of that *Lebensphilosophie* which is the typical form of irrationalism in the imperialist period. Yet of Dilthey himself Lukács always speaks with a remarkable respect. He acknowledges the profundity of Dilthey's scholarship, even though he did not have the light of Marxist theory to give him the true interpretation of his facts. He acknowledges Dilthey's honest desire to escape from subjectivism and irrationalism, though in fact he failed to escape from either. He recognizes that Dilthey would have been horrified if he could have foreseen the Nazis, even though in fact his writings were among the causes which made the Nazi doctrines possible. Nowhere else does Lukács distinguish so clearly between his judgment on a philosophy as an incident in the social struggle and his judgment on the philosopher himself as a man and a thinker.

He begins his account of Dilthey with a discussion of his epistemology, his attempt to refute idealism and establish a realist theory of knowledge. Dilthey is one of those philosophers who claim that objectivity cannot be obtained by any purely intellectual process, not even by the application to sense-data of Kantian categories, but can only be found in the experience of resistance, the experience of coming up against things. There is quite a succession of philosophers who take this view; Dilthey himself refers back to two of his predecessors in the line, Fichte and Maine de Biran. He holds that life (*das Leben*) is experienced fundamentally as a continual interaction between the self and the not-self. From this experience, beginning in the womb in tactual and kinaesthetic terms, is derived the schema of self and not-self into which, after birth, the deliverances of the senses and (still later) the discoveries of abstract thought are fitted. He also holds that the categories upon which our later thinking depends are not given to us *a priori*, in Kantian fashion, but are read off by us from the various aspects of the dynamic relationship between self and not-self.

Unfortunately, as Lukács rightly points out, although Dilthey says *das Leben*, you always find that he means *das Erlebnis*; that is, he talks of life, but he means lived experience. His account of the experience of frustration is enough to show this. I myself in my book *The Philosophy of Wilhelm Dilthey* went into this matter more fully than Lukács does here, but the result is only to confirm Lukács' verdict. In the *Beiträge zur Lösung der Frage vom Ursprung unseres Glaubens an die Realität der Aussenwelt und seinem Recht* (1890) Dilthey analyses the experience of meeting with resistance very interestingly, but he does not succeed in finding in it a genuine apprehension of a not-self. The self interprets its own frustration in terms of a frustrating agent, a counter-self in its own likeness; but this is a projection, not an apprehension, and that is all that Dilthey in the end can offer. Not only so, but there is a good deal in his other writings, early and late, which casts doubt upon the value of this conception of the object as a counter-self. There are passages where Dilthey seems to be a pure phenomenalist after all. If the true philosopher's business is to work out a convincing realist theory of perception, then Lukács is right in saying that Dilthey fails to do so.

The truth is that the whole question means much less to Dilthey than it does to a Marxist. He wanted to refute idealism in order to block the way to a metaphysic of the transcendental self or the Absolute, with the preconceptions which such a metaphysic would impose upon the philosophy of history. But he did not want to put a materialist metaphysic in its place. He wanted to have no metaphysic, no ontology at all, in order to be free to get on with his real work, which was to construct a philosophy of history. For, as Lukács rightly says, his real concern throughout his life was to be the Kant of the historical and social studies. Kant wrote a book which he called a critique of pure reason, but it was really a critique of natural science. What he did not write, and what Dilthey was going to write, was a critique of historical reason, a *Kritik der historischen Vernunft*. All his philosophical works are intended to be contributions to this.

Dilthey generally begins his argument with an attack on the methods of the positivists and the historians influenced by positivism: on Comte, Spencer and Taine. For, he says, they try to account for the facts of history and culture in terms of physiology and theories about the nervous system, in terms of biology and theories about the basic instincts, and in terms of other matters such as present themselves to persons trained in the natural sciences. With categories like these you cannot begin even to describe, much less to make intelligible, the facts of historical life. This is true, but what does Dilthey give us instead? During the greater part of his career, until the last eight years or so of his life, he tells us that the *grundlegende Wissenschaft*, the foundation-science of all the *Geisteswissenschaften*, is a special kind of psychology; not experimental psychology, and of course not the associationist psychology of the earlier British school, but something which he calls descriptive (*beschreibende*) as against explanatory (*erklärende*) psychology. It is to draw its information from common experience, from the facts of mental life and activity as they disclose themselves to a gifted observer and introspector, and it is to take as much guidance as it can get from poets and novelists and religious writers, who have often been gifted observers and instrospectors. From all this it is to put together a description of the kinds of experience (*Erlebnisse*) which constitute the conscious life of man. Lukács speaks of this psychology as 'anti-causal', and Dilthey does in fact inveigh against the giving of causal explanations in a certain sense. Of course he does not deny that history is a story of causes and effects, if by causes we mean stimuli consciously received and reacted to by human agents. The stimulus-and-reaction process pattern on the introspectable level is part of what descriptive psychology is to describe. What Dilthey rejects is the attempt to explain conscious processes by causes which cannot be verified in inner experience, whether they be material or transcendental. His point is not primarily that such explanations are false, but that they are irrelevant to what a historian or philosopher of history needs to know.

Lukács as a Marxist cannot agree with this; to him it seems like condemning oneself from the outset to superficiality and subjectivity.

Dilthey is well thought of as a historian. He wrote a great deal of history, mostly not political history but cultural history, especially history of literature and philosophy. In these fields he is an historian of great learning and great merit, and Lukács acknowledges this; but still, since Dilthey has no suspicion of the nature of the economic substructure of society, but only looks at the cultural superstructures which he finds reflected in his written sources, without ever suspecting how the surface consciousness conceals and distorts the underlying reality, therefore his description, though vivid, and perfectly honest according to the sources upon which he bases it, is subjective in selection, emphasis and interpretation. It is the interpretation placed upon cultural history by a German Professor of Philosophy, full of good will but imperfectly equipped, in the late nineteenth and early twentieth century.

The reality of history as Dilthey conceives it is lived experience (*Erlebnis*), and it is made known to us through the various forms of expression which are the culture historian's data, the books, statues and buildings, social institutions, systems of religious doctrine and the like, which Dilthey lumps together under the name of 'objective mind'. The theory of historical knowledge must therefore consist in an account of how the observer of the objective expressions of the human soul can get from them to an understanding (*Verstehen*) of the experience which they express. Dilthey's attempts to write the theory of such understanding, which are mainly concentrated in his last ten or fifteen years, are to many of his admirers the most significant and valuable part of his philosophy, but to Lukács they appear as an open surrender to irrationalism. Of course understanding involves conceptualizing, and the historian is failing in his work if he does not give us a rational account of the events with which he is concerned. Dilthey has much to say about the methods used in this rationalizing process. But he always ends by declaring that lived experience cannot be fully expressed in rational terms, and that understanding includes re-experiencing (*das Nacherleben*). No one can understand cultural monuments and expressions unless he has in himself the kind of experience which they express. And when it comes to understanding a complex expression such as a work of literature, there is need of an intuitive gift which he calls 'divination', a gift which some men have and some have not. Here we have two of Lukács' bugbears, the appeal to the intuitive knowledge because of the alleged incompetence of reason, and the theory of an epistemological élite.

Again, Dilthey finds himself involved in an antinomy which he confesses himself unable to resolve, between the historian's knowledge of the changefulness of human types and the descriptive psychology which is his foundation-science, and which gives him a limited number of fixed types. Dilthey's descriptive psychology says that there are fundamentally only three types of human character: the types in which intellect, feeling and will respectively prevail, and since these types are based on the three fundamental factors of human nature which do not change, the types themselves do not change. There is of course a great variety of transitional and combined types, but the three fundamentals are fixed. Yet he says in one place that 'the type: Man, dissolves in the course of history', and between the historical relativism expressed in that sentence and the absolute validity of his three types he cannot reach a final decision. He became more and more unhappy about his psychology in later years, but he never found the courage to disown it. In manuscripts which he wrote in his final year, he still says that he adheres altogether to what he has previously said on the subject.

Finally, there is the matter of Dilthey's *Weltanschauungslehre* or theory of world-outlooks. It was Dilthey who first introduced the word *Weltanschauung* into the philosophical vocabulary. It

Georg Lukács

was later vulgarized in a regrettable way, but in Dilthey it had a clear meaning. A *Weltanschauung* is a comprehensive view of the nature of the universe, and the nature and capacities and destiny of man. Everyone who is not wholly unimaginative has a *Weltanschauung* (though he may not be conscious of what it is or what it is based on), and you cannot be a reflective person without somehow formulating your *Weltanschauung*. *Weltanschauungen* find expression normally in three ways, in religion, in art and in philosophy. And there are three fundamental types of *Weltanschauung* corresponding to the three fundamental human types. The type of man in whom intellect predominates tends to go to the naturalistic *Weltanschauung*, in which mathematics or natural science is the prevailing influence. The type of man in whom will is the determinant factor, dominated by the consciousness of freedom and responsibility, goes for a kind of philosophy which Dilthey calls the idealism of freedom, or libertarian idealism. The kind of man in whom feeling rules goes for objective idealism, the doctrine that the universe is an organic whole, and that you can get a kind of unity with it through feeling. Any two of these three types can combine, but not all three, so Dilthey says, and many interesting philosophers can be shown to be the product of such combinations; Descartes, for instance, and Kant, are notable examples of the first existing in tension with the second.

It will be seen that a *Weltanschauung* is not a product merely of intellectual curiosity and speculation, but is a projection of one's entire personality. Consequently different types of people are predestined to have different *Weltanschauungen*, and the *Weltanschauung* in every case is the personal vision of the one who has it. Looking at it this way, and appealing no further than to his descriptive psychology, Dilthey deprives himself of the possibility of seeing how *Weltanschauungen* are also historical and social phenomena and are ultimately to be explained by the economic substructure of society. Furthermore his typology, so ridiculously simple, is totally unable to contain the known facts of the history of religion, art and philosophy, even as they appear to one who does not know about the substructure. But the worst thing of all in this connection is the question that worried Dilthey almost to death: how to reconcile the three *Weltanschauungen* in a single consistent body of truth.

Some of Dilthey's latest writings are concerned with this but none of them find the reconciliation, for indeed his analysis shows that no reconciliation is possible. In one late writing entitled *Traum* he describes how once, visiting a friend's house, he was given a room where there was a reproduction of Raphael's School of Athens, and he went to sleep with the vision of those assembled philosophers in his mind. He went off into a dream in which the philosophers who lived after Raphael's time came and joined those who were there already, and then they began to sort themselves out. First the naturalistic and positivistic thinkers came together around Archimedes and Ptolemy; then the idealists of freedom gathered around Socrates and Plato; and the objective idealists formed a group around Pythagoras and Heraclitus. Descartes and Kant, who were at first among the mathematicians and scientists, left that group and joined the idealists of freedom. Then the three groups began to recede from one another, great fissures appeared in the ground between them, and 'a dreadful hostile alienation seemed to separate them– I was seized by a strange anxiety, that philosophy seemed to exist in three or possibly more different forms – the unity of my own being seemed to be rent, as I was longingly drawn now to this group, now to that, and I struggled to retain it'. I sympathize with Dilthey; for the experience symbolized in that dream has been part of my waking life for the last forty years. One who is open to all the possibilities of interpretation, to all that is there in the history of philosophy, is bound to be faced in one way or another with the urgent need to reconcile the irreconcilable. Dilthey tried to persuade himself that it could be done by saying that, while the three *Weltanschauungen* are indeed incompatible if expressed as metaphysical doctrines, for then they contradict one another, if you do not assert them as doctrines but simply understand them as points of view they each represent a perfectly genuine way of looking at the universe, a way of tasting and feeling life, and it is possible to understand and enjoy and alternate them in oneself. Naturally one will always have one's inherent affinity and preference; but one can escape from one's limitations to the extent of seeing what the other life-interpretations are, and thus achieve a kind of wholeness of vision and freedom from dogma which is the ultimate gift of philosophy. But though Dilthey puts forward this solution bravely, there are indications that he was not wholly satisfied with it.

In *Wilhelm Dilthey: an Introduction* I ventured to suggest that the next step beyond Dilthey's position here might be to a philosophy of deliberate self-commitment to a point of view, such as we find in Kierkegaard. Dilthey himself had no such idea, and Lukács would not have thought any better of him if he had. But something like it is implicit in the *Lebensphilosophie* which followed on from Dilthey, and finally in Jaspers and Heidegger the existentialist doctrine is openly proclaimed. We have seen what Lukács thinks of this line of thought.

I think Lukács' account of Dilthey, though severely critical, is substantially fair. Dilthey had great merits, which Lukács acknowledges. He also had many weaknesses, which Lukács legitimately points out. He asked deep questions which neither he nor his successors could answer satisfactorily. Those who are not at one in doctrine with Lukács may perhaps be readier to own that Dilthey got into some of his difficulties through his honesty in facing awkward facts. Like Siger, he

sillogizzó invidiosi veri

Karl Mannheim (1893–1947) is more a sociologist than a philosopher, though he is something of both; and in philosophy he regarded himself as a disciple of Dilthey. In spite of his name he is not a German but a Hungarian; but he taught in Germany and was one of those who had to leave that country when Hitler came to power. I have heard him speak with pride of the fact that none of his erstwhile pupils had become a Nazi. Lukács has less to say about him than about Dilthey, and that is just, for he is a lesser figure. At the same time Lukács' treatment of him shows an asperity and (I think) an unfairness which I do not find in his treatment of Dilthey.

Lukács begins with Mannheim's 'sociology of knowledge', which is his version of what in most philosophies is called simply the theory of knowledge. Like Dilthey, Mannheim wanted to avoid subjectivism, and he also wanted to avoid the relativism which since Dilthey's time had been so widespread in philosophy and the social sciences. His way of doing so was to adopt what he called relationalism. The difference is that relativism is a kind of scepticism, suggesting that because standpoints differ they are all untrustworthy, whereas relationism is a simple recognition that everyone has a point of view and sees things from this point of view. That does not mean that different points of view must contradict or invalidate one another; they may amplify one another. He went on to conclude that objectivity as often understood, as involving impersonality and standpointlessness, is not merely impossible, but inconceivable, and at the same time unnecessary.

This is another *invidioso vero*. It is easy to see what an unsympathetic commentator can do with it.

Mannheim went on to accept the Marxist contention that consciousness in all its form is socially conditioned, adding that this applies to Marxism too; and he showed how in Marx's teaching there is an interesting combination of genuine rationalism with a kind of messianism whose ultimate source can be found in the Old Testament. Therefore he could not accept Marxism as being simply the truth. It was full of insights into truth which were of the greatest value, but it had this inbuilt messianism to which it owed its mass appeal; and since it is characteristic of messianism to believe uncritically in the near approach of the Kingdom of Heaven, to ignore difficulties and practicalities and to expect and demand quick results from strong action, it was a force tending to encourage dictatorship and therefore socially dangerous. In short, Marxism was convicted also of being, on one side of itself, an organized movement of irrationalism, even while it claims to be true scientific thinking. But if the stronghold of reason is not there, where is it? Mannheim sought to find somewhere in society a group of people who could be at least to some extent free from the intellectual blindness and emotional pressures which lead to such irrationalist doctrines and movements. He thought he found this in the intelligentsia, who were, so he contended, as nearly classless as it is possible to be in a society like ours. But then the problem was to persuade the intelligentsia to understand their role in society and to work in concert to fulfil it.

I hardly need say how all this appears to Lukács. The analysis of Marxism and the appeal to the intelligentsia (the bourgeois intelligentsia, be it noted) are obvious propaganda for the wrong side in the struggle of our time.

In one of Mannheim's latest books, *Diagnosis of Our Time*, where he brings together a number of papers which he wrote for various groups of people, the last of the papers has a footnote saying that he had written it for a small private group of Christian thinkers who used to meet four times a year for a week-end conference. I was a member of that group; Mannheim and I were both members of it from 1938 until his death in 1947. It was a group of about a dozen people who met, as he says, three or four times a year for a week-end. What was the meaning of the group and why was Mannheim in it?

It was a group of people of extraordinarily varied background and character, all but two of whom were Christians in some sense of that very elastic word, and all were concerned about the gap which has opened between the Christian tradition in its present form, both doctrinal and institutional, and the social life of our time. Mannheim and his friend Adolf Löwe, a political economist, not being Christians, were invited into the group to give us the benefit of their sociological insights. They were supposed to teach us to see ourselves as others saw us.

That is why Mannheim was invited into the group; but why did he consent to come? What meaning had it for him? His reasons were sociological reasons. He was deeply conscious of the irrational forces in human nature, which in a broad way are obvious to everyone, but which have been explored especially by Freud and Jung. In particular Mannheim had adopted from Jung the doctrine of the archetypes, the images which crystallize so much of the force of the irrational drives, and which can take possession of people's minds, wills and souls and drive reason out. It seemed to him that generally speaking, in the course of history, it has been the function of religion to canalize the

primitive drives, to civilize them and give them a genuine satisfaction in ways which support and do not threaten the social
fabric. But today the prevailing religion of Europe has broken
down, its archetypal images and symbols no longer cast their
beneficent spell, and no other satisfaction has been offered to
the primitive in man except through coloured shirts and march-
ing columns and mass rallies and messianic myths. It was thus
he explained the terrific power, the 'demonic' power as we called
it in those days, that went into fascism and also into communism;
and he wondered whether in a country like this, where the social
fabric is not so badly deteriorated, where the class conflict is
not yet so desperate, it might be possible for the religious forces
yet to reform and revivify themselves, and yet again to perform
their ancient civilizing function.

As I look back upon it now after twenty or twenty-five years,
it seems to me an astonishingly naïve expectation, that twelve
men plus Mannheim could somehow contrive to set going a
process like that, but we took it from him in those days and it
was an interesting adventure. Be that as it may, this was his
conception; the reality of the irrational, which is no mere by-
product of hostility to progress, but a fundamental, strong and
dangerous fact of human nature. The history of man can be seen as
the history of the attempt to civilize the irrational, and today it is a
question of finding fresh means of civilizing it and keeping it
civilized in a world where science, industry and urban society
have robbed the old archetypes and symbols of their power.
Hence Mannheim's interest in helping that Christian group.
Hence too his interest in the reform of education, his theories
about how to create an élite, and how to bring about a revolution
by democratic planning instead of by violence.

Lukács says that Mannheim, like all ideologists, was far more
frightened of a genuine socialist revolution than of a return of
fascism, and that he was throughout hostile to democracy.
That seems to me to be a perversion of the truth. Mannheim
always pointed to the dangers of mass society. What Lukács
has done is to equate 'mass society' with the 'toiling masses'
and socialist democracy with a communist dictatorship, and
draw the conclusion which then follows. This however is true,

that if you did talk to Mannheim about the necessity of social-ism, meaning by it the public ownership of the means of produc-tion and distribution, he would tell you that that was old hat, that the real danger was not capitalism but totalitarianism, which could spring as easily from socialist as from capitalist soil, and that the way to avoid that was not merely public ownership, but democratic planning. That was Mannheim's teaching as I knew it, and I think Lukács' account of him is notably further from the truth than his account of Dilthey. Mannheim, of course, is a generation later than Dilthey, and roughly a contemporary of Lukács himself.

4 Lukács on the Central Category of Aesthetics

G. H. R. Parkinson

1

Since 1957, Lukács has been devoting himself to the completion of major works on aesthetics and ethics. The first product of these labours has been *Die Eigenart des Ästhetischen,* which was published in 1963. This two-volume work on the specific nature of the aesthetic is only the first part of a longer treatise on aesthetics; Part Two is to discuss in more concrete form the structure of the work of art, and Part Three will be concerned with art as a socio-historical phenomenon (*Die Eigenart des Ästhetischen,* Vol. i, pp. 14–15. Hereafter, references to this work will be made by simply citing volume and page number). However, it is in order to discuss Part One without waiting for Lukács' complete aesthetics, since he states (i. 13) that this part is a self-complete entity.

A work as long and complex as *Die Eigenart des Ästhetischen* cannot be discussed adequately in a single paper; what will be discussed here is only one of the many themes of the work. It is, however, a major theme – namely, the category of *Besonderheit,* which Lukács declares to be the central category of aesthetics, that category in which the 'structural essence of the aesthetic' (ii. 193) is most adequately expressed. The subject is dealt with at length in Chapter 12, though this has to be supplemented by what is said elsewhere in the book. Occasional reference will also be made to some articles belonging to a group which Lukács published between 1954 and 1956,[1] chiefly

[1] These are: 'Kunst und objektive Wahrheit.' *DZP* II, 1954, pp. 113 ff.
'Die Frage der Besonderheit in der klassischen deutschen Philosophie.' *DZP* II, 1954, pp. 764 ff.

in the *Deutsche Zeitschrift für Philosophie* (abbreviated, *DZP*).

Before the central category of Lukács' aesthetics can be discussed, there are two obvious questions that have to be answered. The first is this: what, broadly, does Lukács regard as the tasks of aesthetics? Second, when he speaks of a 'category', what does he mean by this term? The answer to the first of these is that *Die Eigenart des Ästhetischen* attempts to answer a traditional question of aesthetics, namely 'What is a work of art?' Lukács tries to put the making and the appreciation of works of art in the whole context of human behaviour; he tries to distinguish art from everyday thinking and from scientific thinking, from magic and from religion. The reference to magic may cause some surprise, but in explaining its presence we touch on a basic idea of Lukács' aesthetics, and indeed of his philosophy in general. Reality, Lukács says, is essentially historical (i. 24–5), by which he means that we have to regard what exists, not as something static, but as something which constantly changes and develops. If, therefore, we are to understand the structure of anything, place it in the right categories, then we must know how it began. So when Lukács tries to explain what art is, he does so by showing how art developed out of something else (cf. i. 80), and it is his belief that art develops out of magic (i. 377–411). Nothing will be said here about Lukács' account of the origin of art, but it is necessary, before going further, to look more closely at the question which this account is meant to answer. The question is, 'What is the nature of art?' Now, it is a commonplace that words like 'art'

'Das ästhetische Problem des Besonderen in der Aufklärung und bei Goethe'. *Festschrift Ernst Bloch*, ed. R. O. Gropp (Berlin, 1955), pp. 201 ff.

'Das Besondere im Lichte des dialektischen Materialismus.' *DZP* III, 1955, pp. 157 ff.

'Das Besondere als zentrale Kategorie der Ästhetik.' *DZP* IV, 1956, pp. 133 ff.

'Zur Konkretisierung der Besonderheit als Kategorie der Ästhetik'. *DZP* IV, 1956, pp. 407 ff.

One may take these as throwing light on *Die Eigenart des Ästhetischen*, since Lukács refers to the second, third and fourth of these in the work itself (ii. 193 n.) and reproduces large sections of the fifth without alteration (compare *DZP* IV, pp. 138 ff. with ii. 255 ff.).

and 'work of art' are used with varying degrees of liberality. In one sense, things that are hung on the walls of what are called 'art galleries' are works of art, but there is another sense in which something may be on a wall of such a gallery, duly framed and catalogued, and yet be said by some not to be a work of art. Similar distinctions are made in the case of special types or genres of art; for example, a librarian may have no hesitation in classifying a certain book as a novel, whilst a critic may say that the author of the work is not really a novelist. One may mark this difference by distinguishing (as, for example, does Morris Weitz in 'The Role of Theory in Aesthetics', *Aesthetic Inquiry,* ed. by M. C. Beardsley and H. M. Schueller, Belmont, 1967, pp. 9–10) between the 'descriptive' and the 'evaluative' use of words such as 'art'. Broadly speaking, the cataloguer and the auctioneer will tend to use the word 'art' in its descriptive sense. On the other hand, the critic will tend to use it in its evaluative sense; when he says 'This is a work of art', he is praising something. This distinction is perhaps over-sharp; for example, when one says that something is a work of art in the evaluative sense, one can in principle *describe* the features that make it praiseworthy.[1] Conversely, for something to be counted as a work of art in the descriptive sense it must be praiseworthy in some respects – e.g. a certain level of technical accomplishment. However, the distinction may serve our purposes. Now, it is the view of those who are commonly called 'linguistic philosophers' that the philosopher's business is the analysis of the ways in which words are used. They would say that aesthetics, in so far as it is a branch of philosophy – and they would probably add that much of what has been counted as aesthetics does not really belong to philosophy – is concerned with stating the rules that govern the use of words like 'art'. Most of those who try to do this would probably agree with Professor Weitz (op. cit., p. 10) that the analysis of the evaluative use is more difficult and interesting than that of the descriptive use; and

---

[1] It is possible that Professor Weitz would agree, for he writes (op. cit., p. 10), 'For many, especially theorists, "This is a work of art" does more than describe; it also praises'. On the other hand on p. 9 he writes, 'We sometimes say, "This is a work of art" to describe something and we sometimes say it to evaluate something'; there is no hint here that we may sometimes do both.

since (as has just been said) the former use is typically that of the critic, there arises the idea that the chief business of aesthetics is to talk about the critic's language.

Where, then, does Lukács stand in relation to all this? He certainly uses in an evaluative sense words like 'art', and the words for the various genres of art. In his early book on the theory of the novel, he distinguishes between 'the novel' and 'light reading', where 'light reading' (*Unterhaltungslektüre*) clearly covers many works which a librarian might regard as novels (*Die Theorie des Romans,* 2nd ed., 1963, pp. 71, 101, 105). In *Die Eigenart des Ästhetischen* he draws a line between what is art and what is meant to be art (e.g. ii. 118, 231, 310), and clearly includes under the latter heading works that might appear in art galleries, or on shelves marked 'Novels'. One could say, then, that in asking about the nature of art, Lukács is in effect asking questions about the language of criticism. Lukács himself does not say this, and indeed it seems likely that he would object to this way of viewing his aesthetic theory; judging from the last chapter of *Die Zerstörung der Vernunft*, he shares the widespread communist misunderstanding of, and hostility to, modern linguistic philosophy. Here, however, one may quote against him the motto of *Die Eigenart des Ästhetischen: 'Sie wissen es nicht, aber sie tun es'* – 'They don't know it, but they do it'. But of course it would be wrong to try to make of Lukács a linguistic philosopher *malgré lui*; although there are likenesses, there are also important differences. For example, most linguistic philosophers are not system-builders, but Lukács' aesthetics is a systematic work in the grand manner. Again, modern linguistic philosophers would say that they are free from any metaphysical assumptions, whereas Lukács writes from the standpoint of dialectical materialism, which is a metaphysical theory in the sense of being a general theory about the nature of reality. (That Marxists use the word 'metaphysics' in another sense, in which it is contrasted with dialectics, is not relevant here.) Further, Lukács' historical approach is not typical of linguistic philosophers, who are apt to concentrate on the way in which words are used at present. There is still another difference; this seems to be a chance one, not based on the very nature of linguistic philosophy, but in Lukács' case it is particularly important. Those linguistic philosophers who write about criticism tend to do so as spectators rather than as players; that is, they are not committed to any one critical theory. Lukács, on the other hand, is very much a player, in that he is himself a critic. This has the advantage that he knows what he is talking about; he knows criticism, one may say, from the inside. But it also has a disadvantage. When Lukács talks about the critic's use of the word 'art', he is talking about his own use, whereas he tends to speak as if he were talking about *the* use. One might say, then, that to the extent that Lukács' aesthetics offers a definition of art,[1] it offers what some have called a 'persuasive definition'. That is, it professes to give an analysis of the word 'art' and other allied words, whereas it actually contains a disguised recommendation to use these words in another, non-standard sense. Justification of this assertion will be provided in the main body of this paper; but even granting that the assertion is true, this is by no means the end of the matter, for one still has to ask about the point of the definition, about Lukács' aim in using the word 'art' in the way that he does. To put the matter in another way: it may be that Lukács' definition of art is a disguised linguistic recommendation, yet recommendations are made for certain reasons, and it is these reasons that are important.[2] However, they cannot be discussed until something has been seen of Lukács' definition of art; and before this can be looked at, another word demands attention, namely the word 'category'.

Lukács does not claim to list all the categories of aesthetics, still less all categories absolutely. Here he is in line with standard Marxist theory, which states that categories do not form a closed

[1] Lukács himself would deny that it does. For him, a definition fixes on a partial aspect of what is actually of infinite complexity, and makes a spurious claim to finality. Lukács says that his method is one of 'determinations', *Bestimmungen*, a 'determination' being something provisional and in need of supplementation (i. 29–30). This is only a terminological matter; Lukács' 'determinations' seem equivalent to what would generally be called a 'provisional definition'.

[2] Besides Weitz, op. cit., pp. 10–11, cf. W. E. Kennick, 'Does traditional aesthetics rest on a mistake?', in *Collected Papers on Aesthetics*, ed. C. Barrett (Oxford, 1965), pp. 9 ff.

and immutable system, since as reality develops and knowledge increases, the list of categories must change. (See, e.g. Rozental and Yudin, *A Dictionary of Philosophy*, English trans., Moscow, 1967, p. 68. Cf. G.Wetter, *Dialectical Materialism,* English trans., London, 1958, p. 368.) This is one difference between Marxist categories and those of Kant; another is that Marxist categories are not (as Kant supposed categories to be) imposed by the mind. As Lukács puts it, categories are objective, they are not 'points of view' (i. 193). To talk about categories, then, is to talk about certain general features of objective reality; Lukács expresses this by saying that objective reality contains categories objectively within itself (ii. 264). Some Marxist definitions state that categories are concepts which 'reflect' reality (Wetter, op. cit., p. 367), and this view, too, is to be found in Lukács, who says that categories are 'the most general forms of reflection' (i. 686; cf. i. 56 – categories have both an objective and a subjective history). There is another respect in which Lukács' categories, and Marxist categories in general, differ from those of Kant. Hegel criticized Kant for not trying to establish any connections between the categories; orthodox Marxism, too, insists that categories are not to be regarded as independent of one another (Rozental and Yudin, op. cit., p. 67). What matter here are the connections that Lukács establishes between *Besonderheit* and two other categories, *Allgemeinheit* and *Einzelheit*. First, a word about these terms and their translation. *Allgemeinheit, Besonderheit* and *Einzelheit* (or *das Allgemeine, das Besondere, das Einzelne*) are standard terms of logic. In Kant (e.g. *Critique of Pure Reason,* B 95) they refer to forms of judgment, conventionally rendered as universal, particular and singular – all S are P, some S are P, this S is P. In Hegel they are three forms of the 'Notion' or concept, and are rendered as universal, particular and individual.[1] Both ways of using these terms can be found in the Marxist classics. In

[1] Cf. G. R. G. Mure, *The Philosophy of Hegel* (Oxford, 1965), p. 133. Hegel's distinction between *Allgemeinheit, Besonderheit* and *Einzelheit* is made in Chapter 1 of the first section of Book III of his *Wissenschaft der Logik*, in which he discusses the concept. In Chapter 2, sec. B, Hegel distinguishes between singular, particular and universal *judgements*, and uses different terms, viz. *das singuläre Urteil, das partikuläre Urteil, das universelle Urteil.*

Marx, the words are used as referring to concepts – e.g. the three types of value-form, or the three types of division of labour. Engels uses them as referring to judgments, and also (probably) to concepts.[1] How, then, is one to translate these terms in Lukács? 'The universal' and 'the individual' will render '*das Allgemeine*' and '*das Einzelne*'; one may be tempted to translate '*das Besondere*' as 'the particular', but there are objections to this. Lukács roughly equates *das Partikulare* with *das Einzelne* (ii. 552), and he makes a connection between *Besonderheit* and *die Art* (species);[2] '*Besonderheit*' will be rendered here, therefore, as 'speciality' or 'the special'. Lukács is far from being the only Marxist to regard universal, special and individual as categories;[3] what distinguishes him is the way in which he treats the category of speciality – the way in which he defines it, and the fact that he makes of it the central aesthetic category.[4]

2

Although speciality is said by Lukács to be the central category of aesthetics, it is by no means the starting-point of his aesthetic inquiry, and if one is to understand what he says about speciality

[1] For Allgemeinheit, etc., in Marx and Engels, see

(i) Marx, *Capital*, Vol. I, Chapter 1: Marx & Engels, *Werke*, Dietz ed., Vol. 23, pp. 63 ff.; Everyman trans., London, 1930, pp. 17–43. These pages cited by Lukács, *DZP* III, 1955, pp. 171 ff.

(ii) Marx, *Capital*, Vol. I, Chapter 12, sec. 4. Dietz, Vol. 23, pp. 371–2; Everyman trans., p. 370.

(iii) Engels, *Dialectics of Nature*, Dietz, Vol. 20, p. 493; English trans., Moscow, 1964, pp. 228–9.

(iv) Engels, *Dialectics of Nature*, Dietz, Vol. 20, p. 501; English trans., p. 237. Cf. Lukács, op. cit., p. 176.

[2] *DZP* II, 1954, p. 789. On '*Gattung*' as 'genus', '*Art*' as 'species', see, e.g., Kant, *Critique of Pure Reason*, B 682 ff.

[3] 'Single, particular and general' are discussed by Rozental and Shtraks, in their 'The Categories of the Materialist Dialectic', Moscow, 1956 (G. Wetter, *Dialectical Materialism*, pp. 366–7); these categories are also listed by Tugarinov (Wetter, op. cit., p. 369. Cf. G. Planty-Bonjour, *Les Catégories du Matérialisme Dialectique*, Dordrecht, 1965, p. 58). See also Rozental and Yudin, *A Dictionary of Philosophy*, p. 212, on 'Individual, particular and universal'.

[4] Other categories mentioned by Lukács in *Die Eigenart des Ästhetischen* are 'the typical' (i. 396), 'catharsis' (ii. 693), and 'inherence' (i. 633, 750; cf. Part IV below). He also refers to concepts which occur in standard Marxist lists of categories – form and content, appearance and essence, quality and quantity, contradiction, necessity and chance.

and its related categories they must be put in a wider context. It was said earlier that Lukács regards a category, *qua* concept, as a kind of reflection, and it will be useful to start from this point. It is one of Lukács' basic ideas that a work of art is in some sense a reflection (*Widerspiegelung*: i. 382–3) of reality; that it is a copy (*Abbild*) or imitation (*Nachahmung*) – he often uses the Greek word 'mimesis' in this context.[1] Now, in saying that art is a reflection of reality Lukács has only stated its genus; in his view, everyday thought and scientific thought reflect reality also (i. 22, 35), and he therefore has to be more specific, by saying what kind of reflection a work of art is.

The terms 'copy' and 'reflect' are borrowed from standard Marxist theory of knowledge – in particular, from Engels and Lenin.[2] Although this paper is not concerned chiefly with the theory of knowledge, it will be necessary to say something about Lukács' use of these words, so that it can be seen what he has in mind when he calls a work of art a 'reflection' or 'copy'. In his use of such terms, Lukács is perfectly orthodox. He insists (i. 35, 355ff., 279; ii. 289; cf. i. 547, 566) that we are not to think of a reflection as being like a photograph (cf. Lenin, Collected Works, English trans. Vol. 38 (*Philosophical Notebooks*), pp. 182, 372; also Wetter, op. cit., p. 499). In this connection, Lukács makes two very different points. He notes first (i. 357–8) that a man cannot simply let impressions (*Eindrücke*) of reality work on him; he must react on them. Even at the perceptual level he exercises a certain choice, emphasizing some and neglecting others, learning by practice to separate the essential from the non-essential. Second, Lukács says (ii. 347–8) that when we perceive something, the copy and the original are very different –

---

[1] To be exact, reflection is the genus, of which imitation is a species; to imitate is to transpose (*umsetzen*) the reflection of a phenomenon of reality into one's own activity (i. 352). But when speaking of art, Lukács tends to use 'reflection', 'copy' and 'imitation' interchangeably.

[2] See, e.g., the following:

Engels, on Marx's *Critique of Political Economy*. Dietz, Vol. 13, p. 475; Marx and Engels, *Selected Works* (Moscow, 1950), Vol. I, pp. 338–9.

Engels, *Ludwig Feuerbach and the end of classical German philosophy*. Dietz, Vol. 21, pp. 292–3; Marx and Engels, *Selected Works*, Vol. II, p. 350.

Lenin, *Collected Works* (English trans.), Vol. 38 (Philosophical Notebooks), p. 182.

e.g. vibrations on the one hand, and sensations of colour on the other. He then says, 'But if, say, the colour green appears in consciousness as a physiologically necessary reaction to a determinate frequency of vibrations, then what is it if not the copy of this phenomenon in the human soul?' (Cf. Lenin, Collected Works, English trans., Vol. 14 (*Materialism and Empirico-Criticism*), p. 302). To this one can only reply that this is not the normal use of the word rendered as 'copy' (*Abbild*); rather, Lukács seems to be talking about an effect or result. Still, one must not demand that he always uses words exactly as others do; what has to be determined here is his use of words. Why, then, should Lukács want to call a work of art a 'reflection' or 'copy'? Is he simply following Lenin blindly; or is he at any rate being cautious, offering a sop to orthodoxy? Probably not. First, in borrowing a term from the theory of knowledge and saying that the work of art 'reflects' reality, Lukács is saying that the work of art, though not purely an item of knowledge, does involve knowledge of reality. Second, in saying that a work of art is a copy *of reality*, Lukács wants to stress the fact that it is 'a reaction to the external world' (i. 13). One of his basic critical doctrines is that in a work of art, form and content are inseparable (i. 648, 812); that to produce something which is merely formally interesting is not to produce a work of art, and to attend only to the formal properties of a genuine work of art is to attend only to one aspect of it. (Cf. i. 305: the 'abstract forms of the reflection of reality', rhythm and proportion, are mere 'moments' of a work of art.)

Given, then, that a work of art is a copy or reflection in the sense just explained, what kind of copy or reflection is it? It has already been stated that in Lukács' view, not only does art reflect reality, but so too does science, so does everyday thinking; it may be added that even magic and religion imitate or reflect reality after their fashion (e.g. i. 103ff., 136). True to his view (i. 80) that the nature of art can be discussed only in connection with its genesis, Lukács separates art from the other forms of reflection by showing how they all began to be separable forms of activity. His argument is a lengthy one, and it is not necessary here to follow him as he develops it; it is sufficient simply to present the upshot of his inquiries and state the features which, according to him, mark off aesthetic reflection from the other types. His views about these features, it will be found, do not depend for their truth on the correctness of his account of the way in which art originated.[1]

The first feature is that art is anthropomorphic. Science, in Lukács' view (i. 25), 'tries to represent objects and their relations as they are in themselves, independently of consciousness. Aesthetic reflection, on the other hand, proceeds from the world of man and is directed towards it'. In saying that art is anthropomorphic, Lukács means that in the aesthetic object (the painting, sculpture, play, etc.) there are contained 'all typical relations to human life'; the object appears in a way which corresponds to the contemporary state of the inner and outer development of mankind (i. 26). This means that every work of art has in itself the historical here and now of its origin (ibid., cf. i. 248, 285, 529). Of course Lukács, as an historical materialist, regards every reflection of reality as determined by the time and place at which it occurs; even in the case of mathematical truths, the point of time at which a discovery is made is not a matter of chance (i. 26). Lukács' point is, however, that this does not matter for mathematics; for the mathematician as such, it is

[1] This does not mean that the truth or falsity of what Lukács says about the history, or pre-history, of art is irrelevant. There is no indication that he views his account as some political theorists have viewed the social contract theory of the state – that is, not as a description of historical events, but rather as a myth, a way of answering questions about the nature of political obligation by saying, '*Let us suppose that* the history of society is of such and such a kind.' In saying that art, like all reality, is essentially historical, Lukács is opposing the view that there is a fixed and timeless essence of art (i. 24) which has always been present in man, as a kind of innate idea (cf. i. 80). This must not be misunderstood. Lukács has no objection to talking about the *essence* of art (i. 80); what he objects to is the idea of an essence which is eternal, supra-temporal. It may be objected that Lukács is confused here. He seems to be trying to find a definition which will fit any art, Homer as well as Thomas Mann; but what is this if not a search for a supra-temporal essence? Perhaps, however, no confusion is involved; Lukács may mean that if one is to find a definition which fits art of any period, one must remember that art has a history – otherwise, one may fix on features which are peculiar to one period, and think that they hold of any period. All this is unaffected by Lukács' admission that almost nothing is known about the way in which art began (i. 253). An adequate account of art, he would probably say, must take into account the little that is known about its origins.

unimportant (say) when and where the differential calculus was first worked out. In the case of art, the situation is different; every significant work of art makes alive (whether the artist is aware of this or not) the historical here and now in the moment depicted (ibid.).

The second feature which distinguishes art is one of a set of features which are connected with its evocative character. The work of art, Lukács says, evokes feelings, emotions, passions (i. 281, 283, 298–9, 370, 430). So, of course, do many objects which are not works of art – e.g. objects which have been used by persons whom one loves or admires. In the work of art, however, the feelings evoked are not mere by-products; they are the result of conscious direction, of an evocative intention, on the part of the artist (i. 417; cf. i. 408). This again does not fully distinguish art from other forms of evocation; for example, magic evokes feelings, and may do so deliberately (i. 378, 418), and the same may be said of the words and gestures of everyday life (i. 368). The difference is, according to Lukács, that in the work of art the evocation is the end (i. 281), whereas in magic the evocation serves ulterior ends – e.g. success in battle or in the hunt. Again, in everyday life the evocative is merely an aura (i. 368); what is central is the social function of language and gesture (cf. i. 412). Lukács does not deny that a work of art may have practical effects (i. 429), or that it may be created with such effects in mind (i. 654). He is, however, opposed to the view (ii. 676) that every work of art must have an immediately useful social effect, and says (i. 655) that 'the real strength and depth of artistic evocation is directed above all to the inner side (*das Innere*) of men'.

This reference to art as (by definition) evoking emotions must not be abstracted from the rest of what Lukács says; in his terminology, the evocation of emotions is merely a 'moment', an aspect, of the work of art. If it is abstracted, then it is easy to involve Lukács in an insoluble puzzle. Suppose an artist to paint a portrait of someone's wife; his purpose in painting this is to make a picture which shall evoke suitable emotions in the husband when his wife is absent. Clearly, such a painting need not be a work of art in the evaluative sense – but why not? The difficulty is seen not to be real when one notes that for Lukács, a work of art is not only a copy which evokes emotion, but is also evocative in other ways. This introduces a third distinguishing feature of the work of art. Lukács states that aesthetic images[1] evoke in the recipient the picture of reality which is their basis (i. 383); again, the passage just quoted about the 'inner' side of man (i. 655) continues by saying that, as a result of artistic evocation, there are aroused in a man new experiences which broaden and deepen his picture of himself and of the world with which he has to do. Lukács also speaks (i. 425) of an evocative impression of reality, of the evocation of a world (i. 510; cf. i. 803–4). A further point may be added here, in development of the idea of the evocation of a picture. A picture, of the conventional representative sort, is painted from a point of view; the work of art, too, has its metaphorical point of view. Artistic reflection, Lukács says (i. 248), is not just a matter of the simple reproduction of reality, or even a selection of what is essential; it also involves an attitude (*Stellungnahme*), either positive or negative, towards the object reflected, and this attitude is evoked in the audience (i. 655; cf. i. 568–9 and *DZP* IV, 1956, pp. 427ff., on the *Parteilichkeit* of the work of art).

Another distinguishing feature of the work of art is also linked with evocation. Although, as mentioned earlier, the work of art is not produced for immediate social ends, the picture of the world that it evokes is not evoked for its own sake. In a way rather reminiscent of R. G. Collingwood (whom he does not cite), Lukács says that the work of art is a means to self-awareness (*Selbstbewusstsein*: i. 281, 529). Reverting once more to the passage about the 'inner side' of man (i. 655), it is noteworthy that Lukács says that the experiences aroused deepen a man's picture, not only of the world, but of himself. The connection between self-awareness and the evocation of a picture of reality is an intimate one. Self-knowledge and world-knowledge, Lukács says, constitute a circular movement: 'The correct impulse towards "Know thyself" leads a man into the world,

---

[1] The term translated as 'images' (*Gebilde*) is not defined by Lukács, but clearly does not refer to *mental* images. It seems to be equivalent to 'works of art', and is perhaps used to bring out their picture – (*Bild*) like character.

makes him acquainted with his fellow-men, with the society in which they are active, with the nature, the field of action, and the basis of their activity' (i. 511; cf. ii. 326–7). The artist's work exhibits the unfolding of self-awareness, unfolded through the creation of a world of objects (i. 300; cf. i. 477); the work of art also evokes self-awareness in the audience (i. 281).[1] It was suggested earlier, when discussing art as reflection, that although a work of art is not what might be called an item of pure knowledge, it *involves* knowledge, and it is now possible to see how this is; art implies self-knowledge, which implies knowledge of the external world. Lukács is quite explicit about this: a man can know himself only in so far as he has the power to know the world which surrounds him as it really is (i. 511; cf. ii. 298). This may seem to bring art dangerously close to the social sciences, but it should be remembered that these do not aim at evocation in the way that art does. In the social sciences, Lukács says (ii. 297), the world of man is purely an object, whereas the aim of artistic evocation is that the recipient shall experience an image of the objective world of man as his own concern (*als seine eigene Sache*), that he shall have (ii. 298; cf. i. 396) the experience of *tua res agitur*.

There is one further distinguishing feature of art to which reference must be made. It has already been said that for Lukács, art is anthropomorphic; but so, too, is religion (i. 132, 382), which is another form of reflection. The way in which Lukács differentiates between the two is one of the most striking features of his aesthetics, though it is one about which very little can be said here. Briefly, the difference lies in the man-centred character of art (i. 281, 300, 850–51, ii. 297), its 'this-worldliness' (*Diesseitigkeit*, i. 383, cf. i. 245, 382, 386). Art does not ascribe to its images any objective reality (i. 137); it is concerned with this

---

[1] This paper is not primarily concerned with the antecedents of Lukács' views, and it is unnecessary to do more than note briefly that in stressing the connection between self-awareness and the creation of objects, Lukács is following Hegel – in particular, the chapter on 'Master and Slave' in the *Phenomenology*. The slave, as G. R. G. Mure puts it, 'learns to refashion his dissolved and shattered consciousness to a new self-consciousness by fashioning external things before which he does not tremble' (*The Philosophy of Hegel*, p. 76).

world, whereas religion, like magic, claims to deal with the transcendent.[1] From this it follows, according to Lukács, that 'in its objective intention, art is . . . hostile to religion' (ibid.). Lukács stresses the fact that the 'this-worldliness' of art is *objective*. The artist may think that he is aiming at something transcendent, and his audience may take him to be doing this (i. 245); both may think that the work of art serves religion (i. 382). But the views of artists are to be derived from the nature of their work, not from what they say about it (ii. 703; one recalls D. H. Lawrence's dictum, 'Never trust the artist; trust the tale'), and Lukács claims that it can be seen from the artist's work that he really intends to produce something this-worldly.

3

The theses that have just been sketched outline the general structure of Lukács' theory of art. At first sight they may seem fairly comprehensive, and one may ask what need there is for this 'speciality', of which no mention has been made in this sketch, and which is yet declared by Lukács to be the central category of aesthetics. An answer may be approached by noting that the summary just given turns out, when examined, to have certain puzzling features. Consider again the historical nature (ii. 229) of the work of art. When the anthropomorphic nature of the work of art was discussed above, it was said that, for Lukács, every work of art has in itself the historical here and now of its origin. An example that he gives will help to clarify this. A still life by Chardin, he says (ii. 230), does not just represent a number of objects, but rather the way in which the French bourgeois of the mid-eighteenth century stood in relation

---

[1] It is not suggested that this view is peculiar to Lukács. For example, the *Dictionary of Philosophy* edited by Rozental and Yudin states (pp. 31–2) that the task of art is 'the artistic portrayal of the world. It is for this reason that man . . . is always in the centre of any work of art'. A similar view had been expressed by Dilthey, whom Lukács studied before the First World War. According to Dilthey, the artistic mind seeks 'to understand life in terms of itself', and not in terms of the supernatural. (Cf. H. A. Hodges, *Wilhelm Dilthey: An Introduction* (London, 1944), p. 94.

to his surroundings. One has only to compare it with a Dutch still life from the seventeenth century, or one by Cézanne from the nineteenth, to read off (*ablesen*) from these painted objects the historical changes in everyday bourgeois life over two centuries. It is important not to misunderstand the nature of this 'reading off'. It is not like deciphering a document, nor is it like interpreting (as an art historian may do) the meaning of visual symbols of a past age. In the case under consideration the 'essential artistic content' gives us, Lukács says, an answer to our questions that can be experienced directly (ibid.). Now, the fact that the 'here and now' cannot be removed from any work of art means that it cannot be governed by the category of universality. On the other hand, in so far as the here and now becomes (ibid.) the mouthpiece (*Sprachrohr*) of a socio-historical phase of the development of mankind, the work of art does not remain purely individual, but contains some element of generalization. In sum, the work of art does not reflect or evoke mere individuals, viewed as so many isolated entities, nor does it evoke or reflect purely universal laws; it seems to contain elements of both individual and universal. There is a problem, then, as to the category under which it is to be placed.

This is one approach to the category of speciality; another is by way of Lukács' views about the evocative nature of the work of art. He has said that such a work evokes, gives a picture of, a world. He also puts the point by saying (ii. 231–3) that a work of art is a totality – i.e. it is a whole – and that it also reflects a totality. Lukács distinguishes two sorts of totality, 'extensive' and 'intensive'; he says that reality consists of both sorts, but that the work of art aims at evoking only an intensive totality – indeed, it is such a totality (ii. 231, 233). By an 'intensive totality' Lukács seems to mean those objects and relations that concern human beings. The intensive totality which is a work of art, he says, is a reflection of the world of man, from the standpoint of man, and for man (ii. 232, cf. *DZP* II, 1954, p. 123). Now, the work of art is a self-enclosed, perfect totality, whereas the intensive totality that it seeks to evoke is infinite (ii. 231, 233). How, then, can a work of art picture or evoke an infinity? It cannot be compared with a scientific theory. Science, according

Georg Lukács

to Lukács, also aims at reflecting the infinite – presumably he means that the ultimate aim of science is the comprehension of the whole universe – but the essence of such reflection is that it only approximates to its object, with the result that a scientific theory can be superseded by later theories (ii. 231, 233–4; cf. *The Historical Novel*, English trans., London, 1962, p. 91). The work of art, on the other hand, is (as has been seen) self-contained and complete, and it is not superseded by what comes later. Newtonian physics supersedes Cartesian physics; but Bach is not superseded by Mozart. The work of art, then, does not lay claim to universality, in the way that science does. But neither is it governed by the category of individuality; for if one is to see the infinite in objects, these must be generalized, in such a way that they can fit into a system (ii. 233). Once again, therefore, it seems that the work of art falls neither under the category of the universal nor under that of the individual, but contains elements of both.

Lukács' name for the category under which art falls – intermediate between the universal and the individual – is 'speciality'. It must be made clear, however, that speciality is by no means restricted to works of art; art is a sub-form of the category. It is necessary, then, to look first at the category in general. As mentioned in part 1 of this paper, in traditional logic the term '*Besonderheit*' is used to refer to the 'particular' judgment, 'Some S is P', which may be regarded as standing between the universal and the singular judgment.[1] Lukács' concept of speciality is not wholly divorced from this idea; certainly, he cites as an example of speciality what is in fact a particular judgment.[2] If one asks what the particular form of judgment has to do with works of art, Lukács would probably reply that so far the matter has been considered too abstractly; it

[1] To be logically precise, it must be added that this assumes that the universal judgment has existential import.
[2] Cf. *DZP* II, 1954, p. 785. Discussing some of Hegel's works belonging to the Frankfurt period, Lukács notes that for Hegel, the state of the *ancien régime* claims to represent society as a whole (to be a universal), but in fact serves the interest of the ruling feudal classes (logically, the special). The revolutionary class of this period, the bourgeoisie, represent the interests of other classes also (the special becomes universal).

is necessary to move from formal logic to dialectical logic, and in particular to the notion of mediation. In the course of an account which owes much to Hegel, Lukács asserts (ii. 197) that our immediate relations with reality take the form of contact with individuals, by which he seems to mean that our sense-experience is always of an individual or of a complex of individuals. But the merely individual, the mere 'this', cannot be expressed; to *say* anything, one has to say *what* 'this' is referred to, which involves stating the qualities and relations of the 'this' (ibid.). This does not mean that individuals are in any way irrational or untrue; although a pure 'this' could not be expressed, in fact there are present in every individual all its determinations and its relations to others, and these are the basis of our being able to say what the individual is (ii. 198). We cannot, however, give a complete account of any individual, because its determinations are infinite in number; all that we can do is to approximate (ii. 199). This process of saying what something is, of specifying it, may be viewed as a movement either from the individual to the universal, or from the universal to the individual (ii. 196). Lukács expresses this by saying (ii. 201) that the way of thought and knowledge is a constant up and down; as an example of what he means he cites a passage, obviously influenced by Hegel, from Marx's *Grundrisse der Kritik der politischen Ökonomie* (Moscow, 1939, Vol. i, p. 21). Marx is here describing economic method. The starting point, he says, is the real and concrete; but this is, in its immediacy, a mere abstraction, unless its component parts are generalized and brought to the universal concept. From this point, however, thought must retrace its steps, until it again comes to the real and concrete, 'but now, not as a chaotic representation of a whole, but as a rich totality of many determinations and relations'. Lukács notes that the movement from individual to universal, or the converse movement, has many intermediate stages, consisting of relative generalizations (ii. 196). These, the various 'mediations' between individual and universal, constitute what he calls 'speciality', which is (ii. 205) a 'field of mediations'. These three categories – individual, special and universal – must be regarded dynamically rather than statically, for Lukács says that they change into (*umschlagen*) one another (ii. 196, 202, 204).[1]

Much of this is obscure – in particular, the assertion that the three categories change into each other. Lukács may mean that, for example, to see what being a man is, we must know about various species of men, and finally about individuals; to know what *this* man is, we must bring him under universals of varying degrees of generality; to know what being a German philosopher is, we must be able to move both ways, towards individual and universal. The 'movement' involved here is related to the fact that no one of these is intelligible without the rest, so that if we are to understand any of them, we must move from it to the others. But this concerns knowledge, the reflection of reality, and Lukács insists that he is also describing an objective process – the mediations, as he puts it, are real (ii. 207; cf. ii. 225: speciality is not a mere product of consciousness, but is a reflection of reality). This seems to be a case in which a conceptual apparatus which suits an idealism such as Hegel's does not suit a materialist doctrine. However, the topic of this paper is not Lukács' general theory of dialectic, but his philosophy of art, and the general drift of what he says seems clear enough – clear enough, at any rate, for it to be seen why he should say that the 'speciality' that belongs to a work of art is one form of a wider category. How, then, is the speciality of the work of art distinguished from other types of speciality? It has already been noted (part 2 above) that both scientific and artistic reflection aim at providing an adequate copy of the same reality (cf. ii. 206); the differences between them spring from the fact that the one is anthropomorphic and the other is not. One might think that this is sufficient for Lukács' purposes, but he clearly thinks that more precision is required. What he says, broadly, is (ii. 206) that in the aesthetic sphere speciality is not

---

[1] Cf. Lukács on Hegel's theory of the concept, *D Z P* II, 1954, pp. 801–3. For Hegel, the process of determination is always the way from the universal to the special. The latter is not a stable mediating category between universal and individual, but rather 'the self-moved movement of a moving process of specification'. Lukács adds that in Hegel's attempt at seeing concept, judgment and inference in dynamic movement, there is something positive and forward-looking.

simply a mediation (*Vermittlung*) between universal and individual, but is an organizing mean (*Mitte*). In the case of knowledge, we move from universal to individual, or conversely; in the case of art, speciality is the beginning and end of the corresponding movements. In other words, one is not concerned here with a cross-movement between the two extreme categories, but with a movement between centre and periphery.

This is meant only as a summary account, not wholly clear in itself, and Lukács now tries to explain his meaning more fully. It has already been mentioned that the 'mediations' of which he speaks are objective (ii. 207); in his view, the connection of objects in the external world rests largely on mediations. A 'mean', it appears, is not something other than a mediation, but is simply a mediation of a certain kind, one which has an 'objective superiority' (*ein sachliches Übergewicht*, ii. 209, cf. ii. 207) over the extremes. Lukács cites an example from Hegel. If I plan to plough a field, the plough is a 'mean' between myself and my object. But this 'mean' is something rational, and in a sense higher than the ends – e.g. the pleasures of eating – which it serves (ii. 209, quoting Hegel, *Logik, Werke*, Berlin 1841, Vol. V, p. 220). Perhaps Lukács' meaning is clearer in the case of what he calls 'ethics' (*Ethik*), which he later declares (ii. 570; cf. ii. 582) to have a close relationship with the aesthetic, and which he discusses in *Die Eigenart des Ästhetischen* in order to clarify the concept of the mean (ii. 213). Although Lukács rejects Hegel's ethical theory (ibid.) as being too closely linked with the social and political philosophy of his late (i.e. conservative) period, Lukács' own account of ethics owes much to the *Rechtsphilosophie*. As Lukács uses the term, 'ethics' refers to a form of activity, perhaps better rendered as 'ethical conduct'; it is to be distinguished from moral philosophy, which operates with universal concepts (ii. 224). Like art, ethics is a 'mediating mean' in the system of human activity (ibid.); to be more exact, it is a mean between purely objective law (*Recht*) and purely subjective morality (*Moralität*). (There are obvious connections here with Hegel's account of the relations between abstract right, morality and ethics (*Sittlichkeit*).) One may put Lukács' point crudely by saying that ethics stands midway

Georg Lukács

between the idea of law as a set of universal rules, and the individual conscience of the private person. But (and this is the important point) it is not simply mid-way between the two, as in the case of the typical knowledge-process, but exercises 'sublating and therefore modifying functions' on the two extremes (ii. 213). The word translated as 'sublate' is '*aufheben*'; Lukács has in mind the Hegelian view that thesis and antithesis are 'sublated', 'taken up' (*aufgehoben*) into the synthesis.[1] That this is so is made clear when he continues by saying that the two extremes have a deeply based justification as 'moments' (aspects) of social life (ii. 214); it is only when isolated and abstracted that they lead to contradictions – solipsistic anarchism on the one hand, and a separation of law from conscience on the other. Ethics, then, mediates between morality and law. It turns the subjective conscience ('morality') into an ethical consciousness of the whole man, who now sees what he really is – the living totality of the public and the private, of the citizen and the individual personality. As to law, a legal system (ii. 215) cannot function for long if it is completely independent of the ethical views of a people. This may be put in terms of speciality and its related categories by saying that individuality is the decisive category of morality; universality, of law; and speciality, of ethics. Ethics (ii. 216) generalizes the individual acts of conscience, 'sublates' them from the isolation of the moral subject, and widens this subject into a concretely active man among other such men. It stops short at this point, i.e. its dominating category is speciality, for it is important (ii. 233) that the generalization involved should preserve the individual character of the ethical act; otherwise we move too far towards the universal, and are back with the errors of objective law. Lukács adds (ii. 223) that speciality in ethics is again a field. The mean, he says, can be regarded as a kind of harmony, and each individual must have his own kind of harmonious fulfilment.

[1] On 'sublation', cf. Lukács, *Schriften zur Literatursoziologie*, ed. P. Ludz, 2nd ed., Neuwied, 1963, p. 132n (from 'Reportage oder Gestaltung', 1932). See also *The Historical Novel*, English trans., p. 173, and *The Meaning of Contemporary Realism*, English trans., London 1963, p. 85.

It is easy to lose oneself in detail here, but the essential point to remember is that for Lukács, ethics is a mean in that it is a synthesis; it takes up, reconciles, opposing views which, taken in isolation, lead to contradictions, but which can be seen to exist in ethics as aspects of a larger whole. It must now be seen if something comparable holds in the case of the work of art; that is, is the work of art a mean in the sense that it takes up, 'sublates' extremes? Lukács' answer is (ii. 244) that this is so; in the work of art, both the universal and the individual are sublated, in such a way that they are still present, but are now 'moments' of speciality. The way in which universality is taken up into speciality is as follows (ii. 245). In mastering his surroundings, man makes use of universal laws, and it is in this way that the universal makes its appearance in the work of art – namely, as an important 'power of life' (*Macht des Lebens*). Art relates these powers directly to man, by representing them as part of man's fate – indeed, as the fate of concrete men, as opposed to the fate of man in general. When he goes on to consider the way in which art 'takes up' individuality into speciality, Lukács begins (ii. 247) by repeating a point that has already been made when discussing speciality in general, namely that individuality, in its immediate mode of appearance, contains in itself all its determinations, but in an 'undeveloped' (*unentfalteten*: sc. 'unanalysed') form. The sublation of the resulting limitations is the task of both science and art; indeed, even everyday life tries to do this to some extent. Science frees these determinations from their isolation and inserts them into special and universal connections (*Zusammenhänge*). (Incidentally, it is an interesting sidelight on Lukács' use of the term 'reflection' that this is said to be the work of scientific reflection. The non-photographic character of this 'reflection' could hardly be made more clear.) Aesthetic reflection, too, tries to free the relations that are locked up in immediate individuality, but it does so in a distinctive manner – namely, in such a way that the humanly relevant substance (*Ansich*) of the individual now appears, in its new connections in the work of art, more evident, more readily experienced, and more easily understandable than it did in its original form. In other words (ii. 247–8) the aesthetic

Georg Lukács

sublation of the individual stresses the moment of preservation – the preservation of individuality - much more strongly and intensively than science does, and also (Lukács believes) more strongly than everyday thinking. There is, then, a considerable degree of similarity between ethics and art; and the similarity is increased when one notes that there are in aesthetics cases which are comparable to morality and objective law, which, it will be remembered, arise from viewing in isolation and in an abstract way what should be regarded as aspects of a larger, concrete whole. According to *Die Eigenart des Ästhetischen*, the point of view which inclines too much towards the individual is naturalism (ii. 248–9), and that which inclines too much towards the universal is allegory (ii. 252; cf. i. 402–3).[1]

In finding a close relationship between ethics and aesthetics, Lukács is not saying anything new or recondite; it is obvious enough that terms such as 'sincere', 'truthful', 'self-indulgent', 'self-pitying' have a place both in the appraisal of works of art and in the way that we appraise people as moral agents. The interesting questions involved here are two. First, given this close relation between ethics and aesthetics, how does Lukács distinguish between the two? Second, is Lukács right in saying that the similarity between ethics and aesthetics is one of structure – more precisely, of a triadic structure (thesis, antithesis, synthesis) of the Hegelian type? The first question has a short answer; ethics is concerned with action, and art with reflection

[1] If naturalism corresponds to 'morality', one would expect it to be regarded as subjective. In an earlier work, Lukács refers to 'the pseudo-objectivism of the naturalist school and the mirage-subjectivism of the psychologist or abstract-formalist school' (*Studies in European Realism* (1948), English trans., New York 1964, p. 6; *Schriften zur Literatursoziologie*, ed. Ludz, p. 244). This does not necessarily contradict the view that naturalism is subjective, for it will be noticed that Lukács speaks of '*pseudo*-objectivism'. Elsewhere, in a passage written in 1944–5, Lukács states that the principle of naturalism is that of sticking to the reflection of immediately given reality. Naturalism represents the world as it appears directly in the experiences of its characters, and the naturalistic writer does not go beyond the horizon of his characters (Ludz, op. cit., pp. 462–3, quoting *Deutsche Literatur während des Imperialismus*, Berlin, 1945, republished in *Skizze einer Geschichte der neueren deutschen Literatur*, Berlin, 1953). It appears, then, that there is some reason to suppose that Lukács does regard naturalism as a type of subjectivism.

only.[1] (Compare what was said early in part 2 about the difference between magic and art.) The second question cannot be considered fully here, as a full discussion would have to cover ethics as well as aesthetics; however, something will be said of the answer as far as it concerns aesthetics at the end of this paper, when the value of speciality as an aesthetic category is discussed.

In saying (ii. 206) that in the aesthetic sphere speciality is a mean, Lukács might seem to imply that the work of art is in some sense a precise point, mid-way between universality and individuality. Indeed, he does say (ii. 256, 261) that in the case of artistic reflection the special is a mid-point, but he later takes this back (ii. 261), and says that it is more accurate to speak of a space for movement (*Bewegungsspielraum*) round a central point. This expresses (ii. 262) the well-known aesthetic fact that the style, tone, etc., of a work can remain unified, even when there is a decided up-and-down movement within this unity, as certain moments of the work approach the universal, others the individual. Lukács cites as an example Dickens (ii. 263), who in some of his novels characterizes the 'upper class' (*Oben*) by means of satirical generalizations, whilst the 'lower class' (*Unten*) is characterized by means of loving attention to small details of everyday life. According to Lukács, one approaches the essence of art when one thinks of the artistic organization of a 'world' dynamically, as a system of movements, as a system of their tensions and contrasts. The range of movement can be great or small, but there is always a certain tension, even in works which are limited to one particular tone. In aesthetic reflection, then, speciality (ii. 264) is still a 'field' of mediations, as it is in the case of scientific reflection and in the case of ethics.

These various ranges of movement – all within the domain of speciality – differ in respect of their distance from the extremes of the universal and the individual. Lukács finds in this (ii. 256) a

[1] ii. 241; cf. i. 784, ii. 237, 570, 582. Lukács also draws a distinction between ethics and art in terms of their 'exemplary character' (*Beispielhaftigkeit*). He says (ii. 582) that aesthetic reflection, in consequence of its typification, makes every represented action a paradigm to a greater or less degree. But 'this category' (presumably that of the typical) includes everything negative, everything between good and evil, whereas an ethical example must be positive.

justification of the plurality of arts, genres and styles. For example (ii. 257), drama conceives its characters and situations in a more universal way than epic does; individual traits appear in a far less detailed form. In general, then, drama tends to be closer to universality, the epic to individuality. A similar distinction (ii. 258) can be drawn between the classical novella and the novel, the former resembling drama in its tendency to concentrate on greater universality. Even within the sphere of drama there are divergencies – e.g. Racine is closer to universality than Shakespeare is, whereas modern bourgeois drama is closer to individuality.

4

It has now been seen what Lukács means when he says that speciality is a category of aesthetics. Why, then, should he say that it is the *central* category? The answer is complex. As already noted, this category is presupposed by certain things that Lukács says about the work of art – namely, its anthropomorphic character (the element of 'here and now') and its evocation of a world. This, however, is far from exhausting its importance for Lukács; two further features have to be noted. First, speciality is connected with a fundamental concept of his criticism, the notion of the 'type'. This concept is explained clearly in the preface to *Balzac und der französische Realismus* (Berlin, 1952. In *Schriften zur Literatursoziologie*, ed. Ludz, p. 244; cf. *Studies in European Realism*, English trans., p. 6). Here, Lukács connects the type with realistic literature, of which it is both the central category and the criterion. In speaking of 'realistic literature', Lukács is not referring to one particular style of literature among others; as he later expressed himself, realism is the artistic basis of every authentic creation (ii. 840; cf. i. 566, and *The Meaning of Contemporary Realism*, English trans., p. 48). In other words, for Lukács the words 'work of art' (used in their evaluative sense) and 'realistic work of art' have the same reference; to call a genuine work of art 'realistic' is simply to bring out certain features that belong to all such works. Such is the 'realistic literature' with which the type is connected; the type itself is declared by Lukács (*Balzac und der französische Realismus,* loc. cit.) to be a distinctive kind of synthesis, which relates both to character and situation, and unites organically the individual and the universal. What makes something a type is not its average character, nor its individual character, however much this is deepend. Something becomes a type inasmuch as all the humanly and socially essential 'moments' of an historical epoch come together in it; the creation of types exhibits these moments in the stage of their highest development. This can be supplemented by a passage from Lukács' *Einführung in die ästhetischen Schriften von Marx und Engels* (1945; Ludz, op. cit., p. 230), which states that in the representation of the type, in typical art, there are united the concrete and the law, the enduringly human and the historically determined, the individual and the socially universal. In the discovery of typical characters and typical situations, the most important trends of social development receive adequate artistic expression. An example (from *The Historical Novel,* English trans., p. 142) may help to clarify this. In *Anna Karenina* the fate of the heroine is a very individual one, yet it is also typical, in that it reveals in the most powerful terms the inner contradictions of modern bourgeois marriage.

The connection between type and realism is not new with Lukács; it is to be found in one of the classical texts of Marxist aesthetics – Engels' letter of April 1888 to Margaret Harkness. Commenting on her novel *City Girl* – sub-titled 'A Realistic Story' – Engels remarks that the book is not quite realistic enough. 'Realism,' he says, 'implies, besides truth of detail, the truth in reproduction of typical characters under typical circumstances' (Marx and Engels, *Selected Correspondence,* English trans., Moscow, n.d., pp. 478–9). He goes on to say that Miss Harkness' characters are typical enough, but that the circumstances which surround them and make them act are not; in particular, she has not grasped the true, and rebellious, nature of the working class. In another well known passage (to Minna Kautsky, 26 November 1885; Marx and Engels, op. cit., p. 467) Engels makes it clear that a typical character is not such that one can make abstract generalizations from it. Speaking of the characters in Minna Kautsky's novel *The Old and the New*, he says that each of them 'is a type, but at the same time also a definite individual, a *Dieser*, as old Hegel would express himself, and that is how it should be'. All this is (to repeat) familiar, and is not even peculiar to Marxist writers – something similar can be found in Dilthey.[1] What is distinctive is the way in which Lukács inserts these ideas into a wider conceptual framework. At this point we return to *Die Eigenart des Ästhetischen*.

From what has been said so far, it might be supposed that Lukács believes that only the artist creates types. This, however, is not so; in Lukács' view, the types that the artist creates are of a distinctive kind, governed by the category of speciality. Types are not pure creations, but are reflections (ii. 240), and just as there is both scientific and artistic reflection, so both science and art use the notion of a type. The difference, according to Lukács, is that the scientist tries to generalize as far as possible, to sublate the typical into the universal, and this leads to a minimum of types. In the case of art, however, there is a plurality of types, and the type is so understood that the individual is not sublated (ii. 240–41; cf. i. 690–91). So at the basis of artistic reflection there is the unity of the individual with its generalization, with the typical – i.e. with the special (ii. 241).[2] It seems, then, that to talk about 'types' in the work of art is simply another way of talking about the 'speciality' that attaches to art.

A feature of Lukács' account of types that may seem open to criticism is his assertion that art is distinguished from science by the plurality of its types (i. 690–1). It may be objected that scientists recognize thousands of species of living things – and is not this a plurality of types? Lukács can hardly be unaware of this, and it seems probable that what he has in mind when he says that science tends to minimize the number of types is another well known fact – namely, that the scientist often tries

[1] According to Dilthey, the artist 'can single out the essential elements in a thing from the inessentials, and so portray it as to bring out what is typical or truly significant in it' (H. A. Hodges, op. cit., p. 23).

[2] Lukács is careful to relate his views about types to his views about artistic evocation. In each work of art, he says (ii. 242; cf. i. 693) there is a hierarchy of types, which is aimed at the evocation of a 'world'. This hierarchy (ii. 243) is determined by the theme of the work.

to reduce the number of his basic concepts. An example of this would be the reduction of chemical substances to chemical elements, of elements to atoms, and so on. Lukács would be right in saying that there is nothing comparable to this in the arts. It is true that a work of art is sometimes praised for its economy, but this is not what is in mind here. One may, perhaps, sometimes say that one writer achieves in a short story what another fails to do in a novel; but this is not to say that the characters and situations in the novel are *reduced* to those of the short story.

What has just been discussed is one of two features of speciality by virtue of which Lukács calls this the central category of aesthetics. The second of these can most easily be introduced by way of an answer to a possible criticism. One may feel that the theories so far expounded imply that all works of art conform to a single pattern, and that this does not do justice to the uniqueness of each work of art, to the fact that, in a sense, a work of art cannot be repeated. Lukács sees the force of this objection, and tries to meet it by distinguishing between 'subsumption' and 'inherence'. In discussing Kant's *Critique of Judgement*, he says (*DZP* II, 1954, p. 773) that in seeing a 'moment' of chance in the relation of special to universal, Kant has had a glimpse of the truth that what constitutes speciality is not deducible forthwith from the universal, and that a universal cannot be derived forthwith from something special. Elsewhere, Lukács seems to say that Kant did not always realize this. He quotes with approval (op. cit., p. 787) Hegel's attack on Kant's attempt to derive a specific instance of the categorical imperative by saying that the embezzlement of a deposit would lead to contradictions. The real point at issue here, Lukács says, is this: whether in the case of a universal law (such as the categorical imperative) the special cases of its application are to be derived by simple logical subsumption, as Kant assumes, or whether complicated dialectical relations are necessary. This gives some idea of what Lukács means by 'subsumption', and when this is applied to art, it becomes possible to see why he should say that speciality is the central category of aesthetics. To say that it is, he remarks (ii. 260), is not to say that, in the case of a work of art, a universal law is applied to particular cases; indeed, to suppose a simple application of such laws is to destroy the aesthetic essence of such works. He puts the point in this way: when a universal law is applied to particular cases, many exceptions mean that the law must either be rejected, or at any rate drastically modified. But in the case of aesthetics, the exact fulfilment of a law is a sign of artistic worthlessness. The genuine work of art (i. 620) fulfils aesthetic laws in the sense that it makes them wider and deeper; there is no question of a simple subsumption of the individual under the universal, of the 'case' under the law. This applies to the relation of a work of art to the relevant genre and its laws (i. 622), and it also applies to the relation between the genres and art itself; the genres are no more instances or sub-species of the genus art than the individual works are of the genre (i. 631). This last assertion may seem strange, for what are the genres if not *kinds* of art, and therefore species of a genus? What Lukács presumably means, however, is that one cannot derive the genres simply from the concept of art.

All this has been negative, an account of what the genre or the work of art is not. Lukács' name for the relations that do hold between genre and art, or between the work of art and the laws of the genre, is 'inherence'. Inherence is counted by Lukács as a category (i. 633, 750), which is not restricted to works of art. Taken in its most general form, it is said to reflect those moments of the external world that can be grasped immediately; in their essence one can observe a close connection with sensibility, and also with the subjective (i. 634). This is obscure, but Lukács is clearer when he speaks of inherence as a category of artistic form. He takes as an example (i. 635) the relation between individual and social group, and says that as a category of artistic form, 'inherence' refers to an organic unity of the individual, in whom and around whom social forces are active, but which appear immediately as moments of his psychology. 'In the artistic creation, the natural immediate unity of the personality is predominant; the relations to the objective tendencies of society appear in the category of inherence' (ibid.). This is clearly related to what has already been said about the type and about speciality. The relations between inherence and speciality are brought out still more clearly when Lukács says (i. 750) that inherence is that category in which the relations of the individual to those higher orders to which it belongs (species, genus, etc.) become visible, because in aesthetic reflection what is particular and contingent in the individual must never vanish entirely.

Lukács' argument can perhaps be summarized as follows. It is generally agreed that one cannot construct works of art (in the evaluative sense of the word) purely from a set of rules; what is produced in this way will at best be a competent academic exercise. But although a work of art cannot be constructed from rules, it can be brought under rules. Artists can study what others have done, and produce rules from this – for example, rules by which to give form to a musical composition, or universal propositions which state the effects of certain chords or modulations. One may put this by saying that if a work of art were purely individual, if nothing in it were repeatable, artists could not learn from one another. All this confirms Lukács in his view that a work of art does not fall entirely under the category of speciality or under that of individuality. In other words, the concept of inherence leads logically to that of speciality, and the importance of the former concept is another reason why Lukács should regard speciality as the central category of aesthetics.

It may be added that it is also possible that when Lukács speaks of 'inherence' he has in mind a feature of criticism – namely, that one cannot *demonstrate* the excellence of a work of art; rather, one has to work from one's perception of the concrete work. It is true that Lukács says (*DZP* IV, 1956, p. 409) that criticism is a science, not a kind of art. But by 'science' (*Wissenschaft*) he means, not natural science, but a branch of knowledge – a branch governed, of course, by the category of speciality.

5

So far, this paper has merely expounded Lukács' views, and it is now time to attempt some critical comment on them. Such comment may take two forms. It may be asked how much of what has been discussed is really new, and it may be asked how much of it is true. To begin with the first of these lines of comment: in saying that art comes under the category of speciality Lukács is in effect saying that a work of art is something concrete, something individual, which yet has elements of the universal in it. But, it may be asked, is not this a commonplace of romantic aesthetic theory? Walter Pater, for example, believed that in ideal art 'thought and its sensible embodiment are completely fused' (G. Hough, *The Last Romantics,* 2nd ed., London, 1961, p. 163). In this he was typical of late nineteenth-century romanticism, which thought of the work of art as something concrete which was yet suggestive, a means to truth. J. F. Kermode, from whose book *The Romantic Image* (London, 1957, p. 44) this description is taken, notes the connection (op. cit., p. 130) between such ideas and those formulated earlier in the nineteenth century by Schopenhauer, and it may well be thought that Schopenhauer's aesthetics provides the most striking parallel to Lukács' views. Briefly, Schopenhauer's view was that there are certain 'Ideas', eternal essences somewhat like Plato's 'forms', and that it is the function of art to exhibit these. In other words, the work of art, though concrete and specific, communicates something universal. The poem, for example, has its source in experience, but is able to reveal universal truths about the objects or events which it portrays (P. Gardiner, *Schopenhauer*, London, 1963, pp. 213, 223). Again, the portrait painter should not merely produce a faithful copy of his subject; it is his business to 'express the Idea of man in a definite individual manner' (Schopenhauer to Julius Hamel, 1856. Quoted by Gardiner, op. cit., p. 217). This does indeed seems to resemble what Lukács has said; but an important point of difference has been omitted. Schopenhauer states that the Ideas are not governed by the principle of sufficient reason. This principle – which may crudely be expressed as saying that there is nothing without a reason – is said by him to determine the conceptual framework in terms of which we understand our experience (Gardiner, op. cit., p. 88). It follows from this that the kind of knowledge given by a work of art is wholly different from scientific knowledge, or the knowledge of everyday life. This is also typical of the later romantic theorists discussed by Professor Kermode; for them, the work of art is a means to truth 'unrelated to, and more exalted than, that of positivist science, or any observation depending upon the discursive reason' (Kermode, op. cit., p. 44). Now, it is precisely for this reason that Lukács criticizes Schopenhauer's aesthetics (*Die Zerstörung der Vernunft,* Neuwied, 1962, pp. 205–6). He notes that Schopenhauer regards art as a way of contemplating things independently of the principle of reason, and he says that it follows that, for Schopenhauer, knowledge and aesthetic contemplation are diametrically opposite. Lukács contrasts Schopenhauer unfavourably with classical German aesthetics, which regarded knowledge and art as directed towards the same reality, as interrelated ways of conceiving the world. In sum, Lukács will have nothing to do with what he regards as the mystifying attempts of romantic theorists to make of art a kind of knowledge *sui generis.* The artist, he might say, gives us knowledge of a kind, or at any rate knowledge is involved in the work of art; but this knowledge is not wholly different from scientific knowledge.

It seems, then, that Lukács' views do not simply repeat those of Schopenhauer and the late nineteenth-century romantics. It must now be asked whether what Lukács says is true. It is unlikely that many western philosophers will accept readily the general conceptual framework within which Lukács' aesthetics is placed – his view that knowledge is a kind of reflection, and what may be called his philosophical realism, i.e. his belief that a thing's determinations are really in it. However, it has already been argued (cf. part 2) that when it is seen what Lukács means by 'reflection', what he says in terms of this concept seems to be unobjectionable. As to his philosophical realism, it does not seem that he is really committed to the Leibnizian view that a thing's predicates are in it. What he wants to stress is that when it is true that S is P, one must not suppose that it is thinking that makes it so. In short, his 'realism' is opposed to subjectivism, and it seems that any non-subjectivist theory of knowledge would serve his purpose.[1]

In any case, all this concerns a framework; what of the centre of the picture, the idea that speciality is the central category of aesthetics? One may sympathize with Lukács' view that the creation and appreciation of works of art is not a unique and mysterious kind of knowledge, as romantic theorists had supposed; one may agree with him, too, in his rejection of a crudely emotivist theory of art – of the theory that a work of art does no more, and is intended to do no more, than arouse emotions in its audience. Another point in Lukács' favour is his insistence that a work of art is something concrete and sensuous (e.g. ii. 233; *DZP* II, 1954, pp. 123, 130), thus avoiding the Crocean tendency to make of the work of art something other than this painting, this statue, etc. But the theory of speciality as the central aesthetic category claims to do much more than make the fairly familiar points just mentioned, and the question is, whether it can do as much as Lukács thinks it can. The objections that can be brought fall into two main classes. Lukács, it may be said, is a literary critic, and it may be assumed that when he thinks of 'art', it is primarily literature that he has in mind. Now one may ask, first, does his theory of art fit art of a non-literary kind; and second, does it even fit all types of literature?

To begin with the first of these questions: music would seem to be an obvious source of difficulty for Lukács. In what sense is a piece of music governed by the category of speciality, in what sense does it contain elements of both individual and universal? Does music create types? Can one speak of 'realism' in music? Again, it may be recalled that for Lukács a work of art is a copy of reality; but what precisely does music copy? Lukács sees these difficulties, and tries to answer them in a long section (ii. 330–401) of Chapter 14 of *Die Eigenart des Ästhetischen*. His answer to the last question is that music is a double

---

[1]Mention has also been made above (Part III) of obscurities in Lukács' general account of the way in which the categories of universality, individuality and speciality change into each other. But it has also been suggested that these obscurities do not affect Lukács' aesthetics.

mimesis; it is a copy of feelings and emotions, which are themselves copies of reality (ii. 366–7; cf. ii. 355, 363, 368, 376, 378–9, 385, 389, 394, 396). Feelings have their own logic and dynamics (ii. 366), and Lukács seems to regard the structure of a musical work as a copy of these. It will be asked how one copies a feeling, and Lukács' answer is not wholly clear. It has already been seen (part 2 of this paper) that when Lukács says that a sensation of colour is a copy of reality, he means that it is the effect of certain vibrations, and when he says in the present context that an emotion is a 'copy' of reality he must mean that it is an effect of or response to events in the external world. Does he mean, then, that a musical work is in a sense an effect of emotions? It is certainly the case that, when he speaks of music, he moves easily from saying that it copies or imitates feelings to saying that it *expresses* feelings (e.g. ii. 366, 401), and it may be thought that he supposes an expression of a feeling to be caused by that feeling. There are serious philosophical objections to such a view, but it is unnecessary to go into them here, for it is clear that in speaking of music as an expression of feelings Lukács does not mean that it is the end-stage of a causal process whose prior stage is certain feelings that the composer has. He states expressly (i. 435–6) that it is not necessary for the artist, while producing a work, to have the feelings that the work is intended to evoke. He cites from Diderot (*Paradoxe sur le comédien*) the case of actors who do not feel what they act, but act, as we might say, 'from the head' (*aus Reflexion*), and yet are better actors than those who feel their part. It is, therefore, unnecessary to saddle Lukács with the view that a composer who writes a dirge must have funereal feelings. What, then, does he mean when he says that music expresses feelings? It is instructive that in this context he makes a reference to *Klageweiber*, professional mourners (ii. 363–4). These do not express *their own* grief, but they express *grief*. Similarly, it seems, the composer does not (or at any rate, need not) express what happen to be his feelings at the time of composition, but he does express *feelings*.

It must now be seen how Lukács applies this to speciality. (This exposition will follow the account given in Chapter 14, which is clearer than that given in Chapter 12, ii. 254–5.) The musical work is not governed by the category of individuality, in that it contains no element of the purely personal (ii. 367). This may be taken to mean that it is not an expression of (say) just one person's grief. If it is, then it is probably a piece of bad music, i.e. something which is not music in the evaluative sense of the word. On the other hand, music is clearly unable to generalize in the way that the sciences can, and so is not governed by the category of universality (ii. 368). Lukács insists, however, that the language of music is not vague, nor is it an inarticulate stammering of mere bursts of feeling. Music extracts typical traits from each particular phenomenon; it differs from the other arts in that it does not depict the typical in a unified connection with individuals, but rather gives form to the typical as such (ibid.). Lukács means that in the case of the novel, for example, to talk about types is (roughly) to talk about the way in which general social laws are presented through the medium of concrete individuals, but that this does not hold in the case of music. How, then, is music related to the type? Lukács' views on the question of realism in music are relevant here. Such realism, he says (ii. 392), is not the imitation of individual phenomena, by which he means that it is not a matter of an orchestra's making noises like a locomotive or a steel foundry. Neither, again, is it correct (as some adherents of socialist realism have supposed) to conceptualize a musical work, concentrating on its so-called basic idea, and to say that a work is an example of musical realism if this idea is true (ii. 393). Rather (ii. 395), the realistic character of a work is determined by the extent to which it is capable of reproducing and evoking the problems of the moment of its historical origin, from the perspective of its enduring significance in the development of humanity. This appears to be another way of saying that music is able to 'typify', that it 'extracts typical traits' from phenomena. In this case, the phenomena are feelings, which are not merely expressed by music, but are presented by it as the feelings of certain people at a certain stage of human history.

Lukács has made a determined attempt to meet the difficulties mentioned earlier, but it may be doubted whether the attempt is wholly a success. The problems involved are far-reaching, and can only be indicated here. One may ask, for example, whether Lukács is right in saying that the emotions have their own logic, and implying that this is so complex that it is proper to speak of a musical work as 'copying' it. Some philosophers deny that the 'inner life' of feeling has such a degree of richness (e.g. E. Bedford, 'Emotions', *Proceedings of the Aristotelian Society*, Vol. LVII, 1956–7, p. 282); others would agree with what seems to be Lukács' general thesis, and affirm that there is a 'host of qualitatively specific inner feelings' that music can express (R.W. Hepburn, 'Emotions and Emotional Qualities', in *Collected Papers on Aesthetics,* ed. by C. Barrett, Oxford 1965, p. 196). This may seem to be an irreconcilable difference about a matter of fact; however, it may be argued that the latter view involves a confusion. Starting from the quite correct position that music evokes emotions, and that the composer (sometimes, at any rate) has these emotions and expresses them by his music, it makes the assumption that the emotions can be separated from the music. Yet if one tries, for example, to specify the emotions behind the *Eroica* symphony, it is hard to see how this can be done other than by describing the music itself. (Cf. J. Casey, *The Language of Criticism*, London, 1966, p. 25.) Lukács, then, seems to be wrong in thinking that the emotions expressed by music can be described independently. One may also ask whether all music can be regarded as in some way expressing emotion. What emotions are expressed by the 'Musical Offering', for example, or 'The Art of Fugue'?

The second of the questions raised earlier was whether Lukács' aesthetics can be justified if regarded, not as a theory of art in general, but as a theory of literature. Once again it has to be asked whether Lukács' theory covers the whole field. It has often been noted that, as a critic, Lukács is concerned mainly with the novel and drama (especially the former), but that he neglects the lyric. That he should concentrate on the large-scale literary form is not surprising, in view of the emphasis that he lays on the type – the union of individual and universal, of the concrete and of law. Such a union, involving all the socially essential moments of an epoch (cf. part 4 above), seems naturally to demand a large canvas. Lukács is able to bring the short story under his theory of the literary type, by saying that the short story presents central aspects of a type, but not the whole picture of it. (See 'Gorki's Human Comedy', in *Studies in European Realism*, pp. 229–30.) The question is, however, whether his aesthetic theory, and in particular what he says about speciality, can accommodate the lyric.

Lukács would certainly claim that it can. He discusses the problem in Chapter 15 of *Die Eigenart des Ästhetischen*, which deals with problems of natural beauty. He notes first (ii. 637) that the territory of the lyric is governed by subjectivity. The lyric does not represent nature itself, nor even the experience of nature in general (ii. 638); its subject is a man who finds himself in one particular situation. Through the particularity of the situation, nature brings out what is spiritually most important for him at that given moment. The poem, then, displays a unity of inner and outer, in which subjectivity is dominant. In other words (ii. 640), the lyrical form arises out of a synthesis – 'a synthesizing reflection of the interrelations between the whole man of everyday life and the surroundings which awaken in him the relevant experience'. Now, this synthesis is at the same time an aesthetic generalization; for although in many poems the concrete here and now of the cause is preserved, yet the cause and the experience together are raised to the level of speciality, of the typical. In this case the typical is related to the subjective side of man, and not to the part of nature that causes it to be expressed. This shows how the speciality of the lyric is to be distinguished from individuality; Lukács distinguishes it from universality when he notes that the world that is portrayed in the poem makes visible a particular subjectivity and its relation to the human race – not as an abstract 'universally human', but in the concrete form of the given socio-historical moment. He adds that since there is a unity of the man and his natural surroundings, the poet's socio-historical determinations must also become manifest. Paradoxical as it may sound, Lukács remarks, a genuinely poetic representation of spring or winter displays the attitude of the poet to the truly great tendencies and struggles of his time (ii. 640).

Despite the ingenuity of Lukács' account, one may feel that the lyric has been forced into his categories. Is what he says, it may be asked, true of every lyric? Could one, for example, say anything about Wordsworth's politics simply on the basis of reading 'I wandered lonely as a cloud'? Presumably Lukács would reply that if one cannot, then the work is not genuinely poetic; but then what he says about the lyric would be true by definition, and would not be informative. Further, this would not really meet the objection; for the problem was, whether Lukács' aesthetics can account for what are *normally regarded* as lyrics, and there is no doubt that the poem in question is one of these.

In conclusion, we return to a point made in part one of this paper. It was suggested there that Lukács' aesthetics can be regarded roughly as a study of the language of criticism, but that it would be more exact to say that it provides an account of Lukács' own critical vocabulary, which he takes to be *the* vocabulary of criticism; that is, that he gives an account of his own use of words such as 'art', but offers this as an account of *the* use of the words. It has been seen in the course of this paper that this is indeed what he does, so that it is correct to say that in so far as Lukács offers a definition of art, he offers a persuasive definition. This definition, it has been argued, is to be rejected, in that it does not cover all of what would generally be regarded as works of art, in the evaluative sense of the word 'art' – e.g. there are many pieces of music that it does not cover, and much lyric poetry. In other words, the category of speciality does not govern all art; indeed, it does not govern all literature – even when the words 'art' and 'literature' are taken in their evaluative sense, which is narrower than the descriptive sense. This, however, does not mean that Lukács' aesthetics is valueless. His work contains a number of discussions – e.g. his account of the distinction between art and science, and of the relations between works of art and aesthetic 'laws' – which are examples of analysis, and not merely of persuasive definition. Further, it was mentioned in part one that simply to call a definition 'persuasive' is not an end of the matter; one also has to ask about the point of the definition. Here one must make the

Georg Lukács

simple observation that for Lukács, art is something that matters; it is not a mere luxury product (i. 513). The topic of this paper has been one of Lukács' reasons for saying that art matters;[1] it matters (very roughly) in that it presents in concrete, emotionally-evocative form the socio-historical laws that govern human beings. One does not have to agree with Lukács that only a work that does this is properly called a work of art; nevertheless, it seems to the present writer that what Lukács calls 'art' does matter. His aesthetics provides us with a certain way of looking at what are generally regarded as works of art, in the evaluative sense. It would be wrong to regard this as the *only* way, but equally wrong to say that it is not *a* way, and an important one.

[1] It is perhaps worth stressing that what Lukács counts as works of art are regarded by him as important for reasons other than those discussed here. Relevant in this connection is what he says about the relation of art to what may be translated as 'man's totality' (*der Mensch ganz*: see, e.g., i. 659ff., 682, 806ff., 838, 845). But an account of this would require another paper.

5 Georg Lukács: The Concept of Totality

Roy Pascal

The term 'totality' is of crucial importance in Lukács' literary criticism as a criterion of evaluation, but it is also a criterion of life, of reality. For this reason I have to define it in a broad context, and must encroach on fields that are to be more closely examined by other papers in this volume.

Any attempt to weave out of Lukács' judgments a completely integrated theoretical system is beset by the threat of distortion. His critical books and essays arose from particular challenges, in the framework of a Party cultural policy that went through different phases, and his judgments and formulations were always markedly influenced by the particular concerns of the moment. He himself composed a systematic aesthetic only towards the end of his life, and in circumstances that politically and personally were very different from those in which most of his literary criticism was written. In considering this systematic *Ästhetik*, therefore, we have always to ask whether his conclusions fully correspond to his earlier practical work as a critic. Perhaps they in fact represent his thinking at a new stage in what I might call the general (and his personal) communist consciousness, and they were formulated at a time of his own life when, living in retirement and out of favour of the Party, reflexion was more divorced from practical responsibilities than at any time since he joined the Communist Party in 1918.

I believe, however, that to understand Lukács' concept of totality, we should start from the *Ästhetik*, where its general principles are elaborated incomparably more fully and clearly

147

Georg Lukács

than in his earlier writings, and largely in agreement with his earlier usage of the term.

Art is for Lukács one of the great instruments by which man grapples with reality. Reality is man's dialectical being in nature, his self-preservation and self-evolution through work. Science and art are continuing efforts of the mind to contribute to this total anthropological process, through which man changes himself as well as the world in which he lives. Both are rooted in the mental operations involved in all human 'Praxis', in 'everyday life' as he calls it, and are means of developing this Praxis. Both mirror ('*wiederspiegeln*') the reality of which man is part – we note straight away that 'mirror' does not mean surface-reflexion, as the image seems to imply, but means any type of formulation of the relationships in which man stands to the experienced world, so that a flint arrowhead or a scientific formula are 'reflections' of reality.

Both science and art start from experience, from the particular, and both seek a general principle within this particular. The method of science is 'de-anthropomorphization', the elimination of personal immediacy in the search for general laws, for what Lukács calls 'the extensive and intensive totality' governing any particular.[1] It possesses a subjective element too, for its pursuit is governed by choice and intention, just as the operations of everyday life are governed by selective purpose. Distinctions between the more and the less important properties of an object, between the more and the less essential, between 'essence' and 'appearance', are not distinctions in degrees of reality but simply denote different levels of human purpose.[2]

The method of art is on the other hand 'anthropomorphic'. It seeks totality in a double sense. First: Its task is to make a 'totality' out of the reality it is reflecting (this may be a particular object, an event or group of events, a theme or aspect of an event, etc.). Like science it has 'to reproduce the intensive totality, the totality of the essential determinants ("*Bestim-*

[1] G.Lukács, *Ästhetik*, I. i. 237–8. All translations in this essay are my own, and may often be found to vary from the published translations, which are not always as precisely accurate as one needs.
[2] Ibid., 357–9.

148

mungen") of the object', and therefore is not limited to the external appearance of reality; unlike science, however, it does not seek abstract, de-personalized laws, but reproduces the sensuous individuality of objects (events, etc.)[1]. Its peculiar characteristic is that it reproduces in an enhanced form the uniqueness, the particularity, of existence. Like science, it uncovers at the same time a generality within this uniqueness,[2] but its form of generalization is 'the sensuous ("*sinnfällige*") generalization of the whole man', in that what is represented appears as typical – typical of a mode of being, of feeling, etc., typical of a group, class, etc.[3] This typicality is achieved not through intellectual abstraction, but through the form, the order, the style of the work of art.

The work of art is 'total' through another characteristic. It is not a direct expression or copy of an external event, its truth cannot be tested against some particular happening. It is an imitation, an artefact; it is a totality in that it is complete in itself; it is self-enclosed. It can be experienced only by the contemplative mind, temporarily withdrawn from direct engagement in the world. Its effect is therefore not that of direct instruction or exhortation; its object is truth, an insight and understanding that enables the enjoyer 'to change and deepen' his personal participation[4] when he returns from the world of aesthetic contemplation to the practical world.

But totality appears in art in yet another form: as a quality of the 'subject', by which term Lukács means both the creative artist and the recipient, the enjoyer of art. Art brings 'an intensification of subjectivity',[5] and he quotes with approval Klopstock's statement that 'it sets the whole soul in motion'. The outlines of an ontology here appear, on which Lukács is now working. It is 'a basic need of man' for man to feel himself a whole, a more and more urgent need as the division of labour separates his faculties and separates men from one another. Religion and ethics both seek to restore the wholeness of the individual, but the 're-unification of the personality', the 'acknowledgment of the totality, the continuity of the individual-

---

[1] Ibid., 461.   [2] Ibid., 604.   [3] Ibid., 238–44.
[4] Ibid., 428–9.   [5] Ibid., 533.

ity of man' is truly fulfilled only in art.¹ Just as man becomes himself only by engagement in the outside world, so too he becomes a whole only through the creation of the objective totality of art; the two totalities are simultaneous and condition one another.² This intensification of the subject implies however the same sort of generalization as we have seen in respect to the object; in the aesthetic experience, the artist or the enjoyer distance themselves from their ordinary selves to become their essential selves. But Lukács does not allow us to believe that this enhanced subjectivity means we have temporarily transcended our specific historical self and enlarged ourselves to the 'general human'. He insists that the generalization that occurs only means a widening out from our accidental particularity towards identification with the larger self of a social group, class, nation.³

The importance of this second principal form of totality is evident from his comment that, since 'the object of art is the concrete world in which men live, experienced from the standpoint of the whole man', behind all art lies the question: 'How far is this world truly a world of man, that he can affirm as his, as worthy of his humanity?' Art is for him a criticism of the real world through the contrast it establishes between the totality, the wholeness of experience, achieved through the experience of the artefact of the imagination, and 'the narrow and particular sphere of the merely daily'⁴. Repeatedly, in his practical criticism, he asserts that the standard of criticism immanent in the great writers is their vision of wholeness – Balzac for instance is 'inspired with the ideal of the whole man'. But I believe it is true to say that while Lukács' practical criticism expounds systematically the one meaning of totality – the aesthetic reflection of external reality – it only fitfully and gropingly grasps the implications of the second.

In some respects, the distinction Lukács draws between science and art is also that between ideology and art, and some

¹ Ibid., 538, 543–4.
² Ibid., 555.
³ Ibid., 589 *passim*.
⁴ 'Die revolutionären Demokraten' in *Der russische Realismus in der Weltliteratur*, 86 *passim*.

of his most striking criticism demonstrates how, in great writers like Balzac or Tolstoy, their imagination corrects the errors of their ideology. At times, indeed, Lukács suggests that the artistic consciousness is an alternative and corrective to the 'scientific' conclusions even of Marxism, but this elevation of imagination over reason provoked collisions with the Party and with himself. He therefore tends to place dialectical materialism, Marxism, in a unique position, not subject to his general comments on science; or, to put it practically, he accepts the claim of the Party to tell writers what sort of things they should write.

The distinction that the Marxist Lukács draws between science and art is not so very different from the one that the pre-Marxist Lukács drew in *Die Seele und die Formen*, 1911. The realm of science, he stated here, is 'facts and their connections', and of art, 'souls and destinies'.[1] 'Soul' is the term, usual at that time (e.g. Simmel), for the self-fulfilling integral personality, and 'destiny' is a term he continued to use to indicate the dialectical law that embraces teleology and causality, individual purpose and choice, and social and natural law.[2] Both the pre-Marxist and the Marxist definitions might be directly applied, for instance, to the difference between Simmel's scientific analysis of the mental climate of the metropolis (in *Die Groszstädte und das Geistesleben*) and Rilke's description of the 'soul's' encounter with the metropolis in *Die Aufzeichnungen des Malte Laurids Brigge*.

It is worth signalling the relationship of Lukács' terminology, particularly the term totality, to Hegel's, not just because here there is a demonstrable and acknowledged debt, but because Hegel's usage illuminates that of Lukács. Hegel distinguished art from science, from rational understanding, by saying that art does not analyse, but grasps reality 'in its living existence in the particular'; art dwells 'in the substantial entity' that analysis has not broken up.[3] This complex entity of the work of art he calls a 'Totalität', an essential feature of which is its completedness, so that he repeatedly speaks of it as a 'total and free

---

[1] *Die Seele und die Formen*, 7.   [2] *Gespräche*, 60–63.
[3] *Hegel, Ästhetik*, iii. 239.

whole', with the 'independence', or self-sufficiency, that characterizes the work of art.[1] And Hegel relates this self-sufficient totality of the work of art to a basic ontological characteristic of man, his 'interest and need to be a real individual totality and living independent being'. Like his contemporaries, Hegel saw in the ancient Greeks the embodiment of this totality, and attributed its historical disintegration to the division of labour, the stratification of society, and the specialization of professions. The great principle of Goethe and Schiller he considered to have been to 'regain in their poetical works the lost independence of characters', and at the same time to indict the modern world for its failure to make this totality possible in actuality.[2] Totality appears in Hegel (as in Lukács) both as the fulfilment of life, and as the essential characteristic of art.

The similarity with Lukács' conception is evident; it is surprising and significant, however, that Lukács amongst all his copious references to Hegel never, I think, refers to the statement on man's basic need to be 'a real individual totality'. In another respect there is an important difference between their views. For Hegel there are certain great permanent themes of art – e.g. love, the family, power – which determine the limits and define the self-enclosedness of the work of art. They are presented necessarily in a concrete historical form, but in general he considers the historical concretization to be a mere trapping for a general truth.[3] Only when he discusses historical drama does he state that here 'the innermost kernel and meaning of an event' is presented, so that 'the inherent rationality is unfolded and made manifest in its appropriate reality'.[4] Hegel here asserts that the object of historical drama is to capture a total historical situation in such a way that we understand its significance as a stage in the grand process of Reason that is for Hegel the history of mankind.

Lukács was to fasten on to Hegel's interpretation of historical drama as the essential principle of all art. He was to wage a constant campaign against the idea of the 'generally human', the idea that certain great themes incorporate permanent features of the human condition of all times.

[1] Ibid., iii. 239–41.   [2] Ibid., i. 250 ff.   [3] Ibid., i. 359–60.   [4] Ibid., iii. 266.

At the same time as Lukács extends the historicism in Hegel, he also, of course, as a Marxist, gives Hegel's metaphysical system a materialistic interpretation. The grandiose metaphysical evolution of the *Weltgeist* is sobered down. It becomes the evolution of man's mastery over nature, the dialectical process through which the mode of production creates social (ideological) forms that in time come into collision with the further development of production. At the end of this process stands the abolition of class-society, the liberation of man through the socialization of the means of production and exchange. The historic nodal points at which Hegel discerns the decisive advances of the *Weltgeist* are interpreted as stages in this social process, when socio-political revolutions, accompanied by ethical and philosophical revolutions, arise from the contradictions between the economic 'base' and the ideological superstructure. Art for Lukács reflects this process; it does not analyse and generalize, like historical science, but anthropomorphizes and intensifies. Thus *King Lear*, for instance, demonstrates the collapse of feudalism in the image of the family, where the historical process is concretized and intensified through the medium of personal destinies.[1] Art is thus a special way of knowing. 'The science of history [Lukács means Marxism] lays the foundation of our historical consciousness; art awakens our historical self-consciousness and keeps it awake.' Lukács even asserts that we cannot know the past or the present without the peculiar form of consciousness of art: 'As past periods live on in the memory of mankind in the shape given them by the great classical artists, so is it too with our self-knowledge in the present.' Lukács was frequently to assert that the great literature of the past is meaningful to us because it is mankind's living memory of its past, akin to the childhood memories of an individual man.[2]

[1] *Der historische Roman*, 93 (*The historical Novel*, 93–4).
[2] 'Literatur und Kunst als Überbau', *Beiträge*, 425; 'Die revolutionären Demokraten', *Der russische Realismus in der Weltliteratur*, 86; *Gespräche*, 24–5; *Studies in European Realism*, 115.

Totality in Lukács' practical criticism

The first significant use of the term totality in Lukács is in *Die Theorie des Romans*, published as articles in 1916 and as a book in 1920; it was the first outcome of his meeting with Hegel. Correcting his earlier view that art presents 'souls and destinies', Lukács now, concentrating on the distinction between the drama and the novel, agreeing with Hegel claims that the former represents an 'intensive' totality, the latter an 'extensive' one. By an 'extensive' totality, he means, like Hegel, both a totality extending over a large area of time and a number of characters, and one that concerns itself with social relationships, in particular with the 'prosaic reality', as Hegel had called it, of ordinary, modern social life. At this stage Lukács, though already committed to political action, is far from Marxism. He writes of the epic, in fact, in terms that would fit wonderfully well the contemporary works of Kafka: the novel, he says, mirrors a world bereft of transcendental meaning and is the expression of 'the transcendental homelessness of man'. Equally unmarxist is his view that drama gives shape to the 'intensive totality of essentiality', i.e. to a completely unhistorical human essence. The novel is therefore realistic in a way that the drama can never be – 'realistic' in the sense of reproducing the concrete, extensive reality of historical existence.

As Lukács became a Marxist, he was to abandon this absolute distinction between novel and drama, both of which he came to consider reflect a historical social reality,[1] though he was continually and properly concerned with the formal distinctions between novel and drama, and always ready to denote them by the terms 'extensive' and 'intensive' (realism). It is of some significance that his whole terminology is clearly best suited to the novel, and that, though he makes comments of considerable insight on the drama, e.g. on Shakespeare, it is in this area that he also makes some of his most questionable assertions.

It was only after Lukács had entered strenuously into the practical and theoretical work of the Communist Party that the

---

[1] *Der historische Roman*, 146–7 (*The historical Novel*, 140–2).

term totality, like realism, came to play a central role in his literary criticism, and we have to bear in mind one basic principle of his political thought. He was never content simply to restrict his thought to the practical purpose of the victory of the proletariat. Over and over again, in terms that recall the young Marx, he refers to the ultimate human perspective of which the communist revolution is the instrument. Like Marx he revolted in the name of humanity against the exploitation of man by man and the consequent alienation and distortion of man. He saw the ultimate objective as the liberation of man from the distortion and one-sidedness produced by class-society, the social division of labour. He is sustained by a vision of the total human personality, the many-sided, integrated man. 'The great perspective of the socialist revolution is the overthrow of the social division of labour, the great perspective of the all-sided man'.[1] In the *Ästhetik* and the conversations of 1966 Lukács speaks even more emphatically of an ultimate '*Menschwerdung des Menschen*' ('epiphany of man').[2] It was this concern that was in no small degree responsible for his repeated conflicts with the pragmatic, tactically-minded political leadership of the Communist Party.

In the Preface to *Balzac und der französische Realismus* of 1951[3] he puts the matter thus:

> For aesthetics, our classical heritage is that great art that presents the totality of man, the whole man in the totality of his social world ... The goal of proletarian humanism is man in his wholeness, the restoration of human existence in its totality in actual life, the practical real abolition of the crippling fragmentation of our existence caused by class-society. These theoretical and practical perspectives determine the criteria on the basis of which Marxist aesthetics recaptures the classics. The Greeks, Dante, Shakespeare, Goethe, Balzac, Tolstoy, Gorki are at the same time adequate presentations (*Bilder*) of distinct great stages in the evolution of mankind, and signposts in the ideological struggle for the totality of man.

It may be noted that here, as elsewhere, Lukács speaks not

[1] *Karl Marx und Fr. Engels als Literaturhistoriker*, 96.
[2] *Gespräche*, 45, 113. Also *Ästhetik*, I. i. 528.
[3] *Studies in European Realism*, 5.

simply of a future achievement of man, but also of the 'restoration' of man. Like Hegel, Goethe, or Schiller he seems still to have seen in the Greeks (not only Greek art) a human fulfilment sometime to be restored. This nostalgia is also found in Marx and Engels, who held up the Renaissance all-sided man as a lost ideal, and in Rousseau, who talks of the unspoilt man of pre-civilized society. The utopian element reaches back as well as forward.

Hegel had illustrated his notion of the whole man from Goethe and Schiller, and Lukács frequently draws on them for the same purpose, for instance in *Karl Marx und Friedrich Engels als Literaturhistoriker*, or *Essays über Realismus*, or *Goethe und seine Zeit*. He considers the abiding inspiration of their work is the *'Humanitätsideal'*, the ideal of the realization of all human capacities, the overcoming of the division of labour, in its social and its professional sense. The meaning of their imaginative works is, he argues, that they restore in them the lost experience of totality. Realism of the Balzacian type was not appropriate to them, he states, since the petty and provincial German world around them did not focus the great historic issues of the times. Ideal figures remote from any conditions of actuality, Byronic heroes, would not have served their purpose either, for they would have been merely wishful dreams. What Goethe and Schiller did was to invent forms that embodied the potentialities of man at a time when society gave no scope for them. In these forms, however, the idealizing elements always pointed to the social reality from which they sprang. The supple purposefulness of Lukács' criticism appears in many ways. For instance he shows how the narrow world of Goethe's bourgeois provincial idyll, *Hermann und Dorothea*, is lifted into ideality, given a universal significance, by the nobility and elevation of the verse. The best of the essays in the Goethe book is that on *Wilhelm Meister's Apprenticeship*, where all the numerous characters are limited and specific, and necessarily so since each has to adopt a useful role in a society, to be 'educated for reality'. Yet each through the 'free development of his passions' can achieve 'harmony of personality and harmonious co-operation with other free personalities'. The potentialities of man are suggested, a utopian community is adumbrated in which they may be realized, together with the limitations imposed by the particular form of society to which they belong. At the centre stands a somewhat characterless hero, whose chief quality is his educability and capacity for sympathy, and in whom therefore not achievement but potentiality constitutes his claim to be at the centre. The somewhat ironic tone of the style indicates the tentativeness and imperfections of all the personal fulfilments reached. As a whole the novel gives shape to 'the tragic crisis of the bourgeois *Humanitätsideal*, and at the same time the beginning of its – for the time being utopian – emergence beyond the framework of bourgeois society'.[1]

It will be seen that the terms totality, '*Humanitätsideal*', etc., involve social and psychological as well as literary implications. In particular we see that Lukács' evaluation of *Wilhelm Meister's Apprenticeship* rests centrally on the truth of its reflection of a significant moment in human-social evolution, in which the depiction of a particular situation is infused dialectically with criticism of that situation and indications of an emergence from it. Totality applies to the historical import of the content as well as to its artistic form, though the historical import is shaped only in its form and style. We can examine Lukács' procedures more conveniently in the essay on Scott.

Walter Scott

I choose Lukács' criticism of Scott because it illustrates his criticism at its typical best. There are many essays, and many remarks in his essays, that incline to a 'vulgar sociology' of art, and usually one must know the particular situation in which they were written to assess them properly. For instance a remark like: 'Great works mirror in an exemplary way the basis, the productive relations and the fundamental social relations of an epoch' can be properly evaluated only if we know it was made in the course of a public address given in the Hungarian Academy of Sciences in 1951, when Lukács was under severe attack for unorthodoxy, revisionism, etc., and desperately trying to save what

[1] *Goethe und seine Zeit,* 42, 44 (*Goethe and his Age,* 62, 64).

Georg Lukács

he could. The Scott analysis is a chapter of his book *The Historical Novel*, written in 1936–7, in the relatively halcyonic period of the Popular Front, when the Communist Party was making strenuous efforts to win over the progressive bourgeoisie. Lukács was one of its chief spokesmen on the 'cultural front', and he was perhaps never so much at his ease, more himself, than when he was addressing himself to the bourgeois intellectual.

It is 'no accident', says Lukács, that Scott's work was accomplished in early nineteenth-century England. The bourgeois revolution had established the basis here for a 'model' development, a stable 'middle way' along which the bourgeoisie had overcome and reconciled the feudal classes. From the security of this achieved revolution Scott could survey the conflicts of the past without qualms. As a Tory he had a deep sense of identification with the feudal lords, the Scottish clans, and the peasantry, whose forms of life had been shattered and merged in the life of the bourgeois nation, but this identification deepened his sympathies and insight without hindering him from affirming the historical transformation as a whole and identifying himself with the nation as a whole (in this way the artist generalizes his subjectivity). The affinity between his personal character and the historical situation in which he lived made it possible for him to understand history realistically, or 'correctly'.

His genius however lay in his grasp of the literary form in which this historical reality could be expressed. Scott has recognized that the novel does not, like the drama, present 'the violent resolution of conflicts in their most intensified form', but 'the manner in which trends arise and die away'. He finds for the extensive totality of history a form that makes it an aesthetic experience. The great conflicts of the past are presented in a personal form, in the personal relationships of families, friends, small groups, where great issues appear in concrete, personal shape. Local and private as the occurrences and feelings are, they are however always 'typical', that is, they embody 'social trends and historical forces'. Scott does not spread himself indiscriminately, but singles out significant moments, particular

158

situations. He can give these detailed and intensive treatment, and in this way can show the great complexity of the human relationships involved, characteristic of the times of which he writes (as opposed to the world of ancient epic), since society was in those times highly differentiated, and individuals stood in complex relationship to classes, groups, religions, etc. It is this aesthetic and historical insight that is at the root of the profound individuality of Scott's characters and events.

Lukács makes particularly interesting remarks on the central characters of the novels – here helped by remarks of Goethe's on the 'passive', 'retarding' character of the hero of the novel. Scott's central figures are repeatedly rather colourless, men of average ability, not impelled by strong passions, swayed by somewhat indecisive sympathies that pull them this way and that – Lukács is thinking of characters like Waverley or Henry Morton. They have often been criticized as somewhat featureless, but Lukács points out that in their inconspicuousness lies their central artistic function. They properly stand at the heart of the story for they bridge the opposing sides, 'enter into human contact with both camps', and represent the totality, the compromise, the balance struck by the forces engaged in struggle. Their individual destiny is not great and dramatic; they participate modestly in the great events round them. Their survival stands for the continuity of the national community, they represent 'the age-old steadfastness of English development'.

Scott quite properly, Lukács writes, ascribes a secondary artistic role to the great historic figures like Richard Coeur de Lion, Louis IX, Elizabeth, Cromwell, who in the Hegelian sense embody in their own personal ambitions and achievements the substantial interests of their times. These appear in the novels in their completed historical significance, acting their historic role, not as individuals with their own personal story. For this reason they are not suited to be the heroes of novels. They appear as a *deus ex machina*, in the sense that their acts seem to embody the will of history.

The heroic figures of the novels are always leaders of smaller groups, legendary or invented heroes like Rob Roy, Burley,

Jeanie Deans. Their energy and heroism is not abstract-personal or daemonic, like that of the Byronic hero, but is the distillation of the energy of a social group. Within the scope of these smaller groups we are shown in a concrete form the interests moving people. These interests throw up leaders who thus acquire true individuality, and we are therefore also able to understand the historical roots of the great historic figures when they make their decisive appearances. Scott 'portrays the great transformations of history as transformations of popular life'. Thus it is that Jeanie Deans, after rising to heroic action, can return afterwards to the obscure 'preserving life' from which she had momentarily emerged.

Scott's novels are in the deepest sense historically authentic. The historical costume is sufficiently suggestive without being pedantically antiquarian; above all people think, feel, and act according to the environment to which they belong. The novels are rich in accident, like 'prosaic' life itself, but they weave out of accident a meaningful story that is the necessary development of history itself. This necessity has nothing of an 'other-worldly fate' about it, for it is shown to arise out of 'the complex inter-action of concrete historical circumstances in their process of transformation'. Scott does not try to make the past falsely relevant by modernizing it, by introducing anachronistic features. The only anachronism he allows himself is an inevitable one: the writer is more conscious of the significance of the historical events than the characters could have been, and must see the past as the 'pre-history' of his own time.

These are I think the main features of Lukács' chapter on Scott. It will be seen that he scarcely discusses the detail of character drawing, the style; only once or twice does he allow himself criticism, as when he observes a certain philistinism in Scott, particularly in respect to the lack of individuality and passion in the women characters. It would be wrong however to believe that Lukács is not concerned with form; throughout he is concerned with the specific form of the novel, for it is the form that embodies the artist's interpretation of his world. In fact we notice the polemical purpose of justifying Scott's procedures as a prescriptive model for the writers of his own

(Lukács') time. We can sum up, in terms of the concept 'totality', in this way:

1 All art presents a total historical situation, a dynamic one, in which the decisive historical forces and their ideological forms drive through conflict to resolution. Each of Scott's novels centres on such a period and evolution.

2 The totality is grasped in a concrete, individual form, through characters who fulfil their destiny in specific circumstances, and whose personal destiny is rounded off. It is thus a self-enclosed totality, distinct from reality.

3 The totality presented is throughout that appropriate to the novel. History moves through revolutions, but these great changes are prepared by slow disintegrations and accumulations. Tragedy presents the extreme moment of crisis, the novel presents 'the manner in which trends arise and die away'.[1] The novel is therefore prosaic, extensive, and though it borrows dramatic procedures (dramatic occurrences, dialogue) it has to organize them within the flow of its prosaic narrative.

4 This totality is thus something we imaginatively experience, not by divesting ourselves of our modern consciousness, nor by discovering veiled references to a modern situation. All past art, condensing the great historic transformations of the past, is our pre-history, presented as a total, enclosed experience. Its historicity is essential. It is important for us as the embodied memory of our past, of mankind's past, and has the same function for mankind as an individual's memory of the significant moments of his childhood.[2]

The Scott essay is an accomplished demonstration of Lukács' method, but it also illustrates a typical inadequacy of his criticism. Suppose we accept the justice and relevance of all his points: is it a complete criticism? Is it enough to know that Scott's historical insight and his understanding of novelistic form are true and profound? Is this enough to guarantee his greatness as an artist? When we read Scott after reading Lukács, we are startled at the flatness of the writing, the complacency

[1] *Der historische Roman,* 146–7 (*The historical Novel,* 140–2).
[2] *Gespräche,* 24–5; 'Literatur und Kunst als Überbau', *Beiträge zur Geschichte der Ästhetik,* 424–5.

of the tone, at the lack of intensity, exaltation and anguish in our response. Lukács is not unaware of these lacks, but he explains and in essence justifies them as being appropriate to the social compromise reached by Britain in Scott's time. But we ourselves are not content with the knowledge that the novels, in their weaknesses as well as their strength, give an adequate and true image of a historical situation and historical forces.

To express my criticism in terms of Lukács' concept of totality: the concern for the objective totality of the work of art and for its historical categories overshadows that for 'subjective' totality. The latter is not entirely neglected. Lukács does indicate how the social position and personal character of Scott enabled him to grasp the movement of history, and how the formal elements of the novels are organized in such a way as to enable the reader to experience imaginatively this historical movement. But if we can call this an 'intensification of subjectivity', we can do so only in the sense that the reader thereby gains a deeper insight into the mode of historical change and a livelier consciousness of his own part in the social process. The self-directed meaning of subjectivity, what Lukács was in the *Ästhetik* to call the 'reunification of personality', plays no part in this appreciation; it seems scarcely applicable. If it had, Lukács would have had to concentrate much more on features in the novels that promote or hinder the engaged and direct response of the reader. If one reads Donald Davie's *The Age of Scott*, which in several ways links up with Lukács' essay, one will see that Davie rightly concerns himself very seriously with elements that Lukács ignores or brushes aside.

I do not believe that Lukács was so engrossed in cultural politics, or so intellectualistic, that he did not feel this direct response to art; but his criticism generally fails in this respect. If I now turn to his criticism of Kafka it is because here we find elicited from him a rather rare expression of a profound, immediate, aesthetic response, on the basis of which he has to enter into a more complex argument on the meaning of totality.

Totality in the Moderns — Kafka

Throughout the period of his active engagement in the Communist Party, Lukács was relentlessly hostile to all modernist, *avant-garde* literature. This was not due to enforced subservience to Stalin or Zhdanov. As long as Lukács was directly engaged in Party cultural policy he was as convinced as any orthodox socialist realist that modernist literature was decadent, and, by implication if not intention, imperialist or fascist. It was only with *Wider den missverstandenen Realismus* (*The Meaning of Contemporary Realism*) of 1958, after the death of Stalin, the Hungarian rising, and his own forced retirement from the Communist Party and active politics, that his judgment of modernism could free itself from some of the cruder propagandist intentions.

The general features of the imaginative world of Proust, Joyce, Kafka, Musil, Beckett and others are summed up thus: the replacement of the coherent social world of the older realists by an incoherent factuality or a pattern of sense-impressions; the disappearance of any meaningful relationship between man and his social environment; the breakdown of 'character', the disintegration of purpose and will; the isolation and alienation of man; the replacement of objective time by subjective time, the replacement of objective narrative and description by interior monologue, the breakdown of story itself, the tendency to allegory. But Lukács does not now dismiss these features as simply the opposite of realism. The ostensible non-realism of these writers arises, he writes, from a genuine artistic experience of their times, times of the crisis of bourgeois society, of imperialism, fascism, war, from their suffering because of the distortion of man, measured against that intuition and need of wholeness and integrity that is the distinguishing characteristic of the artist. The distortions of reality in modernist works are true reflections of a distorted reality; the chaos and *Angst* that characterize their works are true features of the society in which they live; in fact no modern bourgeois realism is possible unless it embodies chaos and *Angst*.

Georg Lukács

It is of course fully understandable that the experience of modern capitalistic society produces, especially among intellectuals, feelings of *Angst*, nausea, isolation, distrust of oneself and of others, contempt and self-contempt, despair, etc. Yet a portrayal of reality that did not evoke and give shape to such emotions would be untruthful and prettifying.[1]

Lukács' criticism of the modernists lies in the charge that these writers mirror the reality around them too directly, too unreflectively; they remain within the frontiers of bourgeois experience, and therefore cannot see their world whole. He concludes the quotation given above:

The question is not: is all this really there? The question is simply: is this the whole reality? It is not: has all this not to be described? The question is simply: have we to stick at this point?

One of the main themes of his criticism of these writers, and of Heidegger whom he considers to be the central philosophical representative of modernism, is that the specific situation of the modern bourgeois intellectual is presented as if it were a universal and timeless *condition humaine*. We can follow his argument in his criticism of Kafka, whom he takes as 'the very type of modernist art'.

Lukács does not take the easy way of some modern Marxist critics, who rescue Kafka for their cause by interpreting the intention of the novels as subtly disguised social criticism. Social criticism is there, he acknowledges, but it is only incidental to Kafka's ontological intention, the presentation of a universal *condition humaine*, 'a vision of the world dominated by *Angst* and of man at the mercy of incomprehensible terrors'. Lukács recognizes that the search of the heroes of *The Trial* and *The Castle* embodies a deep longing for a transcendental authority, a transcendental meaning, which they preserve despite its continual frustration. Such a judgment would have led the earlier Lukács to conclude that Kafka can have no significance as an artist. But he proceeds to demonstrate the artistic power and integrity of Kafka. He sees how all the features of his vision, events and

[1] *Wider den missverstandenen Realismus*, 85; (*The Meaning of Contemporary Realism*, 76.) (This translation is often loose, sometimes misleading.)

164

actualities, composition and style, belong together. Just as the 'hidden, non-existent God' of Kafka's world is ghostly, so the world in which his heroes move in its 'uncannily genuine detail' is ghostly too. Kafka 'is a genuine artist, who goes beyond the simple evocation of the felt facts of surface data'.

We are aware in these and other remarks of a critical attitude that is closer than is earlier the case to Lukács' definitions in the *Ästhetik*. The objective totality of Kafka's world arises out of the insight into experienced reality, out of the consonance of all parts, the unity of style and structure, so that it forms a total, self-enclosed imaginative world, that reflects the world of reality in that it gets beneath its surface appearances. At the same time it creates a subjective totality that corresponds to, or rather is immanent in, this objective totality. Our subjectivity is 'intensified' since we are seized and transported by the aesthetic experience. Our horror, our fascination, is the measure of the degree in which we are made more acutely conscious of our need for wholeness of personality, for a meaningful existence and world, which are the hidden values that determine the quality and shape of Kafka's vision.

Yet Lukács denies Kafka the full title of realist, by which he means the achievement of true and great art. For Kafka is typical of modernism in that his vision is not total; he is 'stuck fast' in immediacy, and in spite of his insight cannot see reality 'critically', cannot see all the decisive determinants ('*Bestimmungen*').

Franz Kafka is the classic of this situation, arrested at a blind and panic *Angst* before reality. His unique position is due to the fact that he finds a direct and simple expression for this basic experience, without formalistic mannerisms. The basic import in its simple immediacy determines the aesthetic form, and for this reason Kafka seems to belong to the family of the great realistic writers. And – from a subjective point of view – he belongs in a still higher measure to this family, for there are few writers who have been able to grasp and reproduce the world with such originality and naïvety, with such wonder at its utter novelty. Today, at a time when routine, whether experimental or stereotyped, rules the majority of writers as of readers, this vehement impetus must make a tremendous impact.

The intensity of work like this is further heightened not only because the work breathes a rare candour and honesty, but also because the imagined world is correspondingly simple and natural. In this lies Kafka's deepest originality. Kierkegaard says somewhere: 'The more genuine a man is, the more he is at the mercy of *Angst*.' Kafka has the genuine originality to give artistic form to this *Angst* and to what produces it, the (allegedly) corresponding structure and factualness of objective reality. The artistic foundation of Kafka's originality is not his invention of novel formal techniques, but the suggestive and outraging self-evidence of his factual world and the reaction of his characters to it. 'It is not the monstrous uncanniness that shocks,' writes Adorno, 'but its matter-of-factness'.[1]

For all his genuineness and originality, however, Kafka is not a realist. His method and intention are allegorical, and in this too he is representative of modernism. For Lukács, allegory is an aesthetic category that rests on the presupposition of 'a split in the world resulting from the transcendence of its being and final ground, from the abyss between man and reality. Allegory . . . rejects this-sidedness, that immanence of meaning in human existence and human activity which was and is the basis of all artistic work'. Lukács allows some validity to allegory in the plastic arts, and perhaps in the literature of earlier periods when the outlook of immanence had not yet overcome the belief in supernatural forces, but condemns it as an artistic procedure in times when it means abandoning the hard-won philosophical position of immanence, repudiating the profane meaningfulness of reality. He quotes with approval Walter Benjamin's theory of allegory in his study of Barock drama, which he properly understands as a defence of the modernist view and method. In allegory, Benjamin maintains, history appears as 'a frozen primeval landscape', as 'the Passion of the world'; death is the only reality. History is seen not as the process of eternal life, but as a process of decay. Allegory seeks something beyond beauty: 'allegories are in the realm of thoughts what ruins are in the realm of things'. 'The false semblance of totality fades out; the eidos [image] fades, the likeness dies, the cosmos in it withers.' 'Everything, persons, things, relationships can mean anything

[1] Ibid., 86–7 (77–8) – figures in brackets refer to the translation.

you like' – thus the allegorical method means that the 'profane world' is condemned absolutely, and rightly, says Benjamin. Nothing has a specific inherent value. At the same time each particular acquires a new, transcendental value, it is raised to the level of an abstraction in a transcendental system. Lukács sums up: while in realistic (i.e. true, great) literature every particular is both unique, personal, unmistakably itself and at the same time meaningful in the sense that it is typical – typical of a whole historical situation and movement – in allegory every particular is torn out of its real historical context and placed into a transcendental context of meaning; instead of being part of a complex web of reality and itself infinitely complex, it becomes a disparate item, a cipher.[1]

Lukács is here not simply criticizing the *Weltanschauung* of modernism. He has frequently shown how the false *Weltanschauung* of writers such as Balzac, Scott and Tolstoy does not harm their truthfulness as imaginative writers. The great error of allegory is that it is an artistic *form* that embodies a false *Weltanschauung*. The allegorical mode negates realism; or to put it into our own context, it is lacking in totality. And he makes this more precise: it lacks 'perspective' in the sense that the world of allegory lacks the element of time, history, movement, change. This limitation is inherent in the allegorical form of Kafka, for allegory abstracts the particular from the historical process and establishes it as a transcendental absolute. Kafka's imaginative world is an allegory of a 'transcendental nothingness', in which life has frozen into rigidity. It is not Kafka's 'unrealistic' method that deprives his work of totality, not the ghostliness and uncanniness, but the absence of movement. Lukács defends the 'totality' of that other ghostly writer, E. T. A. Hoffmann, who had been condemned by Zhdanov as a decadent, with the argument that Hoffmann's fantastic world is a true reflection of a Germany moving 'from the distortions of feudal-absolutism to the distorted capitalism' of early nineteenth-century Germany; but Kafka lacks this historical import because he turns the reality he perceives into an allegory of a general state of man. What Lukács means by 'perspective' is made clear

[1] *Wider den missverstandenen Realismus*, 41–5 (40–5); *Ästhetik*, I. ii. 727–74.

by the contrast he draws between Kafka and Thomas Mann. Mann also embodies the *angst*, the isolation of modern man in his novels; but he remains resolutely of this world, he defines these features as features of a particular modern situation, a situation that is made and changed by men; and he holds up the 'perspective' of socialism, socialist humanism, as its outcome. Thus Mann's characters, however specific, acquire a general significance as types, not as cyphers of an absolute situation. As types of attitudes and roles characteristic of a particular situation they are not frozen into rigid attitudes, but have the power of decision, of change.

Conclusion

In the course of this paper I have continually encroached on problems that could not be fully dealt with, such as in the last pages the role of the imaginative writer's *Weltanschauung*. I must content myself with a summary indication of what I believe to be the main advantages and disadvantages of the concept of totality and what is implied by it.

1 Underlying the term is a complete aesthetic, itself embedded in a general philosophy, an 'anthropology' in Feuerbach's sense. The nature and function of art in relation to the other main forms of human activity are defined. The great advantage of a comprehensive system of this kind is that it makes judgments possible; without it one is at the mercy of prevailing interests and fashions or private taste, and cannot securely distinguish between art and non-art, great and small art. The disadvantage is, of course, that the validity of judgments depends to some extent on the validity of the general system.

2 I say 'to some extent' because Lukács' aesthetic is not simply deduced from the general tenets of Marxism, but is informed by an alert response to the great works of literature. It was indeed Lukács' keen response to literature that led him in several respects to challenge orthodox Marxism and to correct ideological deductions by empirical experience. In some major instances, however, he is not able to incorporate this direct aesthetic experience into his system – notably lyric poetry, and

works like Goethe's *Iphigenie*. The constant reference to the great works of the past also promotes in him a tendency to conservatism, traditionalism, a blindness to new forms and styles; it led him to underestimate the significance of minor works and experimentation, and hence to be a chilling influence on young and experimental writers, whether socialist or bourgeois.

3 If one accepts the general principles of Lukács' historical materialism and of his aesthetic, and accepting too the general intention of his concept of 'totality', there is I believe a central flaw in his use of the term. I have mentioned the utopian element in this term as it is used to denote a glory achieved in the historic past (in Greece or the Renaissance for instance). The utopian element is still more marked in respect to the future, when Lukács believes that with the disappearance of the 'social division of labour' the all-sided man will re-emerge. It is a deep characteristic of Lukács' work as a Marxist that this dogma hinders any concrete analysis of the existing or future socialist society, and in particular any consideration of the position of the individual in the gigantic organizations within this society. This utopian dogmatism rests on an almost exclusively historical-social interpretation of the term totality, and this is also the great weakness of his use of it as an aesthetic category. What is missing is adequate attention to the ontological function of art, a thorough inquiry into the meaning of art in reference to the self-purpose, self-fulfilment of the individual. He has taken some steps in this direction in the *Ästhetik*, and is now I believe completing an *Ontologie*.

Earlier he shared Marx's suspicion and scepticism of all general definitions and was content to stop at the level of Marx's 'man is the ensemble of social relations'. Only in his last publication, the *Gespräche* of 1966, does Lukács suggest an ontological definition of man – here he calls man 'a responding being', i.e. one with choice within certain historical limits. Yet here as always self-fulfilment, 'wholeness', is thought to be achieved through self-identification with the progressive forces of society, through the fulfilment of the socialist social objectives. He never in his published works goes so far as in a letter to me over my book *Design and Truth in Autobiography* of 7 March 1961, where he wrote: 'I am also in agreement with your definition of the purpose of autobiography. It's a question here indeed of a fundamental problem of human existence: that of the substantiality or lack of substantiality of the human personality . . .'

The degree to which, and the form in which, this self-directedness of the individual appears in art varies greatly in history, but there can be no doubt that it is one of the great motives and motifs of literature, for instance of lyric poetry (which is practically excluded from Lukács' system). In 1903 Simmel writes that 'the deepest problems of modern life arise from the claim of the individual to preserve the independence and identity of his being against the super-powers of society, of his historical inheritance, and of the external culture and technique of life'. Lukács interprets this attitude of his erstwhile teacher only sociologically, as a statement of the bourgeois thinker or artist, and believes this conflict will be completely overcome in socialist society, once the vestiges of bourgeois ideology are obliterated. It is the lack of understanding for this self-purpose of the individual that underlies the crudely political or propagandist character of some of Lukács' interpretations of modern bourgeois and socialist-realist writers, and that makes his conception of totality too limited. It is also, I believe, at the root of his failure to provide an adequate theory of the artist himself, for while he does justice to the mysterious workings of the imagination as a mirror of the external world, and often subtly demonstrates the links between the artist and society, he disregards the artist as a person trying to make a meaning out of personal existence. This concern must promote 'inwardness', and it is true that such inwardness has often led poets to anti-social attitudes and to metaphysical, mystical beliefs; we might sympathize with Lukács for combating these as distorting or limiting the achievement of totality. But he had no right to ignore this function of art, or to condemn it as hostile to art. The great question is: might his general theory have been modified and expanded to embrace it? But, of course, if he himself had tried to do so, it would have meant alienation from orthodox Marxism and from the Party.

[1] G. Simmel, *Brücke und Tür*, 227.

Full titles of works quoted in this paper:
G. Lukács:
 Die Seele und die Formen, 1911.
 Theorie des Romans, 1920.
 Goethe und seine Zeit, 1947. *(Goethe and his Age, 1968.)*
 Essays über Realismus, 1948.
 Karl Marx und Friedrich Engels als Literatur-historiker, 1948.
 Studies in European Realism, 1950.
 Balzac und der französische Realismus, 1952.
 Der russische Realismus in der Weltliteratur, 1952.
 Beiträge zur Geschichte der Ästhetik, 1954.
 Der historische Roman, 1955. *(The historical Novel*, 1962.)
 Wider den missverstandenen Realismus, 1958. *(The meaning of contemporary Realism*, 1962.)
 Ästhetik, one volume in two parts, 1962.
Gespräche mit Georg Lukács, ed. Pinkus, 1967.
Hegel, *Ästhetik*, 3 vols, 1835–8.
G. Simmel, 'Die Groszstädte und das Geistesleben', 1903; in *Brücke und Tür*, 1957.

6 The Marxist as a Literary Critic

A. G. Lehmann

It would be impertinent to offer to survey Lukács' *career* as a literary critic, in the context of this symposium; and it is not certain that it would be a very useful exercise. Implicit in such an exercise would be the study of a great many other people's writing and thinking: there would be a need to discuss both the objects of Lukács' criticism and the criticism itself; and there would be a duty which I do not regard as constructive, namely to draw attention to areas in which one might have expected Lukács to have something to say, but in which he did not, owing to the nature of this career, and the limitations of activity which it implied.

Instead, however, it is permissible to attempt a view of Marxism – Lukács' Marxism – in its relation to the study of literature; and it is possible to do this by way of an examination of a few important and typical critical studies. Naturally, this is in a sense an artificial exercise; Marxism is a large and sprawling matter; it is exceedingly difficult to separate the study of literature from the study of aesthetics, or in other words the groundwork of literary criticism (or metacriticism); and elsewhere in this collection Lukács' aesthetics come specifically under review. Nevertheless, with so encyclopedic and all-round a speculator and writer, a limited contribution on a particular line of argument is liable to prove more positive than a non-committal survey.

It may seem trite, but is none the less essential, to insist at the outset that in the perspective of the history of ideas, Marxism is *not* a single ideology, or body of doctrine, or set of prescriptions of method in the social or human sciences; let alone a number of unambiguous prescriptions for relating theory to practice in dialectical or other ways. Like Darwinism, Marxism is a large intellectual family of alternative versions of all these things. It is so already in the writings of Marx; in the corpus of publications in which Marx and Engels collaborated; and by the beginning of this century there were many exponents of Marxism (whether in exile from Russia, or in various forms of oppositional activities in Europe) whose views, in different areas – whether of dialectical or historical materialism or of the development of these in relation to revolutionary planning – were vastly divergent. The tangle can be briefly pointed to by the rehearsal of some typical names: Bernstein, Lenin, Jaurès, Sorel, Plekhanov, Kautsky, Trotzky, Bukharin . . . From 1924 to 1929 it was even possible in France for a number of highly individualist surrealists to consider themselves communists in a Marxist sense. In Russia after 1924, and in the rest of Europe essentially in the thirties, the exercise of power by a party dictatorship and of influence by the Third International greatly inhibited this kind of diversitarianism, always in the name of party discipline. It was the achievement of General Secretary Stalin to transform debate and dialogue into a one-sided accumulation of rulings, normally in a style which owed its grace and dispassionate clarity to the example of Lenin's *Materialism and Empirio-criticism*. Thus it is mainly during the thirties and for a very short time after 1945, that the *multiplicity of Marxisms* (already pointed to by Sorel at the opening of the century under the name of *decomposition*) was largely lost sight of. Today it is no longer plausible even for Marxists of the strict obedience to overlook the multiplicity; and even those old enough to have observed communism at work under Stalin or to have puzzled over his pronouncements on, say, linguistics, have some difficulty in recalling the vehemence of the party dictatorship in such secondary matters as literary criticism.

Lukács' main writing as a Marxist critic of literature falls largely within that period in which it was most difficult, or even dangerous, to air venturesome thoughts that might not quite fit in with the canon of rigid and fixed rulings about what one should or should not think. It is not easy to assess the extent to

Georg Lukács

which appeals for loyalty to the cause of proletarian revolutionary unity can induce a man to inhibit his natural inclination to
inquire freely and without prejudice in intellectually attractive
fields. It is not easy even to guess at the extent to which, over a
changing life in a changing world, the threatening maxim of
the unity of theory and practice can have become lodged preju-
dicially in a mind grounded essentially in a nineteenth-century
liberal world view.

To recall these facts of history and to append to them these
conjectures is not to exculpate the philosopher, let alone to
applaud him. But Lukács' critical activities did not happen in a
void, and they reflect certain facts about the world he lived in.
During his stay in Moscow, Lukács did not announce his views
through participation in the polemics on Socialist Realism, the
new Russian orthodoxy exported to the rest of Europe via the
network of party organs. He wrote of Tolstoy or Gorky, but not
much of the successors of Sholokhov. He gave as a reason for
this his defective knowledge of the Russian language. He gave
keen attention to the novels of Heinrich Mann, as examples of a
new democratic humanism in the making; but he steered clear of
the entirely orthodox, copy-book 'socialist realist' – even programmatic – early socialist novels of Aragon in France (1935
onwards), though these were written in French. If he had pro-
nounced their sentiments, treatment of themes, and value systems to be 'correct', he would no doubt have had difficulty in
explaining why the novels, as novels, are unremarkable and
tedious; but if he had attempted such an explanation, the results
would have been complicated in other ways. Better then to concentrate on important literature, on major monuments of the
past. This has always the advantage that it is easier to deal with
issues that are not topical: safer too; moreover, the philosopher,
in his search for general principles requires elbow-room, and a
certain calm. Not that for any philosopher eager to contribute to
Marxist thought in the age of Stalin the search for general principles can be an entirely unrestricted quest: Marx, Engels,
Lenin cannot be overlooked (even their particular fancies and
tastes), and a certain number of tenets cannot be allowed to
admit of exceptions ('Realism good, Naturalism bad'). But there

174

remains scope for fresh discoveries within the framework of general guide-lines.

First, then, the guide-lines within which Lukács operated as a literary critic, and notably historical materialism. The intellectual life of a community is a superstructure, determined in large measure, and over the long view, by the socio-economic relations of the members within the community. These relations are themselves largely shaped in analogous fashion by the prevailing means of production (rather than distribution) by which a society lives. Religion, philosophy, law, art and literature, indeed all cultural activities reveal – to those who can read them – the massive underlying social realities, and thence the dialectical process which is history. Not only that: on occasion, these cultural fields are battlefields on which social struggles are enacted – or at least, screens on which the struggles are projected, not always consciously. The struggles between social groups are important when (but only when) the groups are *classes* in the sense Marx attached to that word. A class is not simply what the naïve mathematician means – for instance, the class of positive integers – but a group which can be defined by a common position in the economic productive process; landed proprietors, owners of industrial capital, independent craftsmen, proletarian labourers, and so on. Marx was not dogmatic always in his use of the term; in *The Civil War in France* he notices half a dozen classes. But classifications other than those reflecting productive processes are of subordinate interest, because not integral to the dialectical processes of history.

A specially interesting case arises when a privileged class has reached a point in the historical process where it has no further interest in pressing change, and is therefore conservative. *Then* its systems of beliefs, values, norms, cultural activity in general tend to turn away from the militant search for truth about social reality, which from then on can only hurt it; instead, it becomes the tortuous manufacturer of mystifying and distracting systems of belief or values – *ideologies*. Thus natural law was a mighty engine of discovery in the class war against 'feudalism' but an instrument of reaction in the later, defensive capitalist world.

'Liberty', 'the rule of law', mighty words in 1789, become by 1851 'reactionary' slogans to confuse the enemies of those in power.

Just as it is the business of philosophy, economic analysis, or historiography to search for the truth, and find it, in the 'scientific' application of historical materialism, so it is the business of the artist to apprehend the deepest truth about the social world he inhabits, past or present, and render that. It goes without saying that neither Chaucer, Shakespeare nor Goethe had the advantage of knowing the world in terms of dialectical and historical materialism; but all three lived in societies where the emergence of dynamic new values (on a Marxist judgment) stimulated them to unusual efforts; the values they rehearsed were in a given historical moment the deepest and most important, whether they knew it or not, and thus afforded scope for the highest achievements. Just as in a Christian perspective Socrates, living before Christ, can be given his due by the aid of a doctrine of partial and progressive revelation, so the pre-Marxist artist can be credited with some limited or intuitive understanding of that which it was the business of Marx and others after him to make fully explicit in its historical significance.

Two special cases arise from this argument. The first was seen by Marx and Engels, the second is a later development. On the one hand, the artist who assents to a 'reactionary' ideology, but who is in some sense so powerfully endowed that he is unable to avoid coming face to face with features of uncongenial reality and, like Balaam, rehearses truth – unknowingly or against his conscious inclination. On the other hand, the artist living after the Marxian revelation, who has accepted the challenge to understand society and his place in history, and who, because of the tenet that he who is not for the process of change must be against it, and because also of the Marxist principle of the unity of theory and practice, recognizes his obligation to engage in the class struggle and must therefore make of his art, in some sense, a *weapon*. A hard precept; Aragon wrote brilliantly before he learnt that art for art's sake is part of a reactionary ideology; but dully when he applied himself to promoting Marxist understanding of bourgeois decadence or glorifying tractors in the boundless steppe. '*Avec de bons sentiments on fait de la mauvaise littérature.*' Artistic intuition is not engineered to be on tap like hot water, and Stalin forgot this when he defined artists as 'engineers of souls'. But these cautionary comments are themselves liable to be dismissed as the mark of the bourgeois or the aesthete: the perception of the deepest (and therefore most moving) truths about man – in love, heroism, work or wonder – can for the Marxist *only* arise from a correct standpoint grounded in historical materialism; and he who does not see the love of man shine in the wisdom of the party praesidium or in the symbol of the tractor, is not only a lost soul but a bad or unimportant artist or wordwright.

Some such propositions as these, it appears, would be acceptable to all communists of the strict obedience, and to almost all people to whom the word Marxist would normally be applicable. For the period covered by the rule of Stalin, they are certainly representative. And they serve as a valid backcloth to the criticism of Lukács. They carry with them certain corollaries. (i) The Marxist theses do not add up to a comprehensive programme for explaining *all* that can be observed in a work of literature: the position is not a crude determinist one. There is a no-man's-land between the significant and the insignificant, though the Marxist would tend – reasonably – to make raids into the no-man's-land to try to extend the range of his coherent evidences. (ii) In so doing he is more interested in studying the relation between text and the author's experience of the world (a trend of scholarship and philology highly characteristic of the nineteenth century) than in studying the author's exploration of some autonomous or quasi-autonomous realm of formal resources. A Marxist Wölfflin is just conceivable; a Marxist Worringer is not. No Marxist will be satisfied with an approach to literature which rests heavily upon concern with individual psychology, and no Marxist can consent to an approach which rests upon a neo-Kantian interest in symbolic forms as such. In other words, a Marxist aesthetic, and *a fortiori* a Marxist criticism, must be compatible with historical materialism *and also* with the premiss that social relations (attitudes towards the

Georg Lukács

family, towards class ethic, towards human potential in an enslaved or liberated community) are decisive in their shaping of articulate sensibility. (iii) What is left to the critic? A free hand to analyse and describe, concretely, without procedural rule of thumb save the need (from time to time) for reassuring references to Marx and Lenin; a free hand to consider the suitability of different kinds of literature for different purposes – that is to say, latitude in that branch of criticism which we may call the classification of the arts; provided that this is conducted in a concrete, historical context, not one of eternal forms or ahistorical possibilities.

All these requirements are fully satisfied by the critical writings on literature of Lukács, or at least by those writings which fall within the period between the two world wars. Indeed, in one or two particulars to be examined he seems to be even more of a Marxist than would appear to be necessary on prudential grounds. This can be seen, to begin with, in his important study, *The Historical Novel*, written in Moscow in 1936–7, and published soon after in Russian.[1] The argument of this rich book is not entirely simple; it overlaps in part, but not entirely, with the theses of Lukács' studies in European Realism; and such of it as bears upon the present study may be conveniently summarized as follows.

From a survey of representative novels from Walter Scott to Romain Rolland, Lukács derives a 'classical' age, dominated by Scott and Balzac; a conservative age, after 1848, where all sorts of bad faith and bourgeois ideological retreat is demonstrated in Flaubert, Thackeray, Meyer, Stifter; finally a new dawn, the birth of a new democratic humanism, at the touch of a new revolutionary movement – Feuchtwanger, Heinrich Mann, Romain Rolland bear witness to the possibility of reintegrating the artist in a world which he can find meaningful and *make* meaningful in his interpretation of its real and central social issues. This survey also contains a secondary general argument on the relative potentialities of novel and drama – an argument which although in itself interesting, adds nothing to the con-

[1] English translation from the German, *The Historical Novel*, published by the Merlin Press, London, 1962.

178

clusions on this subject arrived at, even before Hegel, by A. W. Schlegel, Goethe, and a whole era of now forgotten early nineteenth-century criticism.

The most interesting, and by far the most original, part of Lukács' study is that devoted to the rehabilitation of Sir Walter Scott, at first sight a much more unlikely candidate than Balzac for the role of a classical Balaam. Balzac, after all, had already been validated by Marx. Lukács argues that the historical romances of olden times form a series of insignificant and trivial entertainments until the French Revolution generated a lively awareness of historical process (this of course is not true; the awareness was present long before 1789, and indeed Scott himself derived a considerable amount of his insights into Romance and the social significance of chivalry, etc., from such perspicuous and philosophical scholars as Lacurne de Sainte Palaye, whose contributions to the study of vanished or decaying institutions were the opposite of trivial). Change and social transformation was a challenge taken up variously in Europe; in the case of Walter Scott the challenge was taken up, albeit indirectly, in historical novels from *Ivanhoe* onwards. How is this seen? In the following major characteristics of his work:

1 The major novels represent situations in the past in which a major social tension or conflict gives meaning to the action narrated. There is a continuation of the 'great realistic social novel' of the eighteenth century, but with a difference, since the depiction of social conflict introduces a new dramatic dimension.

2 In the choice of 'middling' central characters, Scott's own conservative position *vis-à-vis* the class struggle is revealed, though he never refers to contemporary struggles between 'bourgeoisie' and 'proletariat'. He centres his action on figures who – unlike those of what Lukács calls 'romanticism' – allow typical social processes to be seen without distortion. Thus Waverley allows us to see all sides of the world in which he is involved.

3 This choice enables the novel to enjoy an epic scope. It is really a pity that Lukács lacks the information, based on research, which would permit him to know that Scott lived in a

world which was by no means innocent on the subject of epic, romance, and drama, and their differences: an awareness which is revealed, in however an indirect and curious form, in Scott's earlier interest in ballad, minstrelsy, even the *Lay of the Last Minstrel*. Imposing an anomalous theory on this subject, Lukács quotes[1] Belinsky's dictum that 'the hero of the epic is life itself and not the individual'. It is thus the movement of life itself which is the chief object of attention; unlike the old epic or heroic poem, where the hero concentrates within himself the whole value-system of a society. Scott's Britain is never totally committed to fanatical partisanship, daily life goes on even in wartime, in a subtle relation to the issues being fought over. Perhaps it is a pity that Lukács has never lived in Britain.

4 Hence great historical figures, who stand normally for one principle only, make only incidental appearances, when the situation is ripe for them; as with Hegel, Scott's composed worlds are such that they generate the conflicts and ripen the issues to which the Great Man responds; the middling kind of hero or central figure in these novels, however, is more intimately involved in popular movements.

5 'What matters, therefore, in the historical novel is not the retelling of great historical events but the poetic awakening of the people who figured in those events.'[2] This is not primarily a matter of 'local colour', for which Scott acquired an irrelevant reputation, but the 'portrayal of the broad living basis of historical events in their intricacy and complexity, in their manifold interaction with acting individuals'.[3]

6 This in turn requires that the main figures, though individualized, are also representative of contending classes and strata. *Human greatness* is liberated in the important representatives by the 'historical crises of popular life'. Undoubtedly the French Revolution aroused, consciously or unconsciously, this tendency in literature; 'Revolutions are the great periods of mankind because in and through them such rapid upward movements in human capacities become widespread'[4] (writing today, Lukács would no doubt have to qualify somewhat carefully the

[1] *The Historical Novel*, p. 35.   [2] Op. cit., p. 42.
[3] Op. cit., p. 43.   [4] Op. cit., p. 53.

kinds of revolutions to which such a maxim might with orthodoxy be applied).

7 Scott in fact presents and defends progress arising from contradiction between conflicting historical forces. This faith in progress is grounded in his patriotism. Lukács observes that Scott seldom makes his aristocratic characters 'positive' (this is a term borrowed from the Stalinist vocabulary of socialist realism), though when he does, this arises from their patriarchal relationship with the people. There is in fact an uncanny prescience:

> In this field of theory and historiography, only historical materialism is capable of intellectually unearthing this basis of history, of showing what the childhood of mankind was really like. But what in Morgan [the consecrated darling of nineteenth-century anthropologists – A.G.L.] Marx and Engels was worked out and proved with theoretical and historical clarity, lives, moves and has its being poetically in the best historical novels of Scott[1] . . .

8 Scott thus becomes a great poet of history because he has a deeper, more genuine and differentiated sense of historical necessity than any novelist before him.

Impressed by this approach (of which the foregoing is no more than a sketch) George Steiner writes:

> We do not take Walter Scott altogether seriously. If we care to learn how deliberate an artist Scott was, and how penetrating a sense of history is at work in *Quentin Durward* or *The Heart of Midlothian,* we do best to read a book written in Moscow by a Hungarian critic.[2]

That is easily said, though the claims may be contradicted (and it will shortly be our duty to contradict them). But to begin with, deliberateness of artistry is no guarantee that the product will or should or need interest us; a penetrating sense of history, if it should happen to be exhibited in a novel, is no guarantee that the novel will be readable, let alone reward our search for a powerful imaginative construction. We are recommended to go to Moscow to learn about Scott and about his sense of history: but it is rather facilely accepted that this particular sense of

---

[1] Op. cit., p. 56.
[2] *Language and Silence* (London, 1967), p. 363.

history corresponds in fact to the Marxist's idea of what it ought to represent. It is the last of these doubts which may here be most relevantly expressed. It is one thing to slot Walter Scott into an extension of the Marxist schemata devised according to the slap-happy traditions of a crude brand of nineteenth-century Germanic *Geistesgeschichte*; it is quite another to start with the novels, weigh them according to the more unassuming practices of literary analysis, and then judge the relevance to them of either a Marxist or indeed any other gross hypothetical construct of *Geistesgeschichte*.

It is not quite true that we have to turn to a book written in Moscow by a Hungarian critic to inform ourselves on Scott's sense of history. The following points summarize[1] a rather different point of view. First, the 'middling hero'. The Waverleys, Osbaldistons and Quentin Durwards of Scott are young men of good family. They encounter various adventures in various walks of life. It may be true that they enable an 'undistorted' picture of historical process to be observed, in the sense that they are only very partially involved; it is also the case that they hardly live, hardly grow; and that if on balance they tend to emerge from their adventures sadder and wiser men, this is not the result of any particularly vital processes in which they are a part. It may indeed be argued that this is one of the major weaknesses of the novels in which they appear: this very non-commitment, attributed by Lukács to Scott's conservatism, stifles and stultifies whatever human meaningfulness the survey of social or other conflict might have been expected to develop. But this is still a point which bears on Scott's qualities as a novelist, rather than on his intuition of history.

As for 'Great Men', Scott, who portrays Louis the feudal leader taking his people into war, would hardly have understood Lukács' claim[2] that 'the great historical personality is the representative of an important and significant movement embracing large sections of the people'. There is equivocation

[1] Amplifying and including observations developed by Miss Eleanor Milburn in *Walter Scott and the Gothic Revival* (M.A. thesis, unpublished) University of Reading.

[2] *The Historical Novel*, p. 38.

here over the word 'movement'. As for the 'broadly drawn social struggles which precede the appearance of the hero', and which 'show how at just such a time such a hero *had to arise* in order to solve just such problems',[1] there is to at least one reader's knowledge no clear example of this in the optic of Scott's novels. And this is not surprising, since for Sir Walter it is natural that a leader should come, quite simply, from the 'leading' classes. Alongside kings and nobles, Lukács undoubtedly classes Cedric and Robin Hood as popular leader figures, 'more historically imposing than the well-known central figures in history'.[2] But it is simply misleading to characterize Lovell as an imposing leader figure, unless one happens to be obsessed with the need to search for such phenomena. The attraction of Robin Hood, the people's hero, is easy to understand; nevertheless, in *Ivanhoe*, the reader must plainly see that Scott's real interest is attached firmly to the far more challenging figure of Richard, warts and all. Robin is a foil to Richard; but also an intriguing piece of picturesque furniture. And if we take in this context the example of Rob Roy, there is little doubt that in the novel of that name Rob Roy far overshadows in interest, as a person and as a portent, all other characters; he is also in a sense a popular or spontaneous hero: but it would be grotesque to argue from this that he can be seen, either by Scott or by Lukács or by any sane reader, as a portent of popular revolutionary stirrings. The Lowlander Scott knew quite enough about his Highlands to avoid the delusion that Rob Roy's movement of revolt was in any sense 'progressive': progress, to the extent that it is here represented at all, is represented (caricaturally) in the person of the baillie. This vivid though imperfect novel conveys what must to the Marxist appear to be a strangely negative, not to say nihilist, view of the historical process on Scott's own doorstep. Yet in the Scott canon, there is nothing unusual or aberrant about it.

The expression, 'the common people', full of equivocation under the Marxist pen, is applied with equal firmness to medieval peasantry and Highland clansmen of piratical propensities, with the possibility always of blurring into craftsman and prole-

[1] Ibid.   [2] Ibid.

tarian all classes save the 'feudal' landowner and the privileged 'capitalist'. Undoubtedly in many novels of Scott they are shown at the mercy of oppressors; but also under the beneficent protection of feudal superiors. A rugged formula to define this contradictory predicament was in fact sought persistently by historians of the eighteenth and early nineteenth century, both Whig and Tory, *philosophe* and conservative. It tantalized but eluded contemporaries of Scott – Guizot, Barante in France, Hallam in England, for example – and Scott himself made a bid in *Anne of Geierstein* to stabilize an essentially puzzling phenomenon:

> In all feudalized countries, an ardent spirit of liberty pervaded the constitution, and the only fault that could be found was that the freedom and privileges for which the great vassals contended did not sufficiently descend to the lower orders of society . . .

For Scott, *pace* Lukács, the 'ardent spirit of liberty' will on no account be required to 'emerge suddenly with colossal force to the surface'; simply because in the medieval novels the 'feudal system' is itself exhibited as being in no great need of serious reform. Rather the opposite, indeed: its virtues are apposite in an age of radicalism and unrest which Scott firmly condemned. Class structures are *not* presented in a way which the unprejudiced reader can find challenging, or portentous of historical change. Not only was Scott himself aware of this, but his contemporaries too. Stendhal not unjustly called him the favourite of the *Ultra* party in France. The Waverley novels had some part in promoting a widespread reversion to esteem for old-established authority, for example by the Oxford Revival.

Such a view of social relations in the novels *could* just be attributed to gross prejudice, universal blindness, generalized bad faith in the first third of the nineteenth century; but only if one is prepared, in this kind of *Geistesgeschichte*, to ignore what one finds uncongenial and discount what one happens not to know. Similarly Scott's own view of what he was doing could be irrelevant, in the light of Engels's convenient principle that the novelist may, like Balaam, convey a perspective different from what he intended. But it is less tortuous to rest in the position that the novels themselves, if read more attentively than there was perhaps time to do in Moscow, convey a general sense not different from the ostensible sense commonly attributed to them, and confirmed by detached and careful reading for their import as novels – i.e. for what they actually exhibit. One can discover new things in Scott; but not beyond the point where the integrity of these careful pieces of writing is itself wilfully set aside or broken down.

We may submit, then, that (i) it is not obvious that social tensions are regulative themes in Scott's evocation of the past; (ii) Waverley and the 'middling hero' are not necessarily signs, therefore, of an attitude by Scott towards the class struggle; (iii) Great Men do not necessarily, on the face of things, symbolize social conflict but are part of an evocation of the past as commonly understood in Scott's day; (iv) the 'awakening of the people' is not obviously or essentially an important feature in Scott's sense of history; (v) and likewise, it is not possible to corroborate the view that the French revolution had any specific impact on his deeper intuition of historical process, revolution, or the release of human energies.

Why, then, should Lukács appear to be perverse in his presentation of Scott as the poet of social change? On the one hand because, writing *Geistesgeschichte*, he is looking for some things – those congenial to Marxist schemata – and not for others. It would be hard to reproach him with having neglected to provide himself with an adequate intellectual and scholarly preparation; but that is what it comes to. The texts of Scott are devoured by a mind ready with the schemata; and this means that the real historical canvas (the historiographical background of Scott) is not considered at any point. On the other hand, though, the texts of Scott, being approached for the purposes just mentioned, cannot be allowed to speak for themselves, fully, at leisure, and with their own equilibrium so to speak – for if a novel is an extended story, it is one in which the balance of emphasis, the balance of tone, of attitude, are themselves part of the story, the representation. (One example, again from *Rob Roy* to which Lukács frequently refers. If it is indeed the case that 'the shrewd merchant and bailiff of Glasgow, Jarvie, clearly sees that it has become a matter of economic necessity for the clans to wage their desperate and hopeless battles on behalf of the Stuarts',[1] what difference does it make that Jarvie is so consistently presented to us as a veritable *caricature* of the bourgeois, an almost Molièresque creation? Has this nuance escaped the Hungarian–Germanic sensibility? Is it of no account? Can it be that Marxist intellectual history can make do with simple abstractions and synopses of novels, rather than stand on the full substance of complex statements, read literally, that is to say, concretely?)

There is a lesson to be drawn, even from the nodding of Homer. Historical materialism requires a tremendous emphasis to be laid upon the primacy of a 'correct' socio-economic analysis of historical process. At all costs, the great artist must be shown to draw his force from that direction: otherwise he is a clown or a sinister ideologist. Witness Flaubert or Dostoyevsky. Naturally one would like to rescue great writers: those just named are beyond reprieve, but Tolstoy can be saved, for his sympathy with the people and unflattering representation of the boss classes. Scott would be nice to save, too; for his European reputation has been much more easily sustained in the continental panorama of foreign language classics, over a century and more, than in the British Isles where he is easier to read. Scott and Byron, indeed, remain two towering figures of genius in the continental schoolbook: '*sacrés ils sont, car personne n'y touche*'. Now nothing in this intelligent Tory gentleman's value-system shows him to be a forerunner of any sort of modern social stirrings: unlike Balzac, who took a great deal from him as a historical novelist (at least between 1826 and 1830). To rehabilitate him, therefore, and to provide a suitably serious ancestry for a form (the historical novel) whose revival Lukács thought he was witnessing in the early decades of the present century, it was necessary to find exactly *why* one can pronounce him a great writer. In such an inquiry, historical materialism imposes very tightly circumscribed limits. The man may be the class enemy incarnate (fortunately, Scott's reputation as that faded and vanished from the view of all but disinterested

[1] Op. cit., p. 58.

scholars); but his works can be searched for evidence that deep down, his hold on reality was great. And this is the task which Lukács the Marxist undertakes. It is a somewhat different task from that which he undertook in 1914, in his *Theory of the Novel*, where Scott is praised for – of all things – his narrative technique, and then dismissed as a utopian aesthete, nostalgic for the past, and with an inner void marked by the absence of any 'idea'.[1]

So much for the positive lesson of historical materialism, in its application to Scott. There is, however, a negative lesson as well – one which brings one, in conclusion, back to the point touched upon already regarding the very uncertain importance of artistic quality to the Marxist viewpoint.

There is, in *The Historical Novel*, an important treatment of the category of *totality*, linked to an allusion to *Besonderheit*.

> Tragedy and great epic thus both lay claim to portraying the totality of the life-process. It is obvious in both cases that this can only be a result of artistic structure, of formal concentration in the artistic reflection of the most important features of objective reality. For obviously the real, substantial, infinite and extensive totality of life can only be reproduced mentally in a relative form.
>
> This relativity, however, acquires a peculiar form in the artistic reflection of reality. For to become art, it must never appear to be relative. . . . But the nature of artistic creation consists in the ability of this relative, incomplete image to appear like life itself, indeed in a more heightened, intense and alive form than in objective reality.
>
> This general paradox of art is sharpened in those genres which are compelled by their content and form to appear as living images of the totality of life . . .[2]

This is perhaps the central aesthetic statement from which Lukács develops his concept of the historical novel as epic (again, not for the first time: from *Ivanhoe* onwards, Scott's novels were a sitting target for European critics inspired by Schlegel's treatment of epic in his *Berliner Vorlesungen*). The thesis recurs explicitly at a later point in Lukács' book, with the following addition:

[1] *Die Theorie des Romans* (2nd ed., Neuwied, 1963), p. 118.
[2] *The Historical Novel*, pp. 91–2.

. . . If this world is to evoke a totality . . . then some form of artistic concentration is again necessary. . . . Accordingly, the novel, like drama, must give central place throughout to all that is typical in characters, circumstances, scenes, etc. . . . The relation of the uniquely individual to the typical is treated in a slacker, looser and more complex fashion in the novel.[1]

So too, drama incorporates reflections of large numbers of 'facts of life', assembled according to 'formal laws' which arise out of 'the material of actual life'. The 'same inner laws of form' operate in many manners, according to periods and styles; they are the same because 'these are the laws of movement of life itself, of which the plays are artistic images'.[2]

Here we see the position, typical of historical materialism, regarding the identification of values and an objective criterion for judging works of literature. Now, in two of these important passages, the term *images* occurs: 'the ability of the relative, incomplete image to appear like life', and again, 'the laws of movement of life itself, of which plays are artistic images'. Clearly, Lukács is not talking about mirror images, but rather of images whose form reflects, by some sort of analogy, features about life with *its* forms, or what he calls laws of movement.

Without trespassing too far on Aesthetics, one point about these images, whether in novels or plays, is important to literary criticism as practised by Lukács. The images, he says, 'appear like life, indeed in a more heightened, intense, and alive form than in objective reality'. All the time he refers to life: 'dramatic life' in Macbeth;[3] 'characters live'; Scott brings a period to 'life'. Art appears – and this of course is as old as Kant and Schiller, even older – as something alive, organic. To condemn bad art, Lukács calls it 'inorganic' or 'mechanical'. When looking for reasons why bad art is 'inorganic', Lukács attempts to discover – and of course succeeds in discovering – an incomplete relationship to the guide-lines of historical materialism. Thus de Coster's *Ulenspiegel* is criticized.

Now to the extent that this mode of discourse can be really understood, it may well be coherent; but its implications for literary criticism would be serious. On the one hand, the Marxist

---

[1] Op. cit., p. 139.   [2] Op. cit., p. 105.   [3] Op. cit., p. 137.

in Lukács is more interested in the relationship between a work of art and the content of historical materialist judgments than in the relationships within a work of art itself. But further, it seems that this preferred relationship is the condition of, if not the actual cause of, the presence in (say) a novel of a quality called living, or organic. The constant recourse by critics since the eighteenth century to synonyms for 'living' or 'organic' has led Suzanne Langer and others to investigate what it is that is being identified by this language; and a fairly normal and not very perverse outcome of this curiosity is the view that a work of literature, novel or other, represents, in a manner which we may conveniently call symbolic, a communicable kind of experience elaborated by a writer. The category of totality could well be accommodated here; so could that of reflection; but historical materialism would be of no direct relevance. A point of view of this kind stems no doubt from a neo-Kantian tradition, not a Marxist one; certainly it does not in any way involve us in judgments about the reflection of objective reality – such things are the business of the public censor rather than of the literary critic. Indeed, it places emphasis rather on the notion that if a novel, in any way, has a 'life of its own', that is because its coherent structure points to or reveals life in a more obvious location – namely its creator, rehearser, or reader.

Such a line of speculation cannot be squared with Lukács' beliefs on the source of excellence (i.e., 'life') in historical novels or any other kind of literature. To be sure, he affirms that 'artistic form is never a simple mechanical image of social life';[1] nevertheless, plays, and novels, are to be regarded as 'artistic images of the laws of movement of life'. In other words, they cannot be credited with integrity – or *not only* with integrity – but require further to conform with some species of configuration as a condition of reflecting its 'life' and acquiring any artistic value. One incidental result of this must be to make judgments of value dependent upon judgments of conformity – conformity with a reality as described by historical materialism. A further incidental result would of course be, that literary monuments cannot be used at all to arrive at hitherto unestablished

[1] Op. cit., p. 106.

judgments of historical reality – only to corroborate those already known in outline. But a graver result seems to be that the Marxist critic, be he Lukács or another, can only see 'life', artistic quality, where he knows or believes it *ought* to reside. He must look for it in the age when capitalism is optimistic and blossoming – and find it in Balzac. He may look, but must not find it, in the age of capitalist 'decline'; and furthermore, when a writer like Zola, a Menshevik and a naturalist, comes under his stern view, he will eagerly accept Zola's (to him) damaging account of how he wrote his novels (mechanically, without objectives of totality), and argue from it that the novels must be bad; overlooking the evidence which a more dispassionate reader would detect of a very real degree of inner 'life'. (To sharpen the irony, Zola's damaging account of his method is now known to be largely untrue; but a more detached critic would not allow it to have deterred him in the first place from seeing whether Zola's novels 'lived'.)

Such are some of the difficulties which Marxism puts in the way of literary criticism. It is not possible to argue that in the characteristic specimen of Lukács' criticism here discussed, he has in any way stirred outside the bounds of customary Marxist procedures.

7 Lukács' Views on How History Moulds Literature

David Craig

Neither so large a question nor Lukács' abundant views on it can be dealt with satisfactorily unless the materials are rich enough to give grounds for the large ideas. Yet the materials available to me have been on the scanty side. Much of Lukács' own work and of the literature he discusses is still untranslated. Books that may well be indispensable for a full understanding of his views of literary history, especially *The Theory of the Novel* and *German Literature in the Age of Imperialism*, are not yet available in English, nor is *Russian Realism and World Literature*. One would hope that this last book dealt faithfully with Russian literature *since* the Revolution,[1] since specific thoughts on this key area are precisely missing from *The Meaning of Contemporary Realism* – the only accessible sample of Lukács' views on the most recent European and American works.

This study then, has had to be based almost wholly on *The Historical Novel, Studies in European Realism* and *Contemporary Realism*. From inside these works it deals mainly with Lukács' interpretation of Scott and Tolstoy and of fiction in general between 1848 and 1917.

Lukács strikes me as seeing through to the very bones and muscles and working organs of the literary tradition where most critics are content to describe its skin; and what enables him to

---

[1] There is one quite specific and suggestive comment on Soviet literature (on the false linking of socialism and an ascetic frame of mind) in *The Meaning of Contemporary Realism* (1963), p. 132; but it seems that Lukács himself has admitted to 'imperfect acquaintance with Soviet literature' (Martin Horváth, 'A Note on the Self Criticism of Lukács' : *Communist Review*, May 1950, p. 156)

get this depth is his historical sense. In this he brings to literary studies something they have been short of for generations. A rare exception these last many years is Christopher Caudwell's *Illusion and Reality* (1937). If Caudwell had not died fighting on the Jarama with the International Brigade in that same year, we might have had an English Lukács. As a teacher of literature I would say that any student of the subject should be able to write out a table like the one in Chapter 6 of *Illusion and Reality*, dividing the history of poetry into periods with brief notes on the historical reasons for each phase coming when and how it did. Yet I am looked on as eccentric, and many of my students are nonplussed or resistant, when such an attempt is made. Hippolyte Taine's profound, endlessly suggestive history of our literary-cum-cultural heritage is now among the great unread. Our experts, even those who do produce bulky volumes in the name of history, tend to detach literature from history at large, even where the links are most plainly integral. For example, in the relevant volume of the Oxford History, Ian Jack bends over backwards to prove that there was no Romantic movement as such in England[1] – although, again, any student should be able to write down three major qualities that all the English poets commonly called Romantic have in common. What is more, a man like Jack is hard to argue with because, since his case is made up of a mass of details, he always knows more than whoever takes issue with him. The empiricist can always find a little something with which to nibble and nag at the bold, groundbreaking generalizations of a pioneer on the plane of theory. Two other typical cases will conclude this point. In an earlier volume of the Oxford History, Douglas Bush denies that the melancholy in the poetry being written at the start of the seventeenth century can be explained by any malaise in the age at large – it is rather 'the religious or the naturalistic pessimism inherent in life itself'.[2] But this is not an explanation; for why did this 'inherent' quality emerge in strength at just that time? Only a scholar either innocent or suspicious of the historical

---

[1] *English Literature 1815–1832* (Oxford, 1963), pp. 406–21.

[2] *English Literature in the Earlier Seventeenth Century* (Oxford, 1962 ed.), pp. 4, 293.

sense could have come out with such an inadvertence. Again,
F.P. Wilson ends his survey of seventeenth-century prose by
remarking comfortably that 'It is no doubt beyond the wit of
any man to say why the novel should have been born in the
eighteenth century and not earlier'[3] – although it seems to me
that quite enough is now known about seventeenth-century
newspapers, printed speeches, 'character'-writing, historical
narrative, and topical printed matter in English to make out a
fairly full case for the theory that what historians now call the
English revolution had engendered both a public for realistic
story-telling and the forms that could readily fuse to create just
such a medium. Time and again in literary studies, historical
explanations so cry out to be invoked as a help with cruxes of
interpretation that the scholar committed to preserving the
'purity' of the literary has to deny the relevance of the historical.
Probably Lukács could explain better than anyone why the
anti-historical form of obscurantism is so prevalent in the west
today.

The philosophy that underlies his own interpretations of
literary history springs from the historical materialism of Marx.
The following is one of Marx's central formulations of this
theory:

In the social production of their life, men enter into definite relations that are indispensable and independent of their will, relations
of production which correspond to a definite stage of development of
their material productive forces. The sum total of these relations of
production constitutes the economic structure of society, the real
foundation, on which rises a legal and political superstructure and to
which correspond definite forms of social consciousness. The mode of
production of material life conditions the social, political and intellectual life force in general. It is not the consciousness of men that
determines their being but, on the contrary, their social being that
determines their consciousness. . . . [As a result of economic change]
the entire immense superstructure is more or less rapidly transformed. In considering such transformations a distinction should
always be made between the material transformation of the economic
conditions of production, which can be determined with the precision
of natural science, and the legal, political, religious, aesthetic or

[3] F.P. Wilson, *Seventeenth Century Prose* (Cambridge, 1960), pp. 21–2.

philosophic – in short, ideological forms in which men become conscious of this conflict and fight it out.[1]

This means so much and has been expanded so fruitfully, yet often so bewilderingly, by Lukács that something must be said about its intrinsic value as an idea. It is so large as to seem almost beyond verification; it is the sort of generality that is easy to assert – or rather to agree with once said, for in its day it was surely difficult to work out. Once said it is easy to repeat, and to 'verify' in a piecemeal way. The test of making it one's own is how one applies it, or (to come closer to the critical act itself) not how one 'applies' it but rather, temporarily ceasing to be aware of Marx's idea, how one goes to work among literature; manages to find, say, family likenesses between works, or main lines of growth inside a trend, or equivalences between a trend or an individual work and things in the main life of an epoch; and *then*, this specifically critical task being done, one may recognize afresh and claim to have confirmed the deep large anterior idea: it is indeed the case at point after point that social being determines consciousness. Any idea that is so large needs a great deal of evidence to confirm it; it must be tested, its application tried out, at a great many points in each of the ideological fields. This essay will try to show how Lukács' work exposes very fully both the fruitful and the risky, or almost unmanageable, aspects of Marx's theory.

I used there the term 'equivalence' between something in art and something in history at large. The term is Plekhanov's; he writes: 'The first task of a critic is to translate the idea of a given work of art from the language of art into the language of sociology, to find what may be termed the social equivalent of the given literary phenomenon.' This is really a condensation, applied to literature, of Marx's 'social being determines consciousness'. It is quoted here from the translators' notes to Lukács' *The Historical Novel*.[2] In this book Lukács works out the social equivalent of Scott's novels in a very full way. Before

[1] Preface to *The Critique of Political Economy*, 1859, in Marx and Engels, *Selected Works* (Moscow, 1958), I, pp. 362–3.

[2] Plekhanov, *The Past Twenty Years*, 1908 ed.: see *The Historical Novel*, 1937 (trans. Hannah and Stanley Mitchell, 1962), p. 11.

going into detail it is best to consider the general issue that is now being raised.

The question is: how does the critic find or identify the social equivalent among the mass of possibles? and, once found, what sort of value can it confer on the work of art? To put the question in terms purely of evaluation (for reasons that will shortly become clear), how is the critic to distinguish between an intelligent conception of an epoch which, however, remains artistically inert and a work which is fully alive and effective in its own medium and thereby succeeds in having, as counterpart to its theme, a social equivalent which is historically important? That this is what Lukács is committed to finding, and evaluating, shows through in many of his theoretical asides. From his Preface to *Studies in European Realism* we can see that he considers the 'personal experience' which is the stuff of literature to be social in its essence:

... the inner life of man, its essential traits and essential conflicts can be truly portrayed only in organic connection with social and historical factors ... every action, thought and emotion of human beings is inseparably bound up with the life and struggles of the community ... whether the humans themselves are conscious of this, unconscious of it or even trying to escape from it ...

In the long Tolstoy essay in the same book he analyses some major examples of this fusion of the social and personal, e.g. Vronsky:

... changes in his external circumstances (retirement from the army, free life abroad) contribute to the loosening-up of Vronsky's rigidity. But even here the dominant factors are the conventional barriers imposed by his position in life. ... When he returns to Russia ... [there begins] his reconversion into a pleasant average aristocrat with perfect manners in whom a great passion is something 'eccentric' and not organically linked with the central interests of his life.[1]

From the following passages we can see how social equivalence operates continuously, inasmuch as individual authors and the characters they create and the forms they use can be taken, if

[1] *Studies in European Realism* (preface dated 1948; trans. Edith Bone, 1950), pp. 8–9, 188.

195

they are seen in line with each other, to represent the mainstream of history. On authors he writes that:

if we regard the classics of the social development that determined the essence of our age, from Goethe and Walter Scott to Gorky and Thomas Mann . . . the development of society moved in a direction which rendered inevitable a conflict between such aspirations of men of letters and the literature and public of their time . . . a society so contradictory in its nature that it on the one hand gave birth to the ideal of the complete human personality and on the other hand destroyed it in practice.

On characters he writes that 'the great characters in literature form a continuous series . . . a certain historical tradition can exist in the creation of great typical characters', for the reason that 'the great objective problems of life do not appear suddenly, like a bolt from the blue', and he instances the series of characters from Pushkin's Onegin through Goncharov's Oblomov and Dostoevsky's Karamazov to a whole cluster of such people in Gorky's stories and novels, some of whom are pathologically lazy, some fatalistic, some resign their responsibility to the Establishment, and all of them throughout this span in the Russian literary tradition represent that tendency to rationalize their social helplessness which persisted until 1917. This also led critics like Virginia Woolf to write as though sadness or indecision were a fixed characteristic of 'the Russian soul'[1]. So much for the historical series of authors and characters. On forms Lukács writes, for example, that 'the historical novel in its origin, development, rise and decline follows inevitably upon the great social transformations of modern times', and *The Historical Novel* is an extended working-out of this theory.[2]

The part of it which I feel best fitted to discuss is the chapter on 'The Classical Form of the Historical Novel', where the main exemplar is Scott. In it Lukács explains both why the historical tendency in European literature arose when it did and the social basis of the Waverley Novels with their special features. The general theory is that the French Revolution, the

---

[1] 'The Russian Point of View', in *The Common Reader* (1925), pp. 222–3.

[2] The series of quotations from Lukács is from: *Studies in European Realism*, p. 13; ibid., p. 218; *The Historical Novel*, p. 17.

wars that followed, and Napoleon's rise and fall 'for the first time made history a *mass experience*'. But it was in Germany, not in France, that 'the problem of the artistic reflection of past ages emerges as a central problem of literature. . . . This conscious growth of historicism . . . has its roots . . . in the discrepancy between Germany's economic and political backwardness and the ideology of the German Enlighteners.'[1] This particularly interested me when I first read it five years ago, because in my *Scottish Literature and the Scottish People* I had explained the well-known cult of the past in Scotland as the attitude of a society intensely aware of its identity, especially its historical aspects, because it was in the act of losing it. I do not think anything in this was actually wrong or false, but it did not reach the root. Lukács' theory applies fully to Scotland. In the later eighteenth century we were backward economically: Scottish engineers invented many of the machines and techniques needed for the Industrial Revolution, but they did so on English soil – James Watt had to go to the iron foundries around Birmingham to find craftsmen skilled enough to bore accurate cylinders for his steam engines.[2] In some coalfields the miners were still chattel-slaves till 1775, and our textile industry was mechanized well after England's. We were backward politically: town councils were self-electing until 1832, and though we had individual Radical heroes, our MPs at Westminster were notoriously a Tory caucus cut off from their countrymen, at whom they sneered from the safety of London.[3] All this was discrepant with our Enlightenment: the rationalism of Hume, the classical political economy of Adam Smith. Scotland's mind was well in advance of its material life, and it seems likely (although detailed verification is still needed) that the resulting tension made us look backward into our past to find the causes of the gap between our ideas and our actuality.

So far so good; but when Lukács turns to the literature itself, he has almost to remould it to make it bear out his thesis. One of the key typical features he finds in the Waverley Novels is the

[1] *The Historical Novel*, pp. 19–25.
[2] T. S. Ashton, *The Industrial Revolution* (Oxford, 1948), p. 68.
[3] Craig, *Scottish Literature and the Scottish People, 1680–1830* (1961), p. 82.

'middling hero' – Morton in *Old Mortality*, Waverley in *Waverley*, Osbaldistone in *Rob Roy*. These he explains as representatives of 'the age-old steadfastness of English [*sic*] development . . . no civil war in history has been so violent as to turn the entire population without exception into fanatical partisans of one or other of the contending camps.'[1] I pass over the view which makes so light of the Civil War in England or the Killing Time in Scotland (a time akin to that of the Black and Tans in Ireland or the village massacres and round-ups carried out by Ngo Dinh Diem in Vietnam during 1957–8).[2] What I am intent on is Lukács' disregard of the opinion most critical readers must have formed on reading *Rob Roy* or *Waverley* or *Old Mortality*: that the heroes are so colourless and unconvincing as to be virtually a gap in the page – not a rendered type of the mediocre or the non-committal but an inadvertent failure of art.[3] *Old Mortality* is about the time of the Covenanters, when these most outright of the Presbyterians were being hunted through the moors of south-west Scotland by Claverhouse's soldiers in a campaign to force them to conform to the established church. Scott repeatedly prompts us to take note of his fair intentions: the hero, Morton, is, from the novelist's point of view, put in specifically to represent the decent, non-partisan '"middle course" asserting itself through the struggle of extremes', as Lukács put it.[4] For example:

> Morton could not but strongly hope that these terms, which comprehended all that was wanted, or wished for, by the Moderate party among the insurgents, might, when thus cleared of the violence of fanaticism, find advocates even among the Royalists, as claiming only the ordinary rights of Scottish freemen.[5]

The trouble is that everything to do with the central conflict in

[1] *The Historical Novel*, p. 37.

[2] Compare I. B. Cowan, 'The Covenanters', in *Scottish Historical Review*, XLVII, 1, No. 143 (Aberdeen, April 1968), pp. 50–1, with Marvin E. Gettleman (Ed.), *Vietnam* (1966 ed.), pp. 232–5.

[3] This objection, and my conclusions from it, which I first suggested in *New Satire*, 4 (Edinburgh, summer 1962), pp. 75–6, have also been put in similar terms by Stanley Mitchell in his searching essay, 'George Lukács and the Historical Novel', in *Marxism Today* (December 1963), pp. 378–9.

[4] *The Historical Novel*, p. 37.

[5] *Old Mortality*, Chapter 27.

the novel is at this level of flatly generalized history. The debates before the decisive battle of Bothwell Bridge bring the main forces together. But where these are not straight history, un-dramatic and laborious, they are set, rhetorical exchanges on which we cannot feel that any outcome depends. They are being rigged towards a simply preconceived notion of the unrelieved bigotry of the extremists, the perfect humanity and good sense of the Moderates. Young Morton stands for decency, but a novelist whose imagination was firing on all cylinders could not have offered such speeches as being addressed by an ener-getic, soldierly young man, at a time of crisis, to tough guerrilla veterans:

'Gentlemen,' said Morton, 'cease this irritating and unavailing recrimination; and do you, Mr Balfour, inform us whether it is your purpose to oppose the liberation of Lord Evandale, which appears to us a profitable measure in the present position of our affairs.'

And Mr Balfour – Burley of Balfour, wild man and leader of the militants – speaks like this:

Thou errest . . . we must work by means, and these worldly men shall be our instruments. At all event, the Moabitish woman shall be despoiled of her inheritance, and neither the Malignant Evandale nor the Erastian Morton shall possess yonder castle and lands though they may seek in marriage the daughter thereof.[1]

One needs no special knowledge of Scottish history to realize that such men would in fact have spoken like a mixture of Cromwell at his most trenchant and our own pithy, vernacular preachers. A copy from the contemporary documents would have been more alive verbally than Scott's wooden efforts. He knew these documents well but his artistic sense was too primi-tive for him to be able to put historical materials to creative use. To Lukács, Rob Roy and Burley are 'monumental historical figures', yet the former is fictionally a sketchy presence, a mere adventurer, barely characterized, and Burley is, as created, a bit of glowering, gnashing melodrama.[2]

I say 'as created' for it may well be that such characters do

---

[1] *Old Mortality*, Chapters 27, 30.

[2] Lukács, *The Historical Novel*, p. 38; Craig, *Scottish Literature*, pp. 183–6.

Georg Lukács

represent some type or conception, visible in Scott's mind as he responded to his age and its past, yet never evolved fully into art (and perhaps more impressive in, say, German translation than in the original). To discriminate between this and the fully achieved thing is precisely the duty of the critic, and one that crops up time and again. For example, we have to say that Hardy's *Tess of the D'Urbervilles* expressed the last gasp of the English village as a self-sufficient community, and that Hardy's melancholy springs, objectively, from the depopulation of the countryside, which hit counties belonging to his 'Wessex' very heavily and earlier than most others.[1] Yet, having said this, we must at once add that this objective or historical theme speaks only half-consciously through Hardy and is not the declared theme of his novel, which is ostensibly about Fate. If we do not add this, we have no way of explaining the novel's serious *longeurs*. The implication of this is that the historical approach is liable to get distorted results unless the critic also remains fully a critic. That is, he must work as much by standards derived from within his own medium as from the historical. In the case of the 'middling hero', one's standard must be in touch with the supreme examples of the type, and one such is Grigory Melekhov, the hero of Sholokhov's *The Quiet Don*. He fights now for the Tsar's army, now for the Bolsheviks, now for the Whites – he can never align wholeheartedly with any side, and he is repeatedly shown to be (like Scott's Morton) agonized by the pressures which in time of civil war force people to take sides.

Large sections of people have always stood between the camps with fluctuating sympathies now for this side, now for the other. And these fluctuating sympathies have often played a decisive role in the actual outcome of the crisis. In addition, the daily life of the nation still goes on amidst the most terrible civil war.

This is Lukács on Scott (*The Historical Novel*, p. 37). But it fits *The Quiet Don* perfectly, with a critical difference that in Sholokhov's novel the scenes are intensely graphic and felt, the characters

[1] John Saville, *Rural Depopulation in England and Wales, 1851–1951* (1957), pp. 54–9 and Table V.

complex though blunt-spoken, and the issues of the struggle never have to be set up for us in explicit didactic exchanges. For example, the devoted Reds, Ilya Bunchuk and Misha Koshevoi, are as fully dramatized as anybody else. The 'daily life of the nation' is unforgettably sensuous and detailed; in Scott it gets in as a few vernacular comic turns. Grigory himself feels everything passionately; Sholokhov has not had to make him a cipher in order to typify the undecided man. On this count it is not necessarily the case that Scott's middling heroes are feeble because they represent the non-partisan man; more probably they are feeble because he was not artist enough to rise above the usual kind of amiable and colourless hero.[1]

My objections to Lukács on Scott may seem so far to be ones of detail, and purely evaluative at that: he admires some things that I do not. But criticism is an integrated activity: if the evaluation differs, so should one's historical explanation of why the work or author in question came upon the scene at all. If historical materialism is valid, it should be able to explain why the historical novel emerged when it did. If we look closely at Scott's own career, we see that first he collected ballads, from the singing of farm folk in the Border hills. Then he imitated ballads, followed by long historical romances in verse. Finally he moved over to prose and wrote his historical novels. In starting as a ballad collector he was very much in the fashion (among 'literary men' rather than among artists), for it is clear from any full list of the important folk-song collections that such work was very rare until after the middle eighteenth century, then it came in a rush: Bishop Percy in 1765-7-75, David Herd in 1769-76, Pinkerton in 1781-3, Ritson in 1783-4, James Johnson (collaborating with Burns) from 1787 onwards, Ritson again in 1791-2-3, Scott himself in 1802-3, and so on thereafter in an

[1] Now that there is a move among the scholars to rehabilitate Scott and treat the low opinion of him as an aberration, it is worth noting that the leading critics have shared this low opinion, e.g. Carlyle: 'your Scott fashions them (his characters) from the skin inwards', etc. (see Craig, *Scottish Literature*, p. 284, n. 1); Taine on Scott's failure to reach the 'foul and fierce' truth of his historical subjects (*History of English Literature*, 1883 ed., III, pp. 434-6); and Leavis on Scott's uncreative failure 'to work out his own form' and break with bad eighteenth-century traditions (*The Great Tradition*, 1948, p. 5, n. 2).

unbroken flow.[1] This particular expression of interest in the common people as history-makers was not at all the result of the French Revolution; it started well before it and continued through it unchanged. It is thus a fact that if one had to draw the family tree that led to Scott's historical novels, it would look like this:

```
        18th c. ballad collecting
                    |
                  imitating
        18th c.     |
        realistic = historical verse
        novel   |     romances
              19th c.
              historical novel
```

This implies that Scott would have written as he did even if the French Revolution had never happened. Well before it did happen, historicism in literature was already growing. What is possible is that this historicism and the Revolution were *cognate* – joint offspring of some trend further back. The implications of this will be returned to. What Lukács distinctly says is that the 'transformation of man's existence and consciousness throughout Europe' as a result of the Revolution 'form the economic and ideological basis for Scott's historical novel' (*The Historical Novel*, p. 31). I cannot see that the facts support this, nor do the intrinsic qualities of the Waverley Novels themselves. Either Scott's interest in the common people was of a post-1789 kind or else it was that of a folk-song-collecting gentlemanly anti-quarian, and the latter is surely the case. What opportunities does Scott seize of catching history at its most fluid, when great numbers of people were most involved? For example, where is his counterpart of what Dickens does with the Gordon Riots in *Barnaby Rudge*, the French revolutionary crowd in *A Tale of Two Cities*, or the militant cotton workers in *Hard Times*? In *Old Mortality* the popular forces are ludicrous fanatics, so exaggerated that it is the novel itself that becomes absurd; and

[1] F.J.Child, *English and Scottish Popular Ballads*, ed. Sargent and Kittredge (1904), pp. 680–1.

the nationalist crowd at the start of *The Heart of Midlothian* has no necessary link with the drama that follows and could be cut without being noticed. This is not to imply that a novel about the people as history-makers must present militant crowds. My own interpretation of *The Heart of Midlothian* is precisely that it deals most faithfully with a national phase by which time the more outright struggles, dilemmas, and testing times were over and the popular religious conscience had turned inwards to private matters, frictions inside families, niceties of personal faith, and the like.[1] It is also (by common consent) much his most interesting novel – the only one, I would have thought, likely to be much read by people who also admire Tolstoy or Conrad or Malraux. And it owes almost nothing to the factors of which Lukács makes much – the middling hero, the masses as history-makers, and the like. In this case we can say that if Lukács had been more of a critic and less of a speculative thinker, he would have perceived the unique quality, for Scott, of *The Heart of Midlothian*; he would then have had to let it count more in his theory; and the theory would have had to alter.

Let us then go back to Lukács' original idea of what caused the rise of historicism in Germany and Britain alike, let us marry it to a critical view of the literature itself, and then see what happens to his theory. Much of it holds. Scotland and Germany are precisely parallel in that, in each, three factors unite to engender historicism: 'economic backwardness' plus 'ideology of the Enlightenment' plus 'patriotism coming up against national divisions in a fragmented country'. The difference between Scotland and Germany is that, for Scotsmen, patriotism was not 'revolutionary' (*The Historical Novel*, p. 22), but backward-looking; the fragmentation of Highlands and Lowlands had been solved by force; and the problem was now no longer practical but purely emotional, the ache of lost nationhood, whereas Germany was struggling towards nationhood. As a result, Scotland's historicism, embodied in all the glory of its extravagant futility by Scott's works and life, is vitiated by a cult of stirring times; a failure to understand (or even

[1] Craig, *Scottish Literature*, pp. 166–74.

take an interest in) recent or contemporary trends: on one occasion Scott refused to write an article on the previous year's events because it was all Radical riots and corn laws – he consoled himself by writing an enormous life of Napoleon; a focus on trappings rather than essentials; and a playing-down of vital and central popular elements in favour of the quaint and the lunatic fringe.[1] The implication of this view of the Scottish historicism is as follows: one's knowledge of the relevant history must be full and detailed, not broadly generalized, if one is to be able to use it in explaining the literature; conversely, one's sense of the literature must be fully critical if one's account of how it evolved (and of its links with history in general) is not to be distorted.

There remains the possibility, mentioned already, that the historicism and the French Revolution were cognate – joint offspring of some trend from further back. I wish to suggest that this is a law of cultural history: things from the sphere that Marx calls 'ideology' which seem parallel or equivalent to things from the sphere of material development are often not caused by the apparent material counterpart, but sprung jointly from a common origin. Consider another key work from that revolutionary watershed, the *Lyrical Ballads* of 1798. These poems are about the middle and lower classes of society and are written in their language, as Wordsworth says in his Preface; and we know that Wordsworth had felt such bliss at the dawn of the Revolution that like many other talented young poets he had rejoiced at the events in France, and had gone there to see things with his own eyes. Yet I can see no sign in those poems that they resulted, any more than the Waverley Novels, from the transformation of existence and consciousness by the Revolution. It can be shown that they resulted from two things. The first was the need to refresh, indeed to renew the style of English poetry, which had become narrowly conventional in the extreme. This point bears out a basic idea of Engels' from the late letters in which he reformulated historical materialism for correspondents all over Europe. On 27 October 1890 he writes to Schmidt (for my argument I have substituted 'literature' for his 'philosophy'):

[1] Craig, *Scottish Literature*, pp. 150–5.

I consider the ultimate supremacy of economic development established in these spheres too [the ideological ones], but it comes to pass within the limitations imposed by the particular sphere itself: in literature, for example, by the operation of economic influences (which again generally act only under political, etc. disguises) upon the existing literary material handed down by predecessors. Here economy creates nothing anew, but it determines the way in which the literary material found in existence is altered and further developed, and that too for the most part indirectly, for it is the political, philosophical, and moral reflexes which exert the greatest direct influence on literature.[1]

Returning to Wordsworth's poetry, we can indeed say that English poetry needed to be refreshed for a deeply historical reason: that the long, unchallenged dominance, from 1688 onwards, of an affluent bourgeoisie had been instrumental in congealing poetry in a narrowly conventional, and especially in a *euphemistic*, mode. And it was to break this class dominance that our Radical movement, our counterpart of the French Revolution, arose. But this confirms from another angle my argument that Wordsworth's recreation of poetry (in which his influence worked along with that of Burns and Blake) is cognate with and develops alongside, rather than results from, the revolution in the political-economic realm. This is confirmed from a third angle if one now considers the second reason for Wordsworth writing as he did, about working people, in a version of their own 'emphatic and forcible' language. As we can gather from many of his best poems of 1797–1803, and as his letter of 1801 to Charles James Fox makes clear, he was writing partly to express his solidarity with a class, the yeomanry or self-employed land workers, who were then being ruined by the sudden intensification of capitalism, in both factories and landowning.[2] This is crucial: because he was sympathizing with the victim, rather

---

[1] Marx and Engels, *Selected Correspondence* (Moscow, n.d.), pp. 506–7: I presume that 'reflexes' would be better translated as 'responses' or 'reflections'. Lukács does endorse this idea of Engels' (*The Historical Novel*, p. 106) but he does not always act on it.

[2] See esp., 'The Brothers', 'Michael', 'The Ruined Cottage' from *The Excursion*, I; and *Letters of William Wordsworth*, ed. Philip Wayne (Oxford, 1954), pp. 38–40.

than moving on to align himself with the new class produced by this change, it was all the easier for him, once middle-age set in, to move into a wholly conservative position and lose even his earlier solidarity with, and cultural root in, common life.[1] In his art, 'the real language of men' drops out once more; he, of all people, reverts to euphemistic and pompous diction, suited only to abstract pieties and bellicose sonnets in the *Morning Post* about the superiority of the English over all other breeds; and his concern with suffering is transmuted into a piously justifying one, of the kind hit off by Blake in his revolutionary period:

> Pity would be no more
> If we did not make somebody Poor
> And Mercy no more could be
> If all were as happy as we.[2]

To draw the conclusions from this case: if one puts too simply Wordsworth's interest in the people – if one puts it as simply as Lukács did Scott's, and with as much playing-down of the reactionary element in it, one is left with no way of accounting historically for the difference between the great art of his poetry from 1797 to 1805 and the banal verbiage thereafter. And this is unnecessary: our knowledge of history is now full enough and our terms and methods of critical discrimination are fine enough for the two to fuse and give rise to insights deeper than either can manage by itself. But each must be present as itself: undiscriminating criticism and over-generalized history obscure what actually happened and do violence to our aesthetic responses. The fatal thing is to make short cuts or speculative jumps when we are trying to trace the links between real foundation and ideology; and this bears out another idea of Engels':

... our conception of history is above all a guide to study, not a lever for construction after the manner of the Hegelian. All history must be studied afresh, the conditions of existence of the different formations of society must be examined individually before the

[1] See the sensitive and thorough argument to this effect in V.G. Kiernan, 'Wordsworth and the People': *Democracy and the Labour Movement*, ed. John Saville (1954), pp. 257–69.

[2] 'The Human Abstract', from *Songs of Experience*.

attempt is made to deduce from them the political, civil-law, aesthetic, philosophic, religious, etc., views corresponding to them.[1]

Since the next stage in the argument will be to dispute two views that Lukács offers of particular works, this essay may have begun to sound so captious as to need justification. Lukács gives grounds for this himself when he calls *The Historical Novel* 'only an attempt, an essay: a preliminary contribution to both Marxist aesthetics and the materialistic treatment of literary history. I cannot sufficiently emphasize that I consider it, all in all, only a first beginning, which others, I hope, will soon extend, if necessary correcting my results'.[2] That is my aim here.

The two particular works are Tolstoy's *Resurrection* (and with it most of his fiction after 1886) and Kafka's fiction. The Tolstoy comes first because the implications here confirm what arose regarding Scott. I have implied that Lukács 'played down the reactionary element' in Scott's view of the people as history-makers. True, in *The Historical Novel* he repeatedly speaks of Scott's 'conservative philistinism' and the like, just as in *Studies in European Realism* he repeatedly speaks of the 'reactionary nonsense' and the like in Tolstoy's world-view. In both cases, however, he barely even stops to consider whether these traits may not have damaged the writer's art. Here he may have been influenced by a well-known idea of Engels', that the royalist Balzac revealed much more about the tendency of his times – the decadence of his own party, the nobility, and the strength of his enemies, the republicans – than did any consciously progressive writer.[3] Consequently Lukács falls over backwards not to allow the conservative tendencies in Scott and Tolstoy to count. In the case of Tolstoy he follows Lenin (correctly, I am sure) in seeing the great Russian novelist as the representative of the peasant revolution with all its vitality and all its shortcomings. But Lukács writes as though these shortcomings – the utopianism, the individualism, the belief that life can be transformed without concerted struggle – could have confined their spoiling effect to

---

[1] To Schmidt, 5 August 1890: *Selected Correspondence*, pp. 496–7.
[2] *The Historical Novel*, Preface to the English ed., p. 15.
[3] To Margaret Harkness, April 1888: *Selected Correspondence*, pp. 479–80.

the writer's ideas, the preaching-moralizing side of him, and left his art unscathed. He has not one adverse criticism to make of any work of Tolstoy's. Would not most readers agree that the fiction of Tolstoy's last twenty years, notably 'The Kreutzer Sonata' and *Resurrection*, is often painfully thin in rendered life and always blatantly moralistic in the sense that episodes happen, not through the likely development of the *données*, but rather to set up and drive home a set of very predictable morals, mostly to the effect that only poor people are good and that the wickedness of man and society must be solved by self-denial and a general 'change of heart'? Lukács shows in an uneasy paragraph in his main Tolstoy essay that there are indeed these adverse points to answer, but he then covers up with extravagant, unargued claims for *Resurrection* as unrivalled in 'all-embracing epic greatness'. In fact he has already quoted a typically clumsy and uncredible moment from the novel in which Nekhlyudov – Prince Nekhludyov – is amazed and horrified to find that there is a certain amount of corruption in the Tsarist legal system.[1]

Lukács himself actually mentions causes for the collapse of Tolstoy's art into forced moralism, for example his closeness to the religiousness of the peasantry and his resistance to socialism: 'There was, of course, one objective possibility of action in the Russia depicted by Tolstoy: but only for democratic and socialist revolutionaries, and to depict such action was precluded for Tolstoy by his philosophy [of non-violence]', and again: '[Tolstoy] cannot and does not wish to bring them [heroes drawn from the gentry] to the point of rupture with their own class' (ibid., pp. 167, 178). In spite of this Lukács can find no fault anywhere in Tolstoy's work, and on his world-view he remarks calmly that Tolstoy looked at Russian society from the viewpoint of the rebellious peasantry 'with all the faults and limits of that movement; but these faults and limits were historically determined and hence could in part become artistically fruitful' (ibid., p. 194). This is the merest truism, for obviously the faults and limits of all movements are historically determined, including the faults and limits of fascism or imperialism; this therefore

[1] *Studies in European Realism*, pp. 195, 165.

constitutes no presumption at all that belonging to such a movement will be fruitful artistically.[1] The effect of the truism is to
veil the real tragedy of the Russian peasantry. To put this with
absurd brevity: if their outlook had not had such faults and
limits, if they had been able to break with the desire for private
land-holding (which of course it was impossible for them to do),
then many hundreds of thousands would not have lost their lives
during the resistance to collectivization of the farms in 1931–2.
Again the effect of Lukács' approach, applied without fine
adjustment, has been to veil history and misevaluate art. Either
truer history could have put him on to the weakness in the
literature or the weakness in the literature could have obliged
him to realize the historical truth.

The point about Kafka has a similar implication. It comes in
The Meaning of Contemporary Realism, which was based on
lectures given in 1955, finished after the Twentieth Congress of
the Soviet Communist Party, at which Khrushchev exposed the
evils of the Stalin period, and first published in German soon
after the Hungarian uprising of autumn 1956. This book is the
most deeply suggestive essay I know on modernism, and I
remember vividly my relief that at last a Marxist had discussed
in an unpropagandist way the kind of thing that Zhdanov and
other bullies had for years been dismissing as 'rubbish', 'empty-
headed and defeatist', 'rotten and decaying', and so on.[2] But
Lukács seriously equivocates in his explanation of Kafka:

... the experience of the contemporary capitalist world does produce,
especially among intellectuals, *angst*, nausea, a sense of isolation, and
despair. ... The diabolical character of the world of modern capitalism, and man's impotence in the face of it, is the real subject-matter
of Kafka's writings ... What he described and 'demonized' was not
the truly demonic world of Fascism, but the world of the Hapsburg
Monarchy. *Angst*, haunting and indefinable, is perfectly reflected in
this vague, ahistorical, timeless world, steeped in the atmosphere of
Prague.[3]

[1] Mussolini used to bewail the artistic sterility of fascism: "'I wouldn't com-
plain if there was even just one good Fascist book. But what have we had?
Ill-written claptrap!'" (Christopher Hibbert, *Benito Mussolini*, 1965 ed., p. 79).

[2] A. A. Zhdanov, *On Literature, Music and Philosophy* (1950), pp. 30, 48.

[3] *Contemporary Realism*, pp. 76, 77–8.

Do we not have to ask: was it not at least as likely that people, whether intellectuals or not, would experience nausea and despair in Stalin's Russia or Rákosi's Hungary as in the Hapsburgs' Prague? And if this is so, in what meaningful sense is it capitalism that has mainly estranged and crushed man in this century? Is it not rather the workings of *all heartless systems*, all administrations, governments, police or military authorities that treat human beings as so much lost property to be pushed around, locked up, sold off, pulped, allowed to rot through decades of imprisonment? Please realize that I do not raise this objection, from my comfortable berth in safe England, in order to taunt Lukács with being insufficiently outspoken. But the effort now must surely be to clear Marxism of the distortions that have grown in through years of desperate compromising. In the case of the modernist *angst*, if the conditions giving rise to it cannot be shown to lie exclusively with capitalism, then they had better not be linked to it – that is, not to it exclusively.

This point is bound to crop up time and again in the work of a critic so closely committed to the struggle in the world from 1918 onwards, when he joined the Hungarian Communist Party.[1] In that Tolstoy essay he writes eloquently about the attack, in *Resurrection*, on 'the Tsarist form of capitalist state. . . . Here the ruling class is already shown as a gang of vicious imbeciles who carry out their functions either with unsuspecting stupidity or malicious careerism and who are by now nothing but cogs in a horrible machine of oppression'.[2] It is unpleasant to think that this was written in a Soviet Union controlled by such men as Beria, Vyshinsky, and Stalin, but at least no flaw results in the argument itself at that point. A little later, however, Lukács again takes up the main historical theme of the essay, which is that 'coldness and harshness in bourgeois existence', from the mid-nineteenth century onwards, opposes 'a rigid resistance to poetic presentation': 'the mechanical and "finished" character of the capitalist world' has so undermined the 'Homeric intensity of the relations between men and the world' that literature becomes 'petrified', and can be kept vital only by certain special

[1] *Studies in European Realism*, p. v.
[2] *Studies in European Realism*, p. 165.

efforts on the part of the great realists (ibid., pp. 155–6, 189). Again, are those words 'bourgeois' and 'capitalist' used correctly? Another formulation of this idea is to the effect that the 'dreary, dull sense' in capitalist society impels the writer to an artificial luxuriance of style that merely veils the 'ever more lifeless, ever more mass-produced lay-figures' who are his characters (pp. 169–70). That automatically derogatory use of 'mass-produced' is characteristic of literary intellectuals, but in this context it raises an awkward point: since the socialist countries too depend on mass-production and most of their people are or soon will be working in mass-production conditions, can the petrifaction of literature properly be confined, as Lukács does, to the cultures of advanced capitalism? Isn't it at least as likely to set in in socialist industrial societies? I don't mean that the answer is necessarily a simple 'yes' or that there are no strong forces favouring more vital sorts of work in those new cultures in eastern Europe, Cuba, and elsewhere (e.g. a decent popular second-order literature seems to arise far more readily there than in the frantic free-enterprise cultures of the west). But Lukács' formulation of the matter is not precise enough to cope with this doubt. My doubt is added to by what I know of the Soviet novel, for although it is an extraordinarily rich tradition, time and time again its best works have looked far back to the Homeric times of 1905 and 1917 and 1922 for their subjects. There cannot be many exceptions to this: the only very remarkable work I have read that presents Soviet normality with full realism is *The Bonfire*, the final novel in Konstantin Fedin's great trilogy.[1] Even there the action starts in 1942, so that almost at once the normality is broken in upon by the Homeric events of the German invasion. The implication here is therefore the same as that of Kafka and *angst*: if the conditions giving rise to the alleged petrifaction of modern culture cannot be proved to lie exclusively with capitalism, they had better not be linked to it exclusively.

This suggestion – that the socio-historical basis for Lukács' account of later nineteenth-century realism is partly invalid –

---

[1] *Early Joys* (1948), *No Ordinary Summer* (1950), *The Bonfire* (? still unfinished); long excerpts can be found in *Soviet Literature*, 1962, Nos. 1 and 2.

will have to be returned to. But since that piece, 'Tolstoy and the Development of Realism' (1936), is much the most wide-ranging, profound, and consistently penetrating section of Lukács' criticism to be available in English, and shows how much his method can explain, it must be discussed in detail, especially since what has been quoted from it already may have made it sound too like the Arnold/Eliot/Holbrook kind of unrelieved lament for 'modern life'. Lukács' argument depends on taking 1848, the year of defeated revolutions and the collapse of Chartism, as a watershed from the hither side of which flow the streams of modern literature, i.e. the expression of the developments that have led immediately to where we are now. There could hardly be a trend more important to understand, and it is typical of the unhelpful orientation of much British work in literary history that much interest has been spent on an earlier (and also vital) watershed, the seventeenth-century 'dissociation of sensibility', and little on the appraisal of how industrial and urban growth have changed sensibility. As a result, insights like the following (not Lukács' but from another Marxist) still come like a flare in the midst of darkness:

> This formal plot element . . . becomes more and more dominant as the book nears its end, while the social critique, though still remaining strong, becomes more and more a by-product of the formal plot. So, artistically, the latter sections of Dickens's novels (for that matter it seems to me the last sections of the vast majority of eighteenth and nineteenth century English novels) tend to fall considerably short of the rest of the book.[1]

Lukács has many similarly bold and suggestive points to make, and since it was stressed at the start that his kind of large idea must be verified in a great many particular applications, I propose, after presenting the basic idea, to show how well it applies to and explains many – indeed most – of the key things in later nineteenth-century fiction.

Lukács expresses his view of the 1848 crux in several ways. In 'The Classical Form of the Historical Novel' he writes:

[1] John B. Mitchell, '*The Ragged Trousered Philanthropists* – Corner-Stone of a Proletarian Literary Culture and of Socialist Realism in English Literature': *Zeitschrift für Anglistik und Amerikanistik* (Berlin, 1962), p. 50.

It was the 1848 Revolution which for the first time placed before the surviving representatives of this epoch the choice of either recognizing the perspectives held out by the new period in human development and of affirming it, even if with a tragic cleavage of spirit, like Heine, or of sinking into the position of apologists for declining capitalism . . .

In 'Russian Democratic Literary Criticism' he writes that, after the defeats of 1848, 'Some writers devoted themselves fanatically to the new gospel. . . Others, the really great writers of the period, sank into a profound depression and hopelessness – like Flaubert and in his later years, Dickens.' And in 'Leo Tolstoy and Western European Literature' he writes that the defeats of 1848, in England as on the Continent, gave rise to a 'depression, sometimes degenerating into nihilism' and 'a universal despairing pessimism'.[1] All I would say about this is that, although 1848 was undoubtedly a European watershed, it is probably a too-political approach to present this watershed as essentially a matter of defeated uprisings. Would it not put the matter on an altogether sounder, and more verifiable, basis if it were put that at this same time the 'second Industrial Revolution' was occurring? The leading industrial countries were taking a leap forward, beginning to manufacture heavy machinery for making machines, completing their railway networks, and (in Britain anyway) carrying out the full enclosure of the land to which Acts of Parliament had for some time entitled landowners, while at the same time living through the last throes of the old self-employed cottage industry. Here, surely, are the actual forces which transform that texture of daily living which the writer has for his stuff and from which he derives his sense of the possibilities and limits of human life. Although it is easy to prove from explicit statements that Elizabeth Gaskell and George Eliot, for example, felt 1848 to be a watershed,[2] the implicit evidence of the creative work itself shows that the bleakness which now overtook literature was already evolving well before 1848. The main example from our own country is Dickens, our

---

[1] *The Historical Novel*, 30; *Studies in European Realism*, p. 98; ibid., p. 246.
[2] *Mary Barton*, Preface; *George Eliot's Life*, ed. J. W. Cross (n.d.), pp. 98–9 (letter in J. Sibree).

most topical great writer, who feels more intensely and quickly than any other the closing in of that iron system which in Lukács' phrase petrified art. And Dickens sensed the petrifaction long before 1848. He perceived the effects of capitalist ideology on human relations as early as 1838, when the results of the New Poor Law (1834) gave him the motive for *Oliver Twist*; and by 1846 he could bring the thing right home to its origins, in the commercial drive for acquisition and efficiency, when he began to serialize *Dombey and Son*. The implications of this case are like those of Scott's historicism and the French Revolution: what occurs around 1848 seems to be a pair of cognate developments, rather than historical cause/ideological effect.

But in the body of his analysis Lukács does not press the 1848 factor too hard and his analytic points are of the greatest subtlety and depth. He writes: 'The lack of action, the mere description of *milieu*, the substitution of the average for the typical, although essential symptoms of the decline of realism, have their origins in real life and it is from there that they crept into literature,' and everywhere we find that particular writers, not mentioned by him, precisely bear out his points. He says that 'The old writers were participants in the social struggle and their activities as writers were . . . part of this struggle', whereas after 1848 'they found nothing they could support wholeheartedly' and so 're-mained mere spectators of the social process'.[1] This applies to the writers' lives and to their art: when Dickens wants to get to the centre of the English conflict, to write *Hard Times*, he has to go to Preston to collect copy, and in pursuit of the same end Disraeli and George Eliot have to read up Blue Books, Parlia-mentary Reports, and back files of *The Times*.[2] When Lukács takes the point further and says that 'The new type of realist turns into a specialist of literary expression, a virtuoso, an "armchair scientist" who makes a "speciality" of describing the social life of the present' (*Studies*, p. 141), he has defined central aspects of writers as different as Flaubert, Henry James,

[1] *Studies in European Realism*, pp. 169, 140–1.
[2] John Forster, The Life of Charles Dicken (n.d.: 'Gadshill Ed.'), II, pp. 147–8; Cross, *George Eliot's Life*, pp. 386, 396; A. Kettle, 'The Early Victorian Social-Problem Novel', in *From Dickens to Hardy*, ed. B. Ford (1957), p. 178.

and Zola, and the peculiar limitations that stem from their detachment – Flaubert's tendency to be clinical about his characters, James's tendency to insist on the rare or special value of his subjects in excess of what he actually describes, and Zola's unwholesome mixture of documentary and melodrama. The typicality of Dicken's work runs like a ground-bass through Lukács' essay although he specifies other writers: for example,

> There is a paradoxical greatness in the fact that while his [Tolstoy's] conscious striving was constantly directed towards the moral and religious overcoming of this rigid division of society into two hostile camps, in his literary production the reality which he depicted with relentless fidelity constantly exposed the impracticability of this the author's favourite dream . . .[1]

Again, on the way in which the great writers were now obliged to find in the cities, however unpromising they seemed, the material for vivid art:

> Naturally this glamour is no longer the clear, bright, simple magic of the infancy of the human race [*sic*], such as we find in Homer. The striving of the great realists to remain true to the realities of life has for its inevitable result that when they portray life under capitalism and particularly life in the great cities, they must turn into poetry all the dark uncanniness, all the horrible inhumanity of it. But this poetry is real poetry: it comes poetically to life precisely because of its unrelieved horror. This discovery and revelation of poetic beauty in the dreadful ugliness of capitalist life is worlds apart from those photographic copies of the surface which use the hopelessness and desolation of the subject as the medium of presentation.[2]

Although this is about Tolstoy's 'Death of Iván Ilých', it at once defines for us Baudelaire and *The Waste Land, Bleak House, Our Mutual Friend* and *The Secret Agent* – the way in which their authors are all able, with the craft of genius, to allow the worst of city life to saturate their art even while they turn against that environment at the level of opinion or outlook. The implicit account of Dickens in relation to the main trend of his age is summed up when Lukács writes:

[1] Compare my Introduction to *Hard Times* (Penguin, 1969), pp. 34–5.
[2] *Studies in European Realism*, pp. 146–7, 158.

Georg Lukács

. . . there is a considerable difference between writers who insistently
stress this tendency of life in their writings . . . and writers who strive
to swim against the current, who do not accept the effects of capitalism
simply and directly as accomplished facts . . . but who depict the
struggle the final result of which (as a rule, but by no means always)
is the coming into being of such prosaic, anti-poetic mediocrity.[1]

Here, precisely, is *Bleak House* and *Great Expectations*, and
Middlemarch, and *The Ragged Trousered Philanthropists*. On
the debit side: 'the few significant characters produced by this
literature [after 1848] were almost all still-life-like, static portraits
of average people' – Flaubert's Emma Bovary, Pip in *Great
Expectations*, Stephen Blackpool in *Hard Times* – 'while the
figures pretending to above-the-average stature . . . could not be
anything but caricature-like pseudo-heroes, empty phrase-
mongers in a grandiloquent and hollow opposition to capitalism'
(*Studies*, p. 169). Here, precisely, are Disraeli's Charles Egre-
mont (in *Sybil*), George Eliot's Felix Holt and Daniel Deronda –
although Lukács seems not to know their work at all.

However, the case can't be left there, for yet again Lukács has
pursued a historical theory which does not hold at sufficient
points. The first idea in the essay is that Tolstoy in Russia and
Ibsen in Norway were able to take realism to new levels, while it
was petrifying in the west, because Scandinavia and Russia were
late in capitalizing their economies.[2] Here he seems to have
taken one of his speculative jumps, for when he draws his critical
conclusions, they don't quite fit the literature. He writes that
Tolstoy 'always gives a dazzling mass of brilliantly observed
small detail; but his presentation never lapses into the empty
triviality of his western contemporaries'.[3] Now, the writers who
demand comparison here are George Eliot and Henry James,
and surely they excel, not only at significant detail, but also at
that for which Lukács has just praised 'The Death of Iván
Ilých':

by sharply contrasting this drearily meaningless life with the stark
fact of imminent and inevitable death . . . [he puts] before us all the

[1] Ibid., p. 189.
[2] *Studies in European Realism*, pp. 134–9.
[3] Ibid., p. 171.

216

features of middle-class life in a bourgeois society ... never over-steps the limits of the commonplace and average and yet gives a complete picture of life as a whole and is not commonplace or average in any of its moments.

This (save for the extraordinary force of Tolstoy's stress on death itself) is precisely *Middlemarch* and *Deronda* and James's *Washington Square* and *In the Cage* and 'The Bench of Desola-tion' – sheer ordinariness of life whose impact on us is as power-ful as the heroic or remarkable; people pressing and struggling against the iron limits of their society before falling back de-feated; gradually congealing lives followed through, with perfect realism, to their very ends. Most of what Lukács wishes to pre-sent as unique in Tolstoy is richly present in one western con-temporary or another, therefore the advanced capitalist develop-ment in the west had not set the limit on art that Lukács' thesis leads him to suppose; furthermore, if it was the still unpetrified life of Russia that produced Tolstoy, why was there no one writer of that quality at the equivalent stage in the west? Lukács has evidently overlooked certain factors such as the size of Russia, the variety of experience inside the one society, and the creative genius of Tolstoy himself, which enabled him to take advantage of that experience. To conclude: what Lukács lacks is a logical system with which to test his hypotheses. One simple test is to suppose the opposite. If this can be proved, then that part of the thesis must be modified or dropped.

This oversight is plainly that of a pioneer, who must at all costs blaze the trail. The gaps in parts of his *historical* knowledge are due mainly to the long cold war that began in 1917, for example the persistent refusal of the west to recognize that there has been a Soviet literature worth the name, and *vice versa*. The weaknesses in parts of his *critical* analysis are perhaps a fault of the over-theoretical Germanic tradition in philosophy. It is now up to us to re-work his theses, free from the fears and evasions of the cold war, equipped with that historiography which has now got to the grass roots of so many key areas,[1] and remember-ing all the time, when reading literature, to discriminate as finely

[1] E.g. E.H. Carr on the Russian Revolution, Edward Thompson on the mak-ing of the English working-class.

as the best of the non-historical critics. We cannot do without Lukács' boldness in making connections and seeing through to causes. Equally we cannot do without the sensitivity to matters of value, detail, and relevance that has been developed by more empirical kinds of literary thinking.

8 Lukács' Concept of 'The Beautiful'

Stanley Mitchell

'The beautiful' sounds an antiquated term today – unscientific, unhard. The structuralist science which in France is replacing the old humanist and rationalist Marxism will have no truck with it. In Russia, on the other hand, compendium after compendium on 'the beautiful', 'the ugly', 'the aesthetic', 'the artistic', 'the artistically-beautiful', 'the naturally-beautiful' are submitted as doctoral theses in a manner and substance powerfully reminiscent of nineteenth-century academicism or an even earlier Polonius-like scholasticism.

Structuralism may be preferable to academicism. But it is no substitute for humanism. Lukács takes his stand with the central humanist traditions of Marxism which look back to Greece and the Renaissance. Engels wrote, of the Renaissance:

> The heroes of that age had not yet been enslaved by the division of labour, the limiting, one-sided effects of which we so often find in their successors. But what particularly characterizes them is that, almost without exception, they live and work at the very heart of their age, of its movements, and of its practical struggles: they take up causes and do battle, this one with sword and pen, that one with dagger, many with both. Hence that plenitude and force of character which made them into whole men. Scholars of the study were the exception: and these were either people of second or third rank or cautious philistines afraid to scorch their fingers.[1]

Georg Lukács is not, and never has been, a cautious philistine. He has always put his beliefs into practice and stood in the cross-

[1] Karl Marx and Friedrich Engels, *Über Kunst und Literatur*, ed. Michail Lifschitz, Bruno Henschel und Sohn, Berlin 1951, p. 173.

fire of the ideological and political movements of his time: political commissar in the Hungarian revolution of 1919, refugee in Vienna, secret agent to Horthy's Budapest, sentenced there to death in his absence, refugee again from Hitler's Germany, imprisoned briefly by Stalin, Minister in Imre Nagy's government of 1956. Lukács has not kept to his study. And his best work, the pathos which underlies that unremittingly abstract style of the precocious Heidelberg don – a style which changed but never left him – breathes the fire of a true revolutionary. Though at present he is engaged on a systematic aesthetics of Hegelian scope, the 'aesthetic' as such has never for Lukács been merely a philosophical category; rather an arm which man has forged in his own defence. The aesthetic, in Lukács' eyes, the aesthetic experience and aesthetic form, declare, as no other capacity, that man is whole, in the Renaissance sense, despite the ravages of the divisions of labour and class societies. Lukács writes in his own *Aesthetics*:

Men's longing for a moral mode of life, in which the ethical command expresses the inmost core of personality and from there out radiates over the entire periphery of affects and sentiments, desires and thoughts, not in a tyrannical-dualist manner, but organically, as the adequate manifestation of the total personality – such longing springs from the very nature of morality. When this longing struggles for adequate intellectual expression – and it will do so particularly in those periods when the ethical ideals themselves are either already or still socially problematic – then it is extremely likely, and often historically inevitable, that such longing will express itself in aesthetic categories, too. For the aesthetic reflection of reality always creates a unity of outer and inner, of content and form, of character and destiny, etc., in which sense and spirit cohere. Even when its subject is a collision, of the kind we have just suggested, the collision will, in the artistic reflection, appear less dualistically split-apart than would normally be the case in life itself. Nor will this be so as a result of any prettifying of life's conflicts, but on the contrary because the aesthetic reflection is so oriented on the world that it may bring out more clearly than life itself the fact that human individuality will retain an ultimate unity throughout and despite the strongest and most insoluble divisions.[1]

[1] Georg Lukács, *Werke,* Lucherhand, Vol. 12, pp. 578–9.

The ethical, argues Lukács, seeks to match intention with result, will with action. Rarely, if ever, can it succeed; for, in the first place, life is too full of accident, and, in the second, the very dialectics of life, what Hegel termed the 'cunning of reason' confronts intention and will with their opposites in practice at each step of social and historical progress. But aesthetic form, Lukács maintains, requires precisely such coincidence: the individual instance achieves aesthetic validity through its symbolic generalization, through the coherence, the dialectical synthesis of 'sense and spirit', i.e. the sensuous and the significant.

Lukács's ontology is the same as Aristotle's: man is *zoon politikon*, a social animal. The Aristotelian dictum, declares Lukács, is applicable to all great realist literature:

Achilles and Werther, Oedipus and Tom Jones, Antigone and Anna Karenina: their individual existence – their *Sein an sich*, in the Hegelian terminology, their 'ontological being', as a more fashionable terminology has it – cannot be distinguished from their social and historical environment. Their human significance, their specific individuality cannot be separated from the context in which they were created.[1]

In his book *The Meaning of Contemporary Realism*, from which this passage is taken, Lukács denounces modernism for treating man as a solitary. He decries such a view as anti-aesthetic because it undermines the social essence of man and hence his very individual identity. Solitariness, explains Lukács, is indeed a very widespread and typical experience in modern capitalist society; in this sense it is a social phenomenon. Yet it is encompassed and transcended by the movement of society beyond capitalism to a more communal life. Thus modern solitariness is specific to modern capitalist society; it must not be turned into a *condition humaine*. It is no more than a partial phenomenon, as Lukács puts it: 'fragment, a phase, a climax or anti-climax in the life of the community as a whole.'[2]

[1] Georg Lukács, *Realism in Our Time*, Harper and Row, New York, 1964, p. 19.
[2] Ibid., p. 20.

In Lukács's aesthetics the beautiful is a special case of the aesthetic, roughly coinciding with Schiller's notion of 'the naïve', as it is expressed in the essay *On Naïve and Sentimental Poetry*. The naïve, according to Schiller, is a condition of spontaneous unity between men and nature; the sentimental is the fragmentation of this condition by social division and its reconstitution in the consciousness of the artist in terms of an ideal. Lukács seeks to provide a Marxist basis for Schiller's theory.

For Schiller 'nature' or natural society is a condition where the personal and the social harmonize without the mediation of legal machinery, where morality is based upon custom, where no duality divides an outer from an inner ethical code. In wrestling with the divisions of modern society Schiller himself becomes dualistic, desperately seeking to reconstitute man's social unity from within, to create as it were an aesthetic state within which it is possible to live independently of the political one. The aesthetic state then becomes a base from which to transform outside social-political reality (by means of personal self-perfection and emulation). (The thinking is not unlike that of Matthew Arnold, whom Schiller undoubtedly influenced; except that Schiller had more excuse for his internal revolutionary programme in fragmented, particularist, semi-feudal, *fin-de-siècle*, eighteenth-century Germany than Arnold in the solid polity of Victorian England with its clearly defined bourgeoisie and proletariat.) Schiller, therefore, is a monist when he discusses the naïve, a dualist when he confronts the sentimental art and consciousness of his own day and society.

Lukács, as a Marxist, preserves his monism throughout. Translated into his terms, the 'sentimental' very much fulfils the function of the aesthetic as such – to uphold the essential unity of man as a social animal whatever the atomizations that dismember him.

Like Schiller Lukács sees the ideal of the beautiful or the naïve embodied in the art and the public life of the Greek city-state. But Lukács offers a Marxist explanation based on later developments in nineteenth-century anthropology: namely that the Greek *polis* represents an especially fortunate example of the dissolution of primitive communism, whereby, particularly through the active survival of myth – and myth of a uniquely anthropomorphizing kind – the citizens of Athens could, despite their own class divisions, recapture a sense of tribal unity. The Golden Age thereby became an ethical and aesthetic ideal; an ideal which has indeed lasted ever since and merged into its polar complementary, the notion of utopia. Marxism itself sprang from utopian Socialism. Its vision of a classless society relies on the notion of an historically inevitable progression from a primitive classless society.

It is between these two poles, between the memory of a class-less society (and such memories are not so very distant in some parts of the world today), and the vision of a classless society, that a Marxist aesthetics must find its tensions and laws. The Marxist notion of beauty, in particular, ineluctably requires this historical faith: namely that the organic unity of individual and society, the fulfilment of the humanist ideal of the whole man is possible only in a classless society.

In Lukács' aesthetics only the whole man is beautiful, or rather beauty lies in the direct, unmediated, uncircuitous representation of the whole man. Hence, following Schiller, Goethe and Hegel, he takes as his artistic ideal and measure that plastic, sculptural, anthropomorphic, anthropocentric character of Greek art which matched its active, public, dramatic social ethos.

Athens was tied by a unique social bond to a preceding gentile society. Where else, in class society, does a Marxist look for 'the beautiful'? Clearly, as the earlier quotation from Engels testifies, in the Renaissance, which not only took its cue from classical Athens, but ushered in a renewed mercantile society. Engels reminds us that the men of the Renaissance still stood free of the shackling and constricting specializations of later bourgeois development; they could still be all-round men. 'The men who founded the modern rule of the bourgeoisie,' remarked Engels in the same passage, 'may have been limited in all sorts of ways, but never in a bourgeois way.'[1]

[1] Karl Marx and Friedrich Engels, op. cit., p. 173.

Georg Lukács

Yet, when Lukács discusses 'the beautiful' in connection with the Renaissance, he names only one figure – and one who is far less typical of that volcanic multifarious energy which excites Engels. He is Raphael. Lukács does no more than name him. Here is the context, which also includes the names of Mozart and Pushkin. It is taken from a discussion of Goethe's classical period in the book *Sketch of a History of Modern German Literature*:

> Classical periods of literature, art or philosophy are usually very short. An aesthetic harmony which refuses to falsify society, to ignore its contradictions, requires social preconditions which can seldom be sustained over a long period. But it is precisely the unity of ruthless veracity with beauty which epitomizes the truly classic as distinct from the classicistic and academic. In general, social contradictions manifest themselves either too abruptly or remain too undeveloped for the relations between men to appear in clear, expressive, beautiful contours. In history, hitherto, therefore, it has been possible to achieve beauty and preserve an unflinching artistic truthfulness only in brief and exceptional circumstances. The chances for the development of an entire period of this kind, for the emergence of a Raphael, a Mozart or a Pushkin, are very slight and never last for more than a brief space of time.[1]

Personally, I find this the most exciting passage in Lukács' entire *oeuvre*. And yet alas how abstract, how general! Lukács suggests here a sociological model for the appearance of 'the beautiful', for the efflorescence in society and art of that human totality, that harmonious unity of personality, that 'normality' which only a classless society promises to fulfil, but which these precious historical moments briefly anticipate.

But what is that magic moment, that dialectical poise between social contradictions, between those which manifest themselves too abruptly and those which fail to develop? Where do we find that balance, that hair-spring stasis which leads the bourgeois aestheticians, whom Lukács despises, to talk grandiosely of the 'eternally human'? Keats symbolized that moment in his *Grecian Urn*:

[1] Georg Lukács, *Skizze einer Geschichte der neueren deutschen Literatur*, Aufbau-Verlag, Berlin, 1955, p. 30.

> Thou, silent form, dost tease us out of thought
> As doth eternity; Cold Pastoral!
> When old age shall this generation waste,
> Thou shalt remain, in midst of other woe
> Than ours, a friend to man, to whom thou say'st,
> 'Beauty is truth, truth beauty' – that is all
> Ye know on earth, and all ye need to know.

The thought is not so very remote from Lukács'. Indeed Lukács includes Keats and Shelley, along with Hölderlin, Goethe and Pushkin as testimonies of a short-lived attempt to renew the classical ideal of beauty in the period following the French Revolution. He writes thus in his Pushkin essay (the only place where he treats at length of 'the beautiful'):

> If alongside Pushkin we think of Hölderlin and Goethe, Keats and Shelley, then we may glimpse, in world-historical terms, an original and monumental attempt, however short-lived, to renew the classical ideal of beauty, as the result of the changes which the French Revolution and Napoleon had wrought in the image of Europe. It was this period – parallel with the English 'industrial revolution' – which raised capitalist production and bourgeois society to real power and which, in Central and Eastern Europe, made it the principal task to be accomplished.

Lukács then goes on to discuss, again alas ever-so-generally, that balance of contradictions of which we have been speaking:

> This period distinguishes itself from the Enlightenment, which had paved the way for the Revolution, by the fact that the basic contradictions of the new society have already come to light, although no-one is as yet properly conscious of them (that is, from an economic and class point of view). On the other hand, they are not yet sufficiently obvious to form the centre of all the manifestations of cultural life. This is brought about in Europe by the July Revolution and the wave of critical realism which ensues thereupon.[1]

Lukács of course draws distinctions between his poets. Keats and Hölderlin he regards as belated Jacobins who cannot come to terms with post-revolutionary reality, elegists who lament the

[1] Georg Lukács, *Der russische Realismus in der Weltliteratur*, Aufbau-Verlag, Berlin, 1953, p. 24.

overthrow of the gods of the Golden Age. Shelley, on the other hand, sees into the future liberation of mankind, the dawning proletarian revolution. The unbinding of Prometheus is but a hymnic version of Shelley's injunction to the workers:

> Sow seed – but let no tyrant reap;
> Find wealth – let no impostor heap;
> Weave robes – let not the idle wear;
> Forge arms – in your defence to bear.

Lukács escapes from any more serious analysis of Shelley than this. For the ethereal Platonizing Shelley hardly meets his demands for tangible, sensuous form. Hence he finds himself much more at home with the more compromising figures of Goethe and Pushkin.

Compromising is a harsh and unjust word to use about Pushkin. The Russian poet experienced the Russian pendant of the French Revolution, the tiny abortive Decembrist revolt of 1826 – which resulted directly from the participation of freethinking aristocratic officers in the Napoleonic wars. Many of his friends responsible for that revolt were either hanged or sent to Siberia. Pushkin himself, already in exile for having written and circulated insurrectionary verse, was recalled to the capital and given back his freedom at the price of being placed under the personal supervision of the new, charming, cruel, obscurantist Tsar, Nicholas I.

During this last decade of his life (he died in 1837), Pushkin's experience of the recalcitrances of Russian history led him to adopt conservative views. And he had a social need of the court and the capital. But spiritually he never compromised. There is not an ounce of the philistine about him.

How different with Goethe! And this difference Lukács makes the basis of an extended comparison between them in his Pushkin essay. The measure he applies to each is his standard of Hellenic beauty, which he derives very largely from Goethe himself. And he finds Goethe wanting – for precisely the reason that bourgeois critics have traditionally praised him: namely that he understood the virtues of compromise, that he was able to overcome his 'titanic' youth and settle down into 'Apollonian' maturity. Lukács' notion of balance in social contradictions therefore escapes identification with the Golden Mean, though it comes dangerously near, particularly in the critic's refusal to see any good at all in any kind of Romanticism (Scott, Byron, Shelley he reclassifies as realists).

Here is the core of Lukács' comparison between Pushkin and Goethe:

We said that beauty rescues man from the distorting effects of capitalist society, of class rule, and that it does so by presenting the whole man in his immediacy. That is, not by roundabout methods, whether these take the form of exciting pity for his downfall, elegizing upon it, or avenging it artistically, say through irony – as happens later in modern bourgeois literature and which already finds its theoretical prognostication in the work of Goethe's contemporary Schiller.

Goethe recognizes this problem very clearly, with all its difficulties, both inside bourgeois society generally and the German society of his time in particular. He has this to say of the possibilities of a modern classical literature: 'When and where does a national, classical author arise? When he finds in the history of his nation great events and their consequences in a happy and significant unity; when in the attitudes of his countrymen he does not fail to discover nobility, or in their sentiments depth and in their actions strength and consequence; when he himself, instinct with national spirit, feels himself empowered by a faculty of genius that resides within him, to sympathize equally with the past and the present . . .' And then, surveying the German scene of his time, he adds with resignation: 'We do not desire the upheavals which in Germany could bring forth classical works.'

'This split,' Lukács comments,

determines every attitude, Goethe's whole poetic and human position: he sees the necessity of a democratic revolution, if German culture is really to be renewed; at the same time he not only considers it impossible for his time, but he recoils from it inwardly, spiritually. Through this divided attitude to revolution come rushing, as through a leak, all the inconsistencies, the vacillations, the dichotomies in Goethe's artistic theory and practice, from which Pushkin's art is so free.[1]

[1] Ibid., pp. 39–40.

Lukács then goes on to show how Goethe attempts to implement the classical ideal of beauty in two opposite ways. The first is that of his epic poem *Hermann und Dorothea*, in which he seeks to transplant a classical form to a provincial corner of modern Germany, where the epic theme, the French Revolution, recedes to a menacing background. What is produced, says Lukács, is not an epic but an idyll (that is, one of Schiller's modern 'sentimental' categories). Goethe's second path is that of *Wilhelm Meister*, a novel, indeed the bourgeois form *par excellence*, where instead of imposing classical models, he attempts to shape contemporary reality round the ideals of bourgeois humanism. Thus, the aim is to discover in each character his specific essence and to lead him, through error, to unfold that essence in its appropriate practical, public context, that is to make it truly generic. Goethe succeeds, but at the inevitable cost (given the Germany of his time) of making his novel utopian.

Pushkin, argues Lukács, avoids the dilemma of the idyllic and the utopian. In his novel-in-verse *Eugene Onegin*, a work which is neither epic poem nor prosaic novel, which is earth of the Russian earth and entirely un–utopian, Pushkin succeeds in embodying the 'beautiful', in creating what Lukács describes as 'the organic unity of contemporary aspirations to beauty'.

The chief repository of this organic unity is Pushkin's heroine Tatiana. She unites, according to Lukács, moral refinement with popular roots, and in this way contrasts with Goethe's heroines who, on the whole, divide themselves between these two qualities: the Leonores and Natalies on the one hand, the Gretchens, Klärchens, Philines on the other. The class divisions between Goethe's women are obvious. Pushkin's Tatiana presents a provincial and then metropolitan aristocratic girl in close and nourished contact with the people, symbolized in the poem by her peasant nurse.

Thus Lukács sees three periods, three balances of class contradictions which make possible 'the beautiful': the Greek *polis*, the Italian city-state of the Renaissance and the period in Europe subsequent to the French Revolution up to 1830. He pays most attention in his critical work to the last of these. His central literary figure is Goethe (despite his admiration for Pushkin), his central philosopher Hegel, both resigned Germans who accommodated themselves to the *status quo*. Lukács' study of Hegel is devoted to the young Hegel and concludes with a chapter on *The Phenomenology of Mind* which he compares there, and more extensively in his Goethe book, with *Faust*. He takes these works as the supreme intellectual and artistic achievements of the age because they attempt to show man as the microcosm of history, Goethe's Faust personifying the travail of the human species, Hegel's Mind displaying the leaps and revolutions of the individual consciousness as subject magnifies itself through externalization and alienation into self-knowing object. Each work is seen to end the classical period of poet and philosopher; and each coincides more or less, with the final collapse, under the guns of Jena, of the decrepit Holy Roman Empire and of that bony grip which had for so long held prisoner both modern Germany and its modern Fausts, its Goethes, Schillers and Hegels – scholars of the study, private tutors, ministers at petty courts. After the *Phenomenology* Hegel becomes a more abstract philosopher. In the second part of *Faust* Faust can represent the human species only allegorically. What Heine called the *Kunstperiode*, the artistic period, a term central to Lukács' aesthetics, is now over. Faust can achieve his dream of 'free men in a free world' only in a vision when he is old and blind. The method he has used to pursue that goal is the Mephistophelean magic of capitalist enterprise and exploitation. Mephisto wins his wager, but history in the symbolic guise of a Catholic heaven intervenes to save Faust, to redeem what Lukács calls his human core. Thus the direct, immediate, presentation of the whole man is no longer possible. The July Revolution of 1830 confirms the collapse of feudalism. Hegel dies in 1831, Goethe in 1832. Only the human core remains redeemable as a humanist talisman for posterity.

We are back to the substance of our earlier quotation where Lukács connects aesthetic form with ethical needs. In the light of our subsequent remarks that passage should now read more interestingly:

Men's longing for a moral mode of life in which the ethical command expresses the inmost core of personality and from there out radiates over the entire periphery of affects and sentiments, desires and thoughts, not in a tyrannical-dualist manner, but organically, as the adequate manifestation of the total personality – such longing springs from the very nature of morality. When this longing struggles for adequate intellectual expression – and it will do so particularly in those periods when the ethical ideals appear either already or still socially problematic – then it is extremely likely, and often historically inevitable, that such longing will express itself in aesthetic categories, too.[1]

It is clear that the notion of ethical ideals which appear either already or still socially problematic is similar to that of social contradictions which manifest themselves either too abruptly or too weakly. It is when there is unevenness in the structure of the social contradictions – and here indeed we might properly begin to speak *structurally* – that is, when the ethical ideals are deeply out of joint with reality, that a cry goes out for the aesthetic vindication of the essentially human. A couple of years back, in the *Times Literary Supplement*, Lukács discussed Shakespeare precisely in these ethical and aesthetic terms, in terms of a scenic humanism that preserved at whatever tragic cost both a sensuous and a generic individuality of personality.[2] *Hamlet* or *Lear* would be obvious examples.

Is Shakespeare, however, to be characterized as 'beautiful' or not? Has Shakespeare passed over the brink of the 'problematic' or does he still contain that 'problematic' within an unyielding totality? Lukács often uses the phrase 'of a truly Shakespearean beauty', but there it is merely a lay phrase without conscious philosophical intention.

I have used the word 'totality', which has been discussed in a previous paper. I must add to it, in order to fill out the components of Lukács' structure of the 'beautiful', that of 'the popular', *das Volkstümliche*. The individual is whole, argues Lukács, if he is seen as part of a larger whole; he is beautiful if he is directly microcosmic of that whole. Thus the characters of

[1] Georg Lukács, op. cit., p. 578.
[2] *Times Literary Supplement*, April 23, 1964.

Greek drama are inseparable from the chorus. The community in which they live, whose support and sympathy they must win and retain, is there with them on the stage, unceasingly.

Shakespearean England is not the Athenian *polis*. But London is a focal city, drawing countrymen like Shakespeare to its urban culture. It has patricians, it has plebs. They are all there in the audience; they appear episodically, in crowd scenes, on the stage. The crowd scene, according to Lukács, is the aesthetic counterpart of the chorus in Greek drama. It preserves, in a more chequered form, that same sense of totality, of a total world participating, of a total range of values, however fragile and self-contradictory these may be compared with those of the Greeks.

Perhaps the natural scenic tangibility of Shakespeare keeps him 'beautiful' in a way that is withheld from the second part of *Faust*, which remains a philosophic – lyric – dramatic poem rather than a performable play. Lukács does not tell us. But we may come near to a possible answer if we examine his essay on Pushkin's drama *Boris Godunov*. For there, and altogether in Pushkin, Lukács singles out two qualities absent in Shakespeare, but which Lukács considers indispensable for 'the beautiful', namely historicism and laconicism. (The inclusion of historicism in a concept of beauty raises a big question-mark, if we think of Greece and the Renaissance. Since Lukács has never written systematically about beauty, it is not a question he has confronted. Yet he has argued that literature can be unconsciously historical long before a historically-conscious age and that this is especially true of the drama because of its natural concern with clashes between past and present.)[1]

The age of Hegel, the dialecticization of rationalism in post-Thermidorian Europe produced a conception of history as a process that moved in leaps and bounds, in zigzags, in spurts and setbacks. Hegel only systematized ideas that had been expressed before the Revolution by such anti-Establishmentarian figures as Vico, Rousseau, Herder. For the first time men could look historically forward as well as back, as the Catholic disguise at the end of *Faust* poetically testified.

[1] See *The Historical Novel*, London, 1962, Chapter 2.

Georg Lukács

Pushkin was a pupil not only of Shakespeare, but of Scott,[1] regarding the past as the necessary prehistory of the present, demonstrating in both a historical drama and a historical novel how history shaped private life. The action of the characters in *Boris Godunov*, argues Lukács, depends much more closely upon the moods of the populace than in Shakespeare. The heroes do not clash, do not achieve their ends, instead they discover themselves victims of forces larger than they themselves. In Goethe and Hegel the awareness of historical forces which submerge the individual casts resignation and abstraction over much of their later work. The owl of Minerva takes wing, wrote Hegel, only when dusk settles on Athens. Herein we see the limits of their bourgeois sensibility. Pushkin was an aristocrat who could declare the Cossack brigand, Sten'ka Razin, the most poetic figure in Russian history. The popular and the historical are much more closely allied in Pushkin. The moral of *Boris Godunov* is that the people must not put their fate in the hands of Tsars and boyars. In Shakespeare and Goethe, whatever appeals are made to the populace, history happens from above. Goethe's historical hero is the brigand knight Götz von Berlichingen, who callously seeks his fortune in the famous German peasant war of the sixteenth century. When Pushkin, in *The Captain's Daughter*, turns to a comparable peasant war in Russian history, he glorifies Pugachov, the Cossack would-be Tsar.

The lack in Pushkin of a bourgeois polity, where talented men publicly clashed and debated, made Pushkin both laconic and lyrical (rather than rhetorical and dramatic). Tsar Boris is never rhetorical like a Shakespearean king. He is, from the outset, statuesquely reflective, guilt-ridden (a Shakespearean counterpart would, in some respects, be Richard II). But the action of the play, which bypasses him, is swift and sudden. A similar configuration holds true for *Eugene Onegin*; and this Lukács catches well:

> The light-moving verse, the candid lyrical utterance of the most subjective attitudes does not for a moment annul the classical tangibility of the figures and situations of *Eugene Onegin*. On the

[1] See *The Historical Novel*, chapter 1, p. 30 for a comparison between Scott and Hegel as the founders of modern historicism.

contrary, it is precisely in this way that the laconicism of the individual moments, of which I have spoken, makes itself felt. Each
figure is tangible and alive, but if we think of the novel as a whole,
we see that only a few really decisive turning points in the lives of the
heroes are actually depicted, and Pushkin condenses these to their
barest essentials.[1]

In the same essay Lukács mentions how Goethe valued laconicism as one of the most precious characteristics of folk-poetry.
And indeed Goethe is one of the most laconic of lyrical poets.
This was the age of the discovery of the ballad, of folk epics; an
age which re-interpreted Homer as a popular bard. It is to this
age that Lukács pays his closest attention, for it is the success
with which writers can assimilate the popular that makes them
talismanic in his eyes for the post-1830 period, a period of
renewed division of labour altogether more enslaving economically than Engels' picture of post-Renaissance Europe.

For this reason Lukács regards Russian literature as *the*
classical literature *par excellence* of the modern age, a literature
which never severed itself from popular life or revolutionary
tasks. He sees the October Revolution as the consummation of a
literary development which Pushkin began. His final criticism of
Pushkin's beauty is therefore the October Revolution itself,
would-be prelude to a classless society where 'beauty becomes a
problem of the day, that is how to portray the fully-developed
man in the new socialist reality'.[2]

The victory of the October Revolution vindicates for Lukács
not merely Pushkin's historical optimism, his sense of perspective (whatever the poet's immediate view of that perspective),
but his very style. And here we must add one final dimension to
Lukács' concept of 'the beautiful': symmetry or proportionality,
one of the most attractive features of Pushkin's style. This symmetry, Lukács maintains, is never formally imposed as in a
traditional, conventional classicism; it is derived from a sense
of history as process. Pushkin, argues Lukács, was never trapped
in his period, never fixated by any particular experience. To
illustrate he compares him with Dostoevsky. Thus Raskolnikov,

[1] Georg Lukács, *Der russische Realismus in der Weltliteratur*, p. 42.
[2] Ibid., p. 49.

hero of *Crime and Punishment*, was drawn from Pushkin's model Hermann, the self-seeking, engineering officer of *The Queen of Spades*. But whereas Pushkin could both capture, and detach himself from, his nascent bourgeois hero, Dostoevsky choked on the ethical problems of Hermann's descendant, turning him into a 'fallen angel', creating for him a religious panacea. For Pushkin, Hermann was no more than a momentarily interesting type.

One sees how each of the components of Pushkin's concept of 'the beautiful' interlocks: the tangible (*das Plastische*), the total, the historical, the popular, the laconic, the symmetrical. Pushkin is the only figure who appears to include all of them. Is it possible to build a theory of beauty upon one artist? We should dearly like to know more about Mozart and Raphael, why these should have been singled out of their age, the configuration of social contradictions which would account for them. For they have often been compared, and their work has often been called 'beautiful'.

There are other questions we must ask of Lukács. He bases his entire aesthetics on Marx's notion of Greece as the 'normal childhood' of mankind. Is it still possible today to speak in these terms?

The history of Greece may present a unique example of a transition from gentile to civic society which bypassed the rule of kings and priests. But why should one consider such a transition 'normal'? And, Marx notwithstanding, what should a Marxist measure of Greek art be: the Apollonian Golden Mean of the Athenian middle-classes or the Orphic cults, the Dionysian eruptions from the underworld of the slaves? Perhaps this is a false antithesis. Lukács would no doubt interpret it so. But what would his answer be? Alas he enters into too little detail about Greek art and literature for us to know. We are left with a very abstract, hazy notion of 'normality'. Nevertheless, it is clear that he is attracted by the more serene sides of Greek art, that, following the Hegelian tradition, he singles out its sculptural and plastic qualities. But this preference very easily turns into a restrictive aesthetic criterion. We have seen how he avoids any serious analysis of so incorporeal a Hellenist as Shelley.

234

The literary kinds which Lukács prefers are the epic and the dramatic, that is the public, bodied-out genres. Lyric poetry occupies a very small part of his critical *oeuvre*, and it is almost always made to appear subordinate and inferior to epic and drama. He appreciates, as we have shown, the relationship between the lyrical-subjective and the epic-objective in Pushkin's *Eugene Onegin*. Yet the sense of totality and universality of that work (which Belinsky described as 'an encyclopedia of Russian life') radiates out not from those spare peripeties which delight Lukács, but from the poet's lyrical personality, from the lyrical digressions.

This philosophical and psychological compulsion to subdue the lyrical-subjective can lead Lukács into the most abstract, tedious, threadbarishly paradoxical writing of the following sort:

> Pushkin's lyricism, tinctured with irony, provides so many concrete social determinants, adds so much to the concrete clarification of the individual and typical features of the characters, to the interweaving of situations which catch and sum up the social and human development, that it is precisely this lyricism which – in seemingly paradoxical fashion – comes to underlie the epic objectivity, the representation of the totality, and thereby – in an entirely unique way – masters the prose of modern life, lending beauty to the faithful reflection of reality.[1]

The revolutionary in Lukács therefore struggles with the bourgeois humanist, with the Heidelberg don. In his account of 'the beautiful' Lukács is more concerned to find a balance in social contradictions than to read the passions of the authors themselves.

[1] Ibid., p. 43.

Selective Bibliography

The most comprehensive bibliography of Lukács' works is that compiled by Jürgen Hartmann, and contained in *Georg Lukács: Festschrift zum achtzigsten Geburtstag,* ed. by F.Benseler (Luchterhand, Neuwied, 1965), pp. 625–96. The bibliography covers works published up to 1965; an enlarged version is scheduled to appear separately in 1969. The bibliography of Lukács in G. Zitta, *Georg Lukács' Marxism* (Nijhoff, The Hague, 1964), pp. 253–87, offers a less complete list of Lukács' works (up to 1957), but adds a select bibliography of works on Lukács. Mention may also be made of two compilations by Ervin Laszlo: 'Works of Georg Lukács in non-Hungarian languages' (*Studies in Soviet Thought,* VI, 1966, pp. 157–61, 228–38), and a short bibliography of Lukács' works in Hungarian in the same author's *The Communist Ideology in Hungary* (Reidel, Dordrecht, 1966), pp. 178, 275–6. A useful bibliography of works by and about Lukács is also contained in *Georg Lukács: Schriften zur Literatursoziologie* (abbreviated, *LS*), ed. by P.Ludz (Luchterhand, Neuwied, 2nd ed 1963), pp. 503–31. *Georg Lukács: Schriften zur Ideologie und Politik* (abbreviated, *IP*), ed. by P. Ludz (Luchterhand, Neuwied, 1967), pp. 783–91, contains a bibliography devoted chiefly to Lukács' German works.

The bibliography which follows is restricted to works by, and about, Lukács written in English, French and German. It does not claim to be complete, even within its own restricted field, but it aims at the inclusion of the more important books and articles. Part 1 (works by Lukács) is arranged chronologically. Part 2 (works on Lukács) is arranged alphabetically. Where a work by Lukács has been published in more than one edition, the work is entered under the year in which it was first published; later editions, and also translations, are mentioned immediately afterwards. To simplify Part 1 of the bibliography, different editions of the same work are mentioned as a rule only when a later edition is a revised version, or has a new preface. As a further simplification, no separate mention is made of essays later published by Lukács in book form. (This explains an apparent gap in Lukács' production between 1933 and 1946.)

Cross references are included to the two anthologies of Lukács' works edited by P. Ludz mentioned above; also to those volumes of the collected edition of Lukács' *Werke*, published by Luchterhand, Neuwied, which have appeared at the time of writing (August 1968) or are expected to appear in the near future. The volumes of this edition (referred to here as *Werke*) which have appeared so far are:

Vol. 5 *Probleme des Realismus II*, 1964.
Vol. 6 *Probleme des Realismus III*, 1965.
Vol. 7 *Deutsche Literatur in zwei Jahrhunderten*, 1964.
Vol. 8 *Der junge Hegel*, 1968.
Vol. 9 *Die Zerstörung der Vernunft*, 1962.
Vols. 11 and 12 *Ästhetik I* (*Die Eigenart des Ästhetischen*), 1963.
Vol. 2 (*Frühschriften II*) is to appear in Autumn 1968; Vol. 4 (*Probleme des Realismus I*) early in 1969; Vol. 10 (*Probleme der Ästhetik*) in Autumn 1968; Vols. 13–14 (*Zur Ontologie des gesellschaftlichen Seins*) in Autumn 1969. Grateful acknowledgment is made to the Hermann Luchterhand Verlag for this advance information.

G.H.R.P.

Part 1: Works by Lukács

1911 *Die Seele und die Formen*. Fleischel, Berlin, 1911.
An expanded version of a book first published in Hungarian in 1910. Excerpts in *LS*, pp. 296–311.
1914 'Zur Soziologie des modernen Dramas', *Archiv für Sozialwissenschaft und Sozialpolitik*, XXXVIII (1914), pp. 303–45, 662–706.
A translation of the introductory chapter of *A History of the Development of Modern Drama*, published in Hungarian in 1911. Excerpts in *LS*, pp. 261–95.

1916 'Die Theorie des Romans', *Zeitschrift für Ästhetik und allgemeine Kunstwissenschaft,* II (1916), pp. 225–71, 390–431. Published separately, Paul Cassirer, Berlin, 1920.
Re-issued in 1963 by Luchterhand, Neuwied, with a new preface (July, 1962) by the author.
Excerpts in *LS*, pp. 81–108.
French translation by J. Clairevoye, *La Théorie du Roman,* Éditions Gonthiers, Paris, 1963.

1917 'Die Subjekt-Objekt Beziehung in der Ästhetik,' *Logos,* VII (1917–18), pp. 1–39.

1919 *Taktik und Ethik* This work was originally written in Hungarian; the German translation (by M. Lezsák) cited here was first published in *IP*, pp. 1–40. Also in *Werke*, Vol. II.

1920 'Zur Frage des Parlamentarismus', *Kommunismus,* I/6 (1920), pp. 161–72. Also in *IP*, pp. 123–35, and *Werke*, Vol. II.
'Die moralische Sendung der kommunistischen Partei', *Kommunismus,* I/16–17 (1920), pp. 482–8. Also in *IP*, pp. 136–43, and *Werke*, Vol. II.

1923 *Geschichte und Klassenbewusstsein.* Malik Verlag, Berlin, 1923. A second edition, with a new preface (March, 1967), is in *Werke*, Vol. II.
Excerpts in *IP*, pp. 41–74, 82–122.
French translation, *Histoire et Conscience de Classe,* by K. Axelos and J. Bois, Éditions de Minuit, Paris, 1960.

1924 'Lenin'. *Das Forum,* No. 21, Berlin, 1924.
Published in book form in the same year (Verlag der Arbeiter-Buchhandlung, Vienna) as *Lenin: Studie über den Zusammenhang seiner Gedanken.*
Published by Luchterhand (Neuwied, 1967), with a new postscript (January, 1967).
Also in *Werke*, Vol. II: excerpts in *IP*, pp. 169–87.
French translation, *Lénine*, published by Études et Documentation Internationales, Paris, 1965.

1925 Review of Bukharin, *Theorie des historischen Materialismus, Archiv für die Geschichte des Sozialismus und der Arbeiterbewegung,* XI (1925), pp. 216–24.
Also in *Werke*, Vol. II, and *IP*, pp. 188–200.
English translation by B. Brewster: 'Technology and Social Relations', *New Left Review*, No. 39, Sept./Oct. 1966, pp. 27–34.
'Die neue Ausgabe von Lassalles Briefen', *Archiv für die Geschichte des Sozialismus und der Arbeiterbewegung,* XI (1925), pp. 401–23. Also in *Werke*, Vol. II, and *IP*, pp. 201–36.

1926 'Moses Hess und die Probleme der idealistischen Dialektik'.

Archiv für die Geschichte des Sozialismus und der Arbeiter-bewegung, XII (1926), pp. 105–55.
Also in *Werke,* Vol. II, and *IP,* pp. 237–89.

1928 *Thesen über die politische und wirtschaftliche Lage in Ungarn und über die Aufgaben der Kommunistischen Partei Ungarns.* (The 'Blum Theses'.)
First published in Hungarian in 1956; an excerpt (in a German translation by M. Lezsák) is in *IP,* pp. 290–322.
Also in *Werke,* Vol. II.

1932 'Tendenz oder Parteilichkeit?' *Die Linkskurve,* IV/6 (1932), pp. 13–21.
Also in *Werke,* Vol. IV, and *LS,* pp. 109–21.
'Reportage oder Gestaltung?' *Die Linkskurve,* IV/7, 8 (1932), pp. 23–30, 26–31.
Also in *Werke,* Vol. IV, and *LS,* pp. 122–42.
'Aus der Not eine Tugend', *Die Linkskurve,* IV/11–12 (1932), pp. 15–24.
Also in *Werke,* Vol. IV, and *LS,* pp. 143–56.

1933 'Mein Weg zu Marx', *Internationale Literatur,* III/2 (1933), pp. 178 ff. *IP,* pp. 323–9.

1946 *Aristokratische und demokratische Weltanschauung,* the German text of a lecture first published in French, *Forum,* Budapest, I/3 (1946), pp. 197 ff.
IP, pp. 404–33.

1947 *Goethe und seine Zeit,* Francke, Bern, 1947.
2nd, enlarged edition, Aufbau-Verlag, Berlin, 1950.
Also in *Werke,* Vol. VII; excerpts in *LS,* pp. 157–74, 383–402.
English translation, *Goethe and his Age,* by R. Anchor, Merlin Press, London, 1968.
French translation, *Goethe et son époque,* by Goldmann and Frank, Nagel, Paris, 1949.
'Freie oder gelenkte Kunst?' A German translation by M. Lezsák (*IP,* pp. 434–63) of a chapter from Lukács' book *Literature and Democracy,* published in Hungarian in 1947.
French translation, 'Art libre ou art dirigé?' in *Esprit,* XVI/9 (1948), pp. 273–92.

1948 *Der junge Hegel,* Europa Verlag, Zürich and Vienna, 1948.
2nd edition, with a new preface, Aufbau-Verlag, Berlin, 1954.
Werke, Vol. VIII.
Essays über Realismus, Aufbau-Verlag, Berlin, 1948.
2nd, enlarged edition, published as *Probleme des Realismus,* Aufbau-Verlag, Berlin, 1955.
Also in *Werke,* Vol. IV; exerpts in *LS,* pp. 198–212, 318–28.
Schicksalswende, Aufbau-Verlag, Berlin, 1948.
2nd, enlarged edition, Aufbau-Verlag, Berlin, 1956.

Excerpts in *IP*, pp. 330–75.

An English version by Roy Pascal of the chapter 'Über Preuss-entum', entitled 'Prussianism and Nazism', was published in *The Modern Quarterly*, I/3 (Summer, 1946), pp. 85–93.

Karl Marx und Friedrich Engels als Literaturhistoriker, Aufbau-Verlag, Berlin, 1948. Also in *Werke*, Vol. X.

Existentialisme ou Marxisme? French translation, by E. Kelemen, Nagel, Paris, 1948.

A part-translation of a work which appeared in Hungarian in 1947. German translation, *Existentialismus oder Marxismus?*, Aufbau-Verlag, Berlin, 1951.

Excerpts in *IP*, pp. 464–505.

1949 *Der russische Realismus in der Weltliteratur,* Aufbau-Verlag, Berlin, 1949.

2nd, enlarged edition, Aufbau-Verlag, Berlin, 1952.

3rd, enlarged edition, Aufbau-Verlag, Berlin, 1953.

4th, enlarged edition, Luchterhand, Neuwied, 1964. (*Werke,* Vol. V.)

Excerpts in *LS*, pp. 403–18, 487–500.

Chapters have been translated into English by Edith Bone as part of *Studies in European Realism*, Hillway, London, 1950; Grosset and Dunlap, New York, 1964.

The last chapter of the fourth edition has been translated into English by M. A. L. Brown, as 'Solzhenitsyn and the New Realism', *Socialist Register, 1965*, Merlin Press, London, 1965, pp. 197–215.

Thomas Mann, Aufbau-Verlag, Berlin, 1949.

A Hungarian version was published in 1948.

5th, enlarged edition, Aufbau-Verlag, Berlin, 1957.

Also in *Werke*, Vol. VII.

English translation of the 5th edition, *Essays on Thomas Mann*, by Stanley Mitchell, Merlin Press, London, 1964.

1951 *Deutsche Realisten des 19. Jahrhunderts,* Aufbau-Verlag, Berlin, 1951.

Also in *Werke*, Vol. VII.

Excerpts in *LS*, pp. 358–82, 476–86.

1952 *Balzac und der französische Realismus*, Aufbau-Verlag, Berlin, 1952.

Also in *Werke*, Vol. VI.

Excerpts in *LS*, pp. 241–53, 329–57.

English translation in *Studies in European Realism*. (See above, under 1949.)

French translation, *Balzac et le réalisme français,* Maspéro, Paris, 1967.

1953 *Skizze einer Geschichte der neueren deutschen Literatur,* Aufbau-Verlag, Berlin, 1953.

3rd edition, with a new preface, Luchterhand, Neuwied, 1963.

Excerpts in *LS*, pp. 452–75.

French translation, *Brève histoire de la littérature allemande,* by L. Goldmann and M. Butor, Nagel, Paris, 1949. (Based on the original articles, published in 1945.)

'Hegels Ästhetik', *Sinn und Form,* VI (1953), pp. 17–58.

First published in Hungarian in 1952.

Re-issued in the edition of Hegel's *Ästhetik* by F. Bassenge, Aufbau-Verlag, Berlin, 1955, pp. 9–46; 2nd ed., Europäische Verlagsanstalt, Frankfurt am Main, 1965, Vol. II, pp. 587–624).

1954 *Die Zerstörung der Vernunft,* Aufbau-Verlag, Berlin, 1954.

Werke, Vol. IX.

French translation, *La destruction de la raison,* 2 vols., L'Arche, Paris, 1958–9.

Beiträge zur Geschichte der Ästhetik, Aufbau-Verlag, Berlin, 1954.

First published in Hungarian, 1953.

Also in *Werke,* Vol. X.

Excerpts in *LS*, pp. 213–40.

'Zur philosophischen Entwicklung des jungen Marx', *Deutsche Zeitschrift für philosophie,* II (1954), pp. 288–343.

Also in *IP*, pp. 506–92.

1955 *Der historische Roman,* Aufbau-Verlag, Berlin, 1955.

Also in *Werke,* Vol. VI.

Excerpts in *LS*, pp. 175–97, 419–51.

English translation, *The Historical Novel,* by Hannah and Stanley Mitchell, Merlin Press, London, 1962; Beacon Press, Boston, 1962.

1956 'Der Kampf des Fortschritts und der Reaktion in der heutigen Kultur', *Aufbau,* XII/9 (1956), pp. 761–9.

Also in *IP*, pp. 603–32.

Partial English translation, 'The Struggle between Progress and Reaction in the Culture of our Times', *Soviet Survey,* No. 10 (1956), pp. 15 ff.

Rede in der philosophischen Debatte des Petöfi-Kreises am 15 Juni 1956 (Auszug).

Translated by M. Lezsák from the original Hungarian, *IP*, pp. 593–602.

Diskussion über die Blum-Thesen.

Translated by M. Lezsák from the original Hungarian, *IP*, pp. 763–74.

1957 *Über die Besonderheit als Kategorie der Ästhetick,* Luchterhand, Neuwied, 1967.

The original German version, based largely on articles in the *Deutsche Zeitschrift für Philosophie*, 1954–6, of which a Hungarian translation appeared in 1957)
Also in *Werke*, Vol. X.

1958 *Wider den missverstandenen Realismus*, Claasen, Hamburg, 1958. Also in *Werke*, Vol. IV.
English translation, *The Meaning of Contemporary Realism*, by John and Necke Mander, Merlin Press, London, 1963. Published in America as *Realism in our Time*, Harper, New York, 1964.
French translation, *La Signification présente du Réalisme Critique*, by M. de Gandillac, Gallimard, Paris, 1960.
Postscriptum 1957 zu: Mein Weg zu Marx.
First published in Italian, *Nuovi Argomenti*, No. 33 (1958), pp. 1 ff. Original German text published in *IP*, pp. 646–57.

1962 *Brief an Alberto Carocci.*
First published in Italian; German version published in *Forum*, X (1963), pp. 335–7, 407–11.
Also in *IP*, pp. 658–80.

1963 *Ästhetik, Teil 1: Die Eigenart des Ästhetischen*, 2 vols., Luchterhand, Neuwied, 1963 (*Werke*, Vols. XI and XII).
'Zur Debatte zwischen China und der Sowjetunion', *Forum*, X (1963), pp. 519–22, 582–5.
Also in *IP*, pp. 681–706.
English translation, 'Reflections on the Sino-Soviet Dispute', by L. Baxandall, *Studies on the Left*, IV/1 (1964), pp. 22–38.
French translation, 'Contribution au débat entre la Chine et l'Union Soviétique', by Briand, *Les Temps Modernes*, XIX (1963–4), pp. 1479–1501.

1964 'Theatre and Environment', *Times Literary Supplement*, 23 April 1964, p. 347.
German version, 'Über einen Aspekt der Aktualität Shakespeares', *Neue Deutsche Hefte*, 105, May/June 1965, pp. 62–8.
Also in *Werke*, Vol. VI.

1967 *Gespräche mit Georg Lukács*, edited by Theo Pinkus, Rowohlt, Hamburg, 1967.

1968 'An Interview with György Lukács (by P. Rényi and P. Pándi)',
New Hungarian Quarterly, IX (1968), No. 29, pp. 74–82.
An English version of an interview which appeared first in Hungarian on 25 December 1967.

Part 2: Works on Lukács

ACZÉL, T. and MÉRAY, T., *The Revolt of the Mind,* Praeger, New York, 1959; Thames and Hudson, London, 1960, 449 pp.

An account of the events that led up to the Hungarian uprising of 1956; pp. 57–80 deal with the attacks on Lukács by Rudas and Révai in 1949.

ADORNO, T. W., 'Erpresste Versöhnung. Zu Georg Lukács: "Wider den missverstandenen Realismus"', *Noten zur Literatur,* Vol. II, Frankfurt am Main, 1961, pp. 152–87. First published in *Der Monat,* November, 1958, pp. 37–49.

A critical but sympathetic account of Lukács' critique of modernism in literature.

ALTHAUS, H., *Georg Lukács, oder Bürgerlichkeit als Vorschule einer marxistischen Ästhetik,* Francke Verlag, Bern and Münich, 1962, 82 pp.

Despite its title, this is in the main a study of Lukács' literary criticism, with special reference to bourgeois German literature.

ARVON, H., *Georges Lukács,* Seghers, Paris, 1968. (*Philosophes de tous les temps,* No. 41), 189 pp.

Subtitled 'Le Front populaire en littérature', this is a brief introduction to Lukács' work as a whole, followed by 74 pages of short excerpts.

BENSELER, F. (ed.), *Festschrift zum achtzigsten Geburtstag von Georg Lukács,* Luchterhand, Neuwied, 1965, 709 pp.

Includes articles on Lukács by F. Benseler, P. Ludz, J. Rühle, W. Hofmann, I. Mészáros, C. Vasoli and G. Aristarco.

DEMETZ, P., 'Georg Lukács as a Theoretician of Literature', Chapter 8 of *Marx, Engels and the Poets,* 2nd ed., University of Chicago Press, Chicago and London, 1967, pp. 199–227.

A survey of Lukács' aesthetics and criticism, from *Die Theorie des Romans* to *Die Eigenart des Ästhetischen.*

DEMETZ, P., 'The Uses of Lukács', *The Yale Review,* LIV (1964–5), pp. 435–40.

A review of *The Historical Novel, Studies in European Realism* and *Realism in our Time.*

DEUTSCHER, I., 'Georg Lukács and "Critical Realism"', *The Listener,* 3 November, 1966, pp. 659–62.

Remarks on Lukács' literary criticism, occasioned by *Essays on Thomas Mann.*

FETSCHER, I., 'Das Verhältnis des Marxismus zu Hegel', *Marxismusstudien,* Series 3 (1960), pp. 66–169.

Includes (pp. 102 ff.) a study of *Geschichte und Klassenbewusstsein* and *Der junge Hegel.*

Georg Lukács und der Revisionismus, Aufbau-Verlag, Berlin, 1960, 340 pp.

A collection of essays critical of Lukács by representatives of the official Communist point of view, including Révai, Szigéti and Fogarasi.

Georg Lukács zum siebzigsten Geburtstag, Aufbau-Verlag, Berlin, 1955, 262 pp.

Includes essays by K. Farner, E. Fischer, H. H. Holz, W. Markov, H. Mayer, O. Morf, and reprints four essays by Lukács, including 'Mein Weg zu Marx'.

GOLDMANN, L., 'Georg Lukács: L'Essayiste', *Recherches Dialectiques* (Paris, 1959), pp. 247–59. First published in *Revue d'Esthétique*, No. 1, January–March 1950.

A study of the essays on the essay and on tragedy in *Die Seele und die Formen*.

GOLDMANN, L., 'Introduction aux premiers écrits de Georges Lukács', *Les Temps Modernes*, XVIII (1962–3), pp. 254–80.

A study of *Die Seele und die Formen* and *Die Theorie des Romans*.

HELLER, ÁGNES, 'Lukács' Aesthetics', *The New Hungarian Quarterly*, VII (1966), No. 24, pp. 84–94.

An authoritative, but somewhat condensed account by one of Lukács' pupils.

HYPPOLITE, J., 'Aliénation et objectivation', *Études sur Marx et Hegel*, 2nd ed., Rivière, Paris, 1965, pp. 82–104.

A review of *Der junge Hegel* by a leading Hegelian scholar.

ILLÉS, L., 'Die Freiheit der künstlerischen Richtungen und das Zeitgemässe', *Littérature et Réalité*, ed. by B. Köpeczi and P. Juhász, Akadémiai Kiadó, Budapest, 1966, pp. 83–100.

An account of Lukács' literary criticism of the thirties.

KETTLE, A., Review of *Studies in European Realism*, *The Modern Quarterly*, VI/1 (Winter, 1950–51), pp. 72–81.

LICHTHEIM, G., 'An Intellectual Disaster', *Encounter*, XX (May, 1963), pp. 74–80.

An attack on Lukács' literary criticism, with special reference to *The Meaning of Contemporary Realism* and *The Historical Novel*. Answers by G. Steiner, A. MacIntyre, Roy Pascal, J. Cumming and G. Carnall, and a rejoinder by Lichtheim, appeared in *Encounter*, XX (June, 1963) and XXI (August, 1963).

LÜBBE, H., 'Zur marxistischen Auslegung Hegels', *Philosophische Rundschau*, II (1953–5), pp. 38–60.

A review of *Der junge Hegel*, and of Ernst Bloch's *Subjekt–Objekt*.

LUDZ, P., 'Marxismus und Literatur – Eine kritische Einführung in das Werk von Georg Lukács', the preface to *Georg Lukács:*

Schriften zur Literatursoziologie, ed. by P. Ludz, Luchterhand, Neuwied, 2nd ed., 1963, pp. 19–68.

MASLOW, VERA, 'Georg Lukács and the Unconscious', *The Journal of Aesthetics and Art Criticism,* XXII (1964), pp. 465–70.

A reply to some comments in an article by John Fizer, 'The Problem of the Unconscious in the Creative Process, as treated by Soviet Aesthetics', *The Journal of Aesthetics and Art Criticism,* XXI (1963), pp. 399–406. The discussion should now be supplemented by Lukács' remarks in *Die Eigenart des Ästhetischen,* ii, pp. 128–48.

MASLOW, VERA, 'Lukács' man-centred aesthetics', *Philosophy and Phenomenological Research,* XXVII (1967), pp. 542–52.

A study of a theme from *Die Eigenart des Ästhetischen.*

MERLEAU-PONTY, M., Chapter 3, 'Le Marxisme "Occidental"' and Chapter 4, 'Pravda', *Les Aventures de la Dialectique,* Gallimard, Paris, 1955, pp. 43–100.

An acute critique of Lukács' concept of dialectic, as developed in *Geschichte und Klassenbewusstsein.*

MITCHELL, STANLEY, 'Georg Lukács and the Historical Novel', *Marxism Today,* December 1963, pp. 374–82.

PASCAL, ROY, Introduction to *Studies in European Realism,* translated by Edith Bone, Hillway, London, 1950.

RIESER, M., 'Lukács' Critique of German Philosophy', *The Journal of Philosophy,* LV (1958), pp. 177–96.

A temperate and informative review of *Die Zerstörung der Vernunft.*

RUNCIMAN, W. G., Chapter 8, 'Social Science and Political Theory', *Social Science and Political Theory,* Cambridge University Press, Cambridge, 1963, pp. 156–75.

Discusses Lukács' views about the relativity of knowledge.

STEINER, G., 'Georg Lukács and his Devil's Pact', *The Kenyon Review,* XXII/1 (1960), pp. 1–18. Reprinted in G. Steiner, *Language and Silence,* Faber and Faber, London, 1967, pp. 355–70.

An account of Lukács' literary criticism. (The 'Devil's pact' is with historical necessity).

THALHEIM, H-G., 'Kritische Bemerkungen zu den Literaturauffassungen Georg Lukács' und Hans Mayers', *Weimarer Beiträge: Zeitschrift für deutsche Literaturgeschichte,* IV (1958), pp. 138–71.

Argues that Lukács underestimates the role of the popular masses in literature.

TÖKÉS, R. L., *Béla Kun and the Hungarian Soviet Republic,* Praeger, New York, and Pall Mall Press, London, 1967, 292 pp.

An account of the Béla Kun régime of 1919, which makes use of recently published material.

VÁLI, F. A., *Rift and Revolt in Hungary,* Harvard University Press,

Cambridge Mass., and Oxford University Press, London, 1961, 590 pp.

A history of the Hungarian uprising of 1956, its antecedents and consequences.

WATNICK, M., 'Georg Lukács: an Intellectual Biography', *Soviet Survey*, 1958–9. In four parts: I, No. 23, 1958, pp. 60–66; II, No. 24, 1958, pp. 51–7; III, No. 25, 1958, pp. 61–8; IV, No. 27. 1959, pp. 75–81. An abbreviated version (omitting much of I and almost the whole of IV) was published as 'Relativism and Class Consciousness' in *Revisionism*, ed. by L. Labedz, Allen and Unwin, London, 1962, pp. 142–65.

A critical survey of Lukács' thought, up to and including *Geschichte und Klassenbewusstsein*.

ZITTA, V., *Georg Lukács' Marxism: Alienation, Dialectics, Revolution*, Nijhoff, The Hague, 1964, 305 pp.

A hostile and imperceptive account of Lukács' thought, up to and including *Geschichte und Klassenbewusstsein*; valuable mainly for its copious documentation.

(Anonymous) 'The Mirror of Reality', *Times Literary Supplement*, 22 September, 1950, pp. 589–91.

A critical survey of Lukács' views on literature.

Index

Abendroth, W., 30
Aczél, T., 27
Adorno, T. W., 166
Ady, E., 40 ff.
Ahlberg, R., 13
Alienation, 10, 16 f., 163
Allegory, 130, 166 f.
Angst, 163 ff., 210 f.
Antal, F., 44
Aragon, L., 174, 176
Aristotle, 31 f., 221
Arnold, Matthew, 212, 222
'Art', senses of, 110 ff.
Arvon, H., 1, 30
Ashton, T. S., 197
Aufhebung, see 'Sublation'
Axelos, K., 26

Balázs, B., 44
Balogh, E., 29
Balzac, 150 f., 155, 167, 178 f., 186, 190, 207
Bartók, B., 44
Beautiful, the, 219 ff.
Bedford, E., 143
Belinsky, V. G., 180, 235
Benedek, M., 2
Benjamin, W., 166 f.
Benseler, F., 2, 23, 237
Besonderheit, see 'Speciality'
Biran, M. de, 98
Blake, William, 205 f.
Bloch, E., 20, 25
'Brains-Trust', 82 ff.
Brecht, B., 25

Bush, D., 192
Byron, 156, 186, 227

Carlyle, T., 201
Carr, E. H., 217
Casey, J., 143
Categories, Lukács', 9, 72, 113 ff.
Caudwell, C., 192
Child, F. J., 202
Class, social, 175
Class-consciousness, 11 f., 14
Co-existence, 28, 50
Cohen, H., 3, 39
Collingwood, R. G., 120
Comintern, 13, 18, 27, 46, 76, 83, 173
Commitment, 38, 104
Communist Party, Nature of, 14 f., 50, 77
Comte, A., 99
Coster, C. de, 188
Cowan, I. B., 198
Criticism, 112 f., 137, 145, 188 ff.
Croce, 86, 89, 92, 140
Cross, J. W., 213 f.

Dante, 155
Darvas, J., 27
Davie, D., 162
Deborin, A. M., 13 f.
Definition, 113, 145
Democracy, 74
Descartes, 88, 102
Deutscher, I., 22
Dialectic, Hegelian, 10, 88, 130

Dialectic, Marxist, 9 ff., 31 f., 34 ff., 96, 175 ff.
Dickens, 131, 202, 212 ff.
Diderot, 141
Dilthey, W., 5, 39, 95, 97 ff., 122, 134
Disraeli, B., 214, 216
Dostoevsky, 5, 59, 186, 196, 233 f.
Drama, 132, 154, 188, 231

Economics, 70 ff., 90
Ehrenburg, I., 25
Eliot, George, 213 f., 216
Engels, 11 ff., 16, 31, 115 f., 133 f., 173, 176, 181, 184, 204 ff., 219, 223, 233
Epic, 132, 159, 179 f., 187, 228, 235
Essence, 118
Ethics, 74, 77 f., 127 ff., 220 f., 230
Evocation, in art, 119 ff., 134
Existentialism, 4, 25, 101
Expression, 141 f.

Fedin, K., 211
Feeling, 141 ff.
Fetishism, 16 f.
Fetscher, I., 17, 22, 31
Feuchtwanger, L., 33, 178
Feuerbach, L., 20, 73, 168
Fichte, 97
Flaubert, 178, 186, 213 ff.
Fogarasi, B., 29 f., 44
Forster, J., 214
Fragmentation, 5, 56 f., 67

Gardiner, P., 138
Gaskell, Elizabeth, 213
Genre, 136
George, S., 56
Gerö, E., 28 f.
Gettleman, M. E., 198
Goethe, 37, 152, 155 ff., 159, 169, 179, 223 ff.

Goldmann, L., 4 ff.
Gorky, 155, 196
Gramsci, A., 50, 82
Graziadei, A., 83
Greeks, Ancient, 152, 155 f., 222 f., 231, 234

Hardy, Thomas, 200
Harkness, Margaret, 133, 207
Hartmann, J., 237
Hauser, A., 44, 57
Hegel, 5 f., 9 f., 13, 16, 20, 22, 31 f., 35, 37, 39, 45, 70, 72, 87 f., 91, 114, 121, 124 ff., 134 f., 151 ff., 179 f., 221, 223, 229, 231 f.
Heidegger, M., 95, 104, 164
Heine, 213, 229
Hepburn, R., 143
Hibbert, C., 209
Historicism, 197, 203 f., 231 f.
Hitler, 21, 26, 86 f., 96, 104
Hodges, H. A., 5, 26, 122, 134
Hoffman, E. T. A., 167
Hölderlin, 225
Holz, H. H., 30
Homer, 215, 233
Horváth, M., 27, 191
Hough, G., 138
Humanitätsideal, 156 f.
Hungarian Soviet Republic, 7 f., 45 f., 60, 75, 220

Ibsen, 216
Ideology, 23, 150 f., 175, 204
Illés, L., 25
Images, 120, 187 ff.
Individuality, 115, 123 ff., 128 ff., 132, 142, 144
Inherence, 135 ff.
Intuition, 4, 89, 91, 101
Irrationalism, 34, 86 ff.

Jack, I., 192
James, Jenry, 215 ff.

Jaspers, K., 95, 104
Joyce, James, 25, 163
József, A., 44
Jung, C. G., 106

Kádár, J., 29
Kafka, 32, 154, 162 ff., 209 ff.
Kamenev, L. B., 13
Kant, 3, 5, 102, 114, 135, 188
Károlyi, Count, 7
Kassner, R., 56
Kautsky, Minna, 133 f.
Keats, 224 f.
Kennan, G., 82 f.
Kennedy, J. F., 82
Kennick, W. E., 113
Kermode, J. F., 138 f.
Kettle, A., 214
Khrushchev, N. S., 23, 28, 209
Kierkegaard, S., 93 f., 104, 166
Kiernan, V. G., 206
Klopstock, F. G., 149
Kodály, Z., 44
Kofler, L., 30
Kommunismus, 8 f.
Korsch, K., 19, 83
Kun, B., 7 f., 18 f., 26 f.
Kunfi, Z., 7 f.

Labour, division of, 149, 169, 219 f., 233
Laconicism, 231 ff.
Landler, J., 18
Langer, Suzanne, 189
Lask, E., 3, 20, 39
Laszlo, E., 30, 237
Lawrence, D. H., 122
Leavis, F. R., 201
Lebensphilosophie, 52, 95 ff.
Leibniz, 139
Lenin, 7, 9, 18, 39, 45 f., 48, 82, 116 f., 207
Lichtheim, G., 1, 14
Lifschitz, M., 20 f.

Linkskurve, Die, 21
Löwe, A., 106
Ludz, P., 3, 6, 15, 237
Lukács, works of:
  Aesthetic Culture, 42, 45, 56, 67
  Aesthetics, see *The Specific Nature of the Aesthetic*
  Aristocratic and the Democratic World -View, The, 24
  Balzac and French Realism, 24, 132 f., 155
  Blum Theses, 18 ff., 61, 76
  Bolshevism as a Moral Problem, 43
  Bukharin's 'Theory of Historical Materialism', 18, 61
  Contributions to the History of Aesthetics, 161
  Conversations, 30, 35, 54, 82, 84, 151, 153, 155, 161, 169
  Debate between China and the Soviet Union, On the, 51
  Destruction of Reason, The, 4, 26, 29 f., 74, 86 ff., 112, 139
  Essays on Realism, 5, 24 f., 33, 73, 156
  Existentialism or Marxism?, 25
  German Realists of the Nineteenth Century, 24
  Goethe and his Age, 24, 156 f., 229
  Historical Novel, The, 24, 33, 124, 128, 133, 153 f., 158, 161, 178 ff., 194, 196 ff., 213, 231 f.
  History and Class-Consciousness, 2, 7 ff., 34, 43, 50, 61, 64 ff., 70, 73, 76 f.
  Introduction to the Writings on Aesthetics of Marx and Engels, 133
  Karl Marx and Friedrich Engels as Historians of Literature, 155 f.
  Lassalle's Letters, 15, 18, 61

Lukács, works of — *contd.*
  Lenin, 15, 18, 43, 61
  Literature and Democracy, 26 f.
  Meaning of Contemporary Realism, The, 28, 31 f., 128, 132, 163 ff., 191, 209, 221
  Moses Hess, 15, 18, 34, 61 f., 70, 72 f.
  New Hungarian Culture, For a, 73
  New Hungarian Lyric Poetry, 41
  Ontology of Social Being, On the, 20, 30, 34, 64, 81, 84, 169
  Parliamentary Question, On the, 9
  Politics of Illusion Again, The, 18
  Postscript (1957) to 'My Road to Marx', 21 f., 27, 36
  Realism in Our Time, see *The Meaning of Contemporary Realism*
  Report or Form?, 10, 25, 128
  Road to Marx, My, 3, 7, 21
  Role of Morality in Communist Production, The, 43, 46 ff.
  Russian Realism in World Literature, 24, 150, 153, 225, 227, 233, 235
  Sketch of a History of Modern German Literature, 25, 130, 224
  Sociology of Modern Drama, On the, 6
  Soul and the Forms, The, 4, 42, 55 ff., 67 ff., 151
  Speciality as a Category of Aesthetics, On, 32, 34, 63, 73
  Specific Nature of the Aesthetic, The, 6, 21, 23, 30 ff., 34, 55, 63 f., 73, 81, 109 ff., 147 ff., 155, 162, 165, 167, 220, 230, 246

  Studies in European Realism, 130, 132, 144, 153, 155, 195 f., 208, 210, 213 ff.
  Subject-Object Relation in Aesthetics, The, 20
  Tactics and Ethics, 8, 43, 60
  Tasks of Marxist Philosophy, The, 66, 74
  Theatre and Environment, 230
  Theory of the Novel, The, 5 ff., 20, 34, 42, 57 ff., 64, 67, 112, 154, 187
  Thomas Mann, 26, 52
  Turning-Point of Destiny, The, 24, 55
  Virtue of Necessity, A, 10, 21
  Young Hegel, The, 4, 13, 17, 20 ff., 24, 30, 34, 61 f., 73, 229
Luxemburg, Rosa, 39
Lyric Poetry, 143 ff., 168, 170, 235
Lysenko, T. D., 86

MacIntyre, A., 1
Magic, 110, 117, 119, 131
Mann, Heinrich, 49, 174, 178
Mann, Thomas, 37, 52, 67, 168
Mannheim, K., 44, 104 ff.
Mao Tse-tung, 50, 82
Marx, 3, 9, 11, 13, 19 f., 31 f., 35, 37, 39, 47, 72, 82, 85, 115, 125 155, 169, 173, 175 f., 179, 181, 193 f., 234
Materialism, dialectical, *see* 'Dialectic, Marxist'
Materialism, historical, 118, 175 f., 181, 186 ff., 193 f.
Mean, 127 ff.
Mediation, 46, 49, 51, 62, 65, 67 ff., 77 f., 81, 125 ff.
Méray, T., 27
Merleau-Ponty, M., 15
Mészáros, I., 2, 4, 6, 23
Metaphysics, 112
Milburn, Eleanor, 182

Mimesis, 116, 141
Mitchell, J. B., 212
Mitchell, S., 198
Morgan, L. H., 181
Mozart, 224, 234
Mure, G. R. G., 32, 114, 121
Music, 140 ff.
Mussolini, 209

Nagy, I., 29, 220
Natorp, P., 3
Naturalism, 4, 24, 68 f., 130
Neo-Kantianism, 3, 5, 43, 177, 189
Nietzsche, 92, 94, 96
Novel, 6, 132, 154, 158, 161, 188, 193
Novella, 132

Objectivation, 17
Ontology, 53 f., 65, 85, 149, 169
Ought, concept of, 42 f., 52 ff., 59, 80, 85

Pascal, R., 6, 32
Pater, W., 138
Perspective, 167 f., 233
Petöfi, S., 41
'Petöfi Circle', 28
Philosophy, history of, 90
Piana, G., 2
Pinkus, T., 30
Planty-Bonjour, G., 14, 115
Plekhanov, G. V., 20, 194
Popular, the, 230 f., 233
Possibility, ojective, 11
Praxis, 11 ff., 17, 148
Proletariat, 10 ff., 14 ff., 46 f., 60, 94
Pushkin, 196, 224 ff.

Racine, 132
Rajk, L., 26 f.
Rákosi, M., 26 ff.
Raphael, 224, 234

Realism, 24, 32, 132 f., 142, 163 ff., 215
Reflection, 17, 21, 114, 116 ff., 126, 129, 134, 139, 148, 187, 189, 220
Reification, 16
Religion, 117, 121 f.
Renaissance, 156, 219, 223 f., 228, 231
Révai, J., 27, 76, 83, 244
Revisionism, 13, 83
Revolutions:
  French (1789), 22, 90 f., 179 f., 185, 196, 202, 204, 214, 225 f., 228;
  of 1830 ('July Revolution'), 225, 229;
  of 1848, 90, 92, 94, 212 ff.;
  of 1871 (Paris Commune), 94;
  Russian ('October Revolution', 1917), 7, 45, 60, 73, 233;
  Hungarian (1956), 28 f., 62, 163;
  see also 'Hungarian Soviet Republic'
Rickert, 3 ff., 89
Rilke, 151
Rousseau, 14 f.
Rozental, M., 114 f., 122
Rudas, L., 13, 27, 244

Sainte Palaye, L. de, 179
Sartre, J.-P., 37
Saville, J., 200
Scheler, M., 95
Schelling, F. W. J., 91 f.
Schiller, 152, 156, 188, 222 f., 227 f.
Schlegel, A. W., 179, 187
Schopenhauer, 92 138 f.
Science, 88 f., 117 f., 123 f., 126, 129, 134 f., 139, 142, 148 f., 151
Scott, Sir Walter, 157 ff., 167, 178 ff., 196 ff., 227, 232
'Sectarianism', 27, 29, 73, 78, 81
Self-awareness, 6, 120 f.

Shakespeare, 132, 153 ff., 230 ff.
Shelley, 225 ff., 234
Sholokhov, M., 200 f.
Simmel, G., 3 f., 39, 59, 95, 151, 170
Social equivalent, 194 f.
'Socialism in one country', 18, 23, 49 f., 79
Solitariness, 163, 168, 221
Sorel, G., 173
Speciality, 62, 71, 109 ff., 187
Spencer, H., 99
Stalin, 13, 18, 22 ff., 26 f., 31, 63, 76, 86, 163, 173, 177, 210, 220
Steiner, G., 181
Stendhal, 5, 184
Subject-object, identical, 10 f., 16, 65, 67
Sublation, 9, 37, 39, 59, 128 ff., 134
Subsumption, 135 ff.
Symbolism, 67 ff.
Symmetry, 233 f.
Szabó, E., 2, 13, 39 f.
Szamuely, T., 8
Szigéti, J., 27, 29 f.
Szilasi, W., 44

Taine, H., 99, 192, 201
Talmon, J. L., 14
'Thalia', 2, 40 f.
Theory and practice, unity of, 11 f., 45, 48, 72, 174, 176
Thompson, E., 217
Tökés, R. L., 2 f., 7 f., 13, 27
Tolnay, C. de, 44
Tolstoy, 133, 151, 155, 167, 186, 195, 207 f., 210, 215 ff.

Totality, 5 f., 9, 12, 46, 57 f., 64 ff., 69 f., 72, 77, 123, 147 ff., 187 ff., 230, 235
Totality, man's, 146
Tragedy, 187
Trotsky, 51
Truth, nature of, 10
Twentieth Congress of the CPSU, 28, 31 ff., 209
Types, 132 ff., 142, 144, 158, 167f., 188

Universality, 115, 123, 125 ff., 132, 144

Váli, F., 26 ff.
Varga, E., 44
Vernunft, 88
Verstand, 88

Watnick, M., 2, 4, 15, 21
Weber, M., 3 f., 20, 39, 43, 95
Weitz, M., 111
Weltanschauung, 95, 101 ff.
Wetter, G., 13, 114 f.
Wilde, J., 44
Wilson, F. P., 193
Windelband, W., 3, 89
Wölfflin, H., 177
Woolf, Virginia, 196
Wordsworth, 145, 204 ff.
Worringer, W., 177

Yudin, P., 114 f., 122

Zhdanov, A. A., 78, 163, 167, 209
Zinoviev, G., 13 f., 18 f., 83
Zitta, V., 8, 237
Zola, 36, 190, 215

Contributors

DAVID CRAIG Senior Lecturer in English, University of Lancaster. Dr Craig has written poetry and a book, *Scottish Literature and the Scottish People*, and has been preparing editions of Dickens' *Hard Times* and Sillitoe's *Saturday Night and Sunday Morning*, and an anthology of poetry of social movements.

H. A. HODGES Emeritus Professor of Philosophy, University of Reading. Author of *Wilhelm Dilthey: an Introduction*, *The Philosophy of Wilhelm Dilthey*, and *Languages, Standpoints and Attitudes*.

A. G. LEHMANN Associate Professor of French Studies, University of Warwick; formerly Professor of French Studies, University of Reading. Author of *The Symbolist Aesthetic in France, 1885–1895*, and *Sainte-Beuve: a Portrait of the Critic, 1804–1842*.

I. MÉSZÁROS Lecturer in Philosophy, University of Sussex. Formerly Lukács' assistant in the University of Budapest; has written on 'Satire and Reality' (Hungarian), 'The Revolt of the Intellectuals in Hungary' (Italian), 'Attila József and Modern Art' (Italian) and on 'Marx's Theory of Alienation' (forthcoming), and has contributed to *British Analytical Philosophy* (ed. by A. Montefiore and B. Williams), *The Proceedings of the Aristotelian Society, Philosophical Books, The Sociological Review*, and to various Hungarian, French, German and Italian books and periodicals.

STANLEY MITCHELL Lecturer in the Department of Literature, School of Comparative Studies, University of Essex. Has translated Lukács' *Essays on Thomas Mann* and (with Hannah Mitchell) *The Historical Novel*.

G. H. R. PARKINSON Senior Lecturer in Philosophy, University of Reading. Author of *Spinoza's Theory of Knowledge*, and *Logic and Reality in Leibniz's Metaphysics*; has edited and translated *Leibniz: Selected Logical Papers*, and is the editor of *The Theory of Meaning* in the 'Oxford Readings in Philosophy' series.

ROY PASCAL Professor of German, University of Birmingham. Author of *Shakespeare in Germany, The Growth of Modern Germany, The German Sturm und Drang, The German Novel, Design and Truth in Autobiography*, and *German Literature in the Sixteenth and Seventeenth Centuries*; editor of an English translation of *The German Ideology*, by Marx and Engels.

VINTAGE POLITICAL SCIENCE
AND SOCIAL CRITICISM

V-428   ABDEL-MALEK, ANOUAR   *Egypt: Military Society*
V-365   ALPEROVITZ, GAR   *Atomic Diplomacy*
V-286   ARIES, PHILIPPE   *Centuries of Childhood*
V-334   BALTZELL, E. DIGBY   *The Protestant Establishment*
V-335   BANFIELD & WILSON   *City Politics*
V-198   BARDOLPH, RICHARD   *The Negro Vanguard*
V-185   BARNETT, A. DOAK   *Communist China and Asia*
V-87   BARZUN, JACQUES   *God's Country and Mine*
V-705   BAUER, INKELES, AND KLUCKHOHN   *How the Soviet System Works*
V-270   BAZELON, DAVID   *The Paper Economy*
V-42   BEARD, CHARLES A.   *The Economic Basis of Politics* and Related Writings
V-59   BEAUFRE, GEN. ANDRÉ   *NATO and Europe*
V-60   BECKER, CARL L.   *Declaration of Independence*
V-17   BECKER, CARL L.   *Freedom and Responsibility in the American Way of Life*
V-228   BELOFF, MAX   *The United States and the Unity of Europe*
V-199   BERMAN, H. J. (ed.)   *Talks on American Law*
V-352   BERNSTEIN, PETER L.   *The Price of Prosperity*, Revised Edition
V-211   BINKLEY, WILFRED E.   *President and Congress*
V-81   BLAUSTEIN & WOOCK (eds.)   *Man Against Poverty: World War III—Articles and Documents on the Conflict between the Rich and the Poor*
V-513   BOORSTIN, DANIEL J.   *The Americans: The Colonial Experience*
V-358   BOORSTIN, DANIEL J.   *The Americans: The National Experience*
V-414   BOTTOMORE, T. B.   *Classes in Modern Society*
V-44   BRINTON, CRANE   *The Anatomy of Revolution*
V-37   BROGAN, D. W.   *The American Character*
V-234   BRUNER, JEROME   *The Process of Education*
V-196   BRYSON, L., et al.   *Social Change in Latin America Today*
V-30   CAMUS, ALBERT   *The Rebel*
V-33   CARMICHAEL AND HAMILTON   *Black Power: The Politics of Liberation in America*
V-98   CASH, W. J.   *The Mind of the South*
V-429   DE CASTRO, GERASSI, & HOROWITZ (eds.)   *Latin American Radicalism: A Documentary Report on Left and Nationalist Movements*
V-272   CATER, DOUGLASS   *The Fourth Branch of Government*
V-290   CATER, DOUGLASS   *Power in Washington*
V-420   CORNUELLE, RICHARD C.   *Reclaiming the American Dream*
V-311   CREMIN, LAWRENCE A.   *The Genius of American Education*
V-67   CURTIUS, ERNEST R.   *The Civilization of France*
V-234   DANIELS, R. V.   *A Documentary History of Communism*
V-235   (Two volumes)
V-237   DANIELS, ROBERT V.   *The Nature of Communism*
V-252   DAVID, et al.   *The Politics of National Party Conventions*
V-746   DEUTSCHER, ISAAC   *The Prophet Armed*

V-747 DEUTSCHER, ISAAC *The Prophet Unarmed*
V-748 DEUTSCHER, ISAAC *The Prophet Outcast*
V-333 ELLIS, CLYDE T. *A Giant Step*
V-390 ELLUL, JACQUES *Technological Society*
V-379 EMERSON, T. I. *Toward A General Theory of the First Amendment*
V-47 EPSTEIN & FORSTER *The Radical Right: Report on the John Birch Society and Its Allies*
V-353 EPSTEIN & FORSTER *Report on the John Birch Society 1966*
V-422 FALL, BERNARD B. *Hell in a Very Small Place: The Siege of Dien Bien Phu*
V-423 FINN, JAMES *Protest: Pacifism and Politics*
V-225 FISCHER, LOUIS (ed.) *The Essential Gandhi*
V-707 FISCHER, LOUIS *Soviets in World Affairs*
V-424 FOREIGN POLICY ASSOCIATION, EDITORS OF *A Cartoon History of United States Foreign Policy—Since World War I*
V-413 FRANK, JEROME D. *Sanity and Survival: Psychological Aspects of War and Peace*
V-382 FRANKLIN & STARR (eds.) *The Negro in 20th Century America*
V-224 FREYRE, GILBERTO *New World in the Tropics*
V-368 FRIEDENBERG, EDGAR Z. *Coming of Age in America*
V-416 FRIENDLY AND GOLDFARB *Crime and Publicity*
V-378 FULBRIGHT, J. WILLIAM *The Arrogance of Power*
V-264 FULBRIGHT, J. WILLIAM *Old Myths and New Realities* and Other Commentaries
V-354 FULBRIGHT, J. WILLIAM (intro.) *The Vietnam Hearings*
V-328 GALENSON, WALTER *A Primer on Employment & Wages*
V-461 GARAUDY, ROGER *From Anathema to Dialogue: A Marxist Challenge to the Christian Churches*
V-434 GAVIN, JAMES M. *Crisis Now*
V-475 GAY, PETER *The Enlightenment: The Rise of Modern Paganism*
V-277 GAY, PETER *Voltaire's Politics*
V-406 GETTLEMAN & MERMELSTEIN *The Great Society Reader: The Failure of American Liberalism*
V-174 GOODMAN, P. & P. *Communitas*
V-325 GOODMAN, PAUL *Compulsory Mis-education* and *The Community of Scholars*
V-32 GOODMAN, PAUL *Growing Up Absurd*
V-417 GOODMAN, PAUL *People or Personnel and Like a Conquered Province*
V-247 GOODMAN, PAUL *Utopian Essays and Practical Proposals*
V-357 GOODWIN, RICHARD N. *Triumph or Tragedy: Reflections on Vietnam*
V-248 GRUNEBAUM, G. E., VON *Modern Islam: The Search for Cultural Identity*
V-430 GUEVARA, CHE *Guerrilla Warfare*
V-389 HAMILTON, WALTON *The Politics of Industry*
V-69 HAND, LEARNED *The Spirit of Liberty*
V-319 HART, H. L. A. *Law, Liberty and Morality*
V-427 HAYDEN, TOM *Rebellion in Newark: Official Violence and Ghetto Response*
V-404 HELLER, WALTER (ed.) *Perspectives on Economic Growth*
V-283 HENRY, JULES *Culture Against Man*

V-465 HINTON, WILLIAM *Fanshen: A Documentary of Revolution in a Chinese Village*
V-95   HOFSTADTER, RICHARD *The Age of Reform*
V-9   HOFSTADTER, RICHARD *The American Political Tradition*
V-317 HOFSTADTER, RICHARD *Anti-Intellectualism in American Life*
V-385 HOFSTADTER, RICHARD *Paranoid Style in American Politics*
V-749 HOWE, IRVING (ed.) *Basic Writings of Trotsky*
V-201 HUGHES, H. STUART *Consciousness and Society*
V-241 JACOBS, JANE *Death & Life of Great American Cities*
V-433 JACOBS, PAUL *Prelude to Riot: A View of Urban America from the Bottom*
V-332 JACOBS & LANDAU (eds.) *The New Radicals*
V-369 KAUFMANN, WALTER (ed.) *The Birth of Tragedy and The Case of Wagner*
V-401 KAUFMANN, WALTER (ed.) *On the Genealogy of Morals and Ecce Homo*
V-337 KAUFMANN, WALTER (tr.) *Beyond Good and Evil*
V-470 KEY, V. O., JR. *The Responsible Electorate: Rationality in Presidential Voting 1936–1960*
V-361 KOMAROVSKY, MIRRA *Blue-Collar Marriage*
V-152 KRASLOW AND LOORY *The Secret Search for Peace in Vietnam*
V-341 KIMBALL & McCLELLAN *Education and the New America*
V-215 LACOUTURE, JEAN *Ho Chi Minh*
V-327 LACOUTURE, JEAN *Vietnam: Between Two Truces*
V-367 LASCH, CHRISTOPHER *The New Radicalism in America*
V-399 LASKI, HAROLD J. (ed.) *Harold J. Laski on The Communist Manifesto*
V-287 LA SOUCHÈRE, ÉLÉNA DE *An Explanation of Spain*
V-426 LEKACHMAN, ROBERT *The Age of Keynes*
V-280 LEWIS, OSCAR *The Children of Sánchez*
V-421 LEWIS, OSCAR *La Vida: A Puerto Rican Family in the Culture of Poverty—San Juan and New York*
V-370 LEWIS, OSCAR *Pedro Martínez*
V-284 LEWIS, OSCAR *Village Life in Northern India*
V-392 LICHTHEIM, GEORGE *The Concept of Ideology and Other Essays*
V-474 LIFTON, ROBERT JAY *Revolutionary Immortality: Mao Tse-Tung and the Chinese Cultural Revolution*
V-384 LINDESMITH, ALFRED *The Addict and The Law*
V-267 LIPPMANN, WALTER *The Essential Lippmann*
V-204 LOMAX, LOUIS *Thailand: The War that Is, The War that Will Be*
V-469 LOWE, JEANNE R. *Cities in a Race with Time: Progress and Poverty in America's Renewing Cities*
V-407 MACK, RAYMOND *Our Children's Burden: Studies of Desegregation in Ten American Communities*
V-193 MALRAUX, ANDRÉ *Temptation of the West*
V-324 MARITAIN, JACQUES *Existence and the Existent*
V-386 McPHERSON, JAMES *The Negro's Civil War*
V-102 MEYERS, MARVIN *The Jacksonian Persuasion*
V-273 MICHAEL, DONALD N. *The Next Generation*
V-19   MILOSZ, CZESLAW *The Captive Mind*
V-411 MINOGUE, KENNETH R. *The Liberal Mind*
V-316 MOORE, WILBERT E. *The Conduct of the Corporation*

V-251	MORGENTHAU, HANS J. *Purpose of American Politics*
V-703	MOSELY, PHILIP E. *The Kremlin and World Politics: Studies in Soviet Policy and Action* (Vintage Original)
V-57	MURCHLAND, BERNARD (ed.) *The Meaning of the Death of God*
V-274	MYRDAL, GUNNAR *Challenge to Affluence*
V-337	NIETZSCHE, FRIEDRICH *Beyond Good and Evil*
V-369	NIETZSCHE, FRIEDRICH *The Birth of Tragedy and The Case of Wagner*
V-401	NIETZSCHE, FRIEDRICH *On the Genealogy of Morals and Ecce Homo*
V-285	PARKES, HENRY B. *Gods and Men*
V-72	PEN, JAN *Primer on International Trade*
V-46	PHILIPSON, M. (ed.) *Automation:* Implications for the Future (Vintage Original)
V-258	PIEL, GERARD *Science in the Cause of Man*
V-128	PLATO *The Republic*
V-309	RASKIN & FALL (eds.) *The Viet-Nam Reader*
V-719	REED, JOHN *Ten Days That Shook the World*
V-192	REISCHAUER, EDWIN O. *Beyond Vietnam: The United States and Asia*
V-212	ROSSITER, CLINTON *Conservatism in America*
V-267	ROSSITER & LARE (eds.) *The Essential Lippmann*
V-472	ROSZAK, THEODORE (ed.) *The Dissenting Academy*
V-288	RUDOLPH, FREDERICK *The American College and University*
V-408	SAMPSON, RONALD V. *The Psychology of Power*
V-435	SCHELL, JONATHAN *The Military Half*
V-431	SCHELL, JONATHAN *The Village of Ben Suc*
V-403	SCHRIEBER, DANIEL *Profile of a School Dropout*
V-375	SCHURMANN AND SCHELL (eds.) *The China Reader: Imperial China,* I
V-376	SCHURMANN & SCHELL (eds.) *The China Reader: Republican China,* II
V-377	SCHURMANN & SCHELL (eds.) *The China Reader: Communist China,* III
V-394	SEABURY, PAUL *Power, Freedom and Diplomacy*
V-220	SHONFIELD, ANDREW *Attack on World Poverty*
V-359	SILVERT, et al. *Expectant Peoples*
V-432	SPARROW, JOHN *After the Assassination: A Positive Appraisal of the Warren Report*
V-388	STAMPP, KENNETH *The Era of Reconstruction 1865-1877*
V-253	STAMPP, KENNETH *The Peculiar Institution*
V-244	STEBBINS, RICHARD P. *U. S. in World Affairs, 1962*
V-374	STILLMAN & PFAFF *Power and Impotence*
V-439	STONE, I. F. *In a Time of Torment*
V-53	SYNGE, J. M. *The Aran Islands* and Other Writings
V-231	TANNENBAUM, FRANK *Slave & Citizen:* The Negro in the Americas
V-312	TANNENBAUM, FRANK *Ten Keys to Latin America*
V-322	THOMPSON, E. P. *The Making of the English Working Class*
V-749	TROTSKY, LEON *Basic Writings of Trotsky*
V-206	WALLERSTEIN, IMMANUEL *Africa:* The Politics of Independence (Vintage Original)
V-405	WASSERMAN & SWITZER *The Vintage Guide to Graduate Study*

V-298 WATTS, ALAN W. *The Way of Zen*
V-145 WARREN, ROBERT PENN *Segregation*
V-323 WARREN, ROBERT PENN *Who Speaks for the Negro?*
V-729 WEIDLE, W. *Russia:* Absent & Present
V-249 WIEDNER, DONALD L. *A History of Africa:* South of the Sahara
V-313 WILSON, EDMUND *Apologies to the Iroquois*
V-208 WOODWARD, C. VANN *Burden of Southern History*

VINTAGE WORKS OF SCIENCE
AND PSYCHOLOGY

V-286   ARIES, PHILIPPE   *Centuries of Childhood*

V-292   BATES, MARSTON   *The Forest and the Sea*

V-129   BEVERIDGE, W. I. B.   *The Art of Scientific Investigation*

V-291   BIEBER, I., AND OTHERS   *Homosexuality*

V-320   BERNSTEIN, JEREMY   *The Analytical Engine*

V-336   BOHR, NIELS   *Essays on Atomic Physics*

V-11   BRILL, A. A., M.D.   *Lectures on Psychoanalytic Psychiatry*

V-168   BRONOWSKI, J.   *The Common Sense of Science*

V-169   BROWN, NORMAN O.   *Life Against Death*

V-419   BROWN, NORMAN O.   *Love's Body*

V-160   BUCHHEIM, ROBERT W. (ed.)   *The New Space Handbook* (revised)

V-172   CHADWICK, JOHN   *The Decipherment of Linear B*

V-338   CHURCH, JOSEPH   *Language and the Discovery of Reality*

V-410   CHURCH, JOSEPH (ed.)   *Three Babies: Biographies of Cognitive Development*

V-156   DUNBAR, FLANDERS, M.D.   *Your Child's Mind and Body*

V-157   EISELEY, LOREN   *The Immense Journey*

V-390   ELLUL, JACQUES   *The Technological Society*

V-348   EVANS, JEAN   *Three Men*

V-413   FRANK, JEROME D.   *Sanity and Survival: Psychological Aspects of War and Peace*

V-236   FREEMAN & MARCH   *The New World of Physics*

V-132   FREUD, SIGMUND   *Leonardo da Vinci: A Study in Psychosexuality*

V-14   FREUD, SIGMUND   *Moses and Monotheism*

V-124   FREUD, SIGMUND   *Totem and Taboo*

V-396   GILSON, ETIENNE   *The Christian Philosophy of Saint Augustine*

V-195   GRODDECK, GEORG   *The Book of the It*

V-404   HELLER, WALTER (ed.)   *Perspectives on Economic Growth*

V-283   HENRY, JULES   *Culture Against Man*

V-397   HERSKOVITS, MELVILLE J.   *The Human Factor in Changing Africa*

V-150   HOOPER, ALFRED   *Makers of Mathematics*

V-268   JUNG, C. G.   *Memories, Dreams, Reflections*

V-436   KAUFMANN, WALTER   *Nietzsche: Philosopher, Psychologist, Antichrist*

V-437   KAUFMANN, WALTER (ed.)   *The Will to Power*

V-361   KOMAROVSKY, MIRRA   *Blue-Collar Marriage*

V-74   KÖHLER, WOLFGANG   *The Mentality of Apes*

V-226   KROEBER & KLUCKHOLN   *Culture*

V-151   KUHN, HERBERT   *On the Track of Prehistoric Man*

V-164   KUHN, THOMAS S.   *The Copernican Revolution*

V-426   LEKACHMAN, ROBERT   *The Age of Keynes*

V-105   LESLIE, CHARLES (ed.)   *Anthropology of Folk Religion* (A Vintage Original)

V-97   LESSER, SIMON   *Fiction and the Unconscious*

V-280   LEWIS, OSCAR   *The Children of Sánchez*

V-421   LEWIS, OSCAR   *La Vida: A Puerto Rican Family in the Culture of Poverty—San Juan and New York*

V-370   LEWIS, OSCAR   *Pedro Martínez*

V-284   LEWIS, OSCAR   *Village Life in Northern India*
V-384   LINDESMITH, ALFRED   *The Addict and The Law*
V-76   LINTON, RALPH   *The Tree of Culture*
V-407   MACK, RAYMOND   *Our Children's Burden: Studies of Desegregation in Ten American Communities*
V-209   MARCUSE, HERBERT   *Eros and Civilization*
V-437   NIETZSCHE, FRIEDRICH   *The Will to Power*
V-462   PIAGET, JEAN   *Six Psychological Studies*
V-258   PIEL, GERARD   *Science in the Cause of Man*
V-70   RANK, OTTO   *The Myth of the Birth of the Hero* and Other Essays
V-99   REDLICH, FRITZ, M.D. and BINGHAM, JUNE   *The Inside Story:* Psychiatry and Everyday Life
V-395   ROKEACH, MILTON   *The Three Christs of Ypsilanti*
V-301   ROSS, NANCY WILSON (ed.)   *The World of Zen*
V-464   SARTRE, JEAN-PAUL   *Search for a Method*
V-289   THOMAS, ELIZABETH MARSHALL   *The Harmless People*
V-310   THORP, EDWARD O.   *Beat the Dealer,* Revised
V-109   THRUELSEN & KOBLER (eds.)   *Adventures of the Mind, I*
V-68   *Adventures of the Mind, II*
V-239   *Adventures of the Mind, III*
V-299   WATTS, ALAN W.   *The Joyous Cosmology:* Adventures in the Chemistry of Consciousness
V-466   WATTS, ALAN W.   *The Wisdom of Insecurity*

A free catalogue of VINTAGE BOOKS *will be sent at your request. Write to* Vintage Books, 457 Madison Avenue, New York, New York 10022.

VINTAGE BIOGRAPHY AND AUTOBIOGRAPHY

V-708   AKSAKOV, SERGEY   *Years of Childhood*
V-159   BEHRMAN, S. N.   *Duveen*
V-250   BURCKHARDT, C. J.   *Richelieu:* His Rise to Power
V-725   CARR, E. H.   *Michael Bakunin*
V-746   DEUTSCHER, ISAAC   *The Prophet Armed*
V-747   DEUTSCHER, ISAAC   *The Prophet Unarmed*
V-748   DEUTSCHER, ISAAC   *The Prophet Outcast*
V-225   FISCHER, L. (ed.)   *The Essential Gandhi*
V-147   GIDE, ANDRÉ   *If It Die*
V-742   HARE, RICHARD   *Pioneers of Russian Social Thought*
V-268   JUNG, C. G.   *Memories, Dreams, Reflections*
V-50   KELLY, AMY   *Eleanor of Aquitaine and the Four Kings*
V-728   KLYUCHEVSKY, V.   *Peter the Great*
V-215   LACOUTURE, JEAN   *Ho Chi Minh*
V-280   LEWIS, OSCAR   *Children of Sánchez*
V-34   LOWENTHAL, M. (ed.)   *Autobiography of Michel de Montaigne*
V-92   MATTINGLY, GARRETT   *Catherine of Aragon*
V-107   NEWMAN, ERNEST   *Wagner as Man and Artist*
V-373   PAUSTOVSKY, KONSTANTIN   *The Story of A Life*
V-744   SIMMONS, ERNEST J.   *Alexander Pushkin*
V-701   SIMMONS, ERNEST J.   *Leo Tolstoy,* Volume I
V-702   SIMMONS, ERNEST J.   *Leo Tolstoy,* Volume II
V-736   SIMMONS, ERNEST J.   *Dostoevsky:* The Making of a Novelist
V-263   ROEDER, RALPH   *Catherine de' Medici* and the Lost Revolution
V-133   STEIN, GERTRUDE   *The Autobiography of Alice B. Toklas*
V-100   SULLIVAN, J. W. N.   *Beethoven:* His Spiritual Development
V-387   TAYLOR, A. J. P.   *Bismarck*
V-82   TOYE, FRANCIS   *Verdi:* His Life and Works
V-256   WILDE, OSCAR   *De Profundis* (Uuexpurgated)
V-122   WILENSKI, R. H.   *Modern French Painters,* Volume I (1863-1903)
V-123   WILENSKI, R. H.   *Modern French Painters,* Volume II (1904-1938)
V-106   WINSTON, RICHARD   *Charlemagne:* From the Hammer to the Cross

A free catalogue of VINTAGE BOOKS *will be sent at your request. Write to* Vintage Books, 457 Madison Avenue, New York, New York 10022.

Date Due